Victorian Short Stories
An anthology

Selected and introduced by
Harold Orel
University Distinguished Professor of English,
University of Kansas

D1514152

Dent: London and Melbourne
EVERYMAN'S LIBRARY

© Selection, Introduction and Notes, J.M. Dent & Sons Ltd 1987
All rights reserved

Typeset by Inforum Ltd, Portsmouth
Made in Great Britain by
Guernsey Press Co. Ltd, Guernsey, C.I. for
J.M. Dent & Sons Ltd
Aldine House, 33 Welbeck Street, London W1M 8LX

First published as an Everyman Classic, 1987

British Library Cataloguing in Publication Data

Victorian short stories : an anthology. —
  (Everyman classics)
  1. Short stories, English
  I. Orel, Harold
  823.01′08 FS   PR1309.S5

No 591 Paperback ISBN 0 460 01591 5

EVERYMAN, I will go with thee, and be thy guide,
In thy most need to go by thy side

HAROLD OREL earned his academic degrees at the University of New Hampshire and the University of Michigan. He is currently University Distinguished Professor of English at the University of Kansas, and the author or editor of fifteen books, several of which deal with late-Victorian figures such as Thomas Hardy, Rudyard Kipling, and William Butler Yeats. His history of the Victorian short story was published by Cambridge University Press in 1986.

To Ed Ruhe

Contents

Introduction   vi

Douglas Jerrold, *Kind Cousin Tom* (1842)   1
W.S. Gilbert, *My Maiden Brief* (1863)   10
Charles Dickens, *George Silverman's Explanation* (1868)   21
J. Sheridan Le Fanu, *Mr Justice Harbottle* (1872)   49
Robert Louis Stevenson, *Thrawn Janet* (1881)   83
Oscar Wilde, *The Sphinx without a Secret* (1887)   93
Rudyard Kipling, *Without Benefit of Clergy* (1890)   99
Thomas Hardy, *The Son's Veto* (1891)   122
Henry James, *The Real Thing* (1890)   137
'George Egerton', *Virgin Soil* (1894)   163
Hubert Crackanthorpe, *Modern Melodrama* (1894)   175
H.G. Wells, *The Cone* (1895)   183
Arthur Conan Doyle, *The Brazilian Cat* (1898)   194
Somerville and Ross, *Great-Uncle McCarthy* (1898)   214
George Gissing, *The Scrupulous Father* (1900)   230
Baroness Orczy, *The Mysterious Death on the
                    Underground Railway* (1901)   243
Joseph Conrad, *Amy Foster* (1901)   260

Biographical Notes   289
Acknowledgments   298

Introduction

All the stories in this anthology were written during Queen Victoria's reign. They illustrate various aspects of nineteenth-century life and manners. They are deeply rooted in circumstantial detail and a sense of fact, despite occasional elements of fantasy, the supernatural, and psychological speculation. Even when the locale is non-English, as in the tales by Kipling and Somerville and Ross, the narratives illustrate characteristic Victorian concerns. Taken singly and collectively, they are entertaining, and possess high literary quality.

The majority of the stories came from the last quarter of the nineteenth century. So high a proportion reflects the fact that the short story matured relatively late as an independent literary genre. Short stories were often used, during earlier decades of the century, to enliven novels (for example, no less than nine tales were added to Dickens's *Pickwick Papers*). It was unclear to many authors where to draw the line between a sketch and a story, or whether, indeed, any distinction applied. Novelists were certain, for a very long time indeed, that short stories, whether published in periodicals or in hard-bound collections, paid less than novels published as three-deckers and read by the patrons of Smith's and Mudie's circulating libraries.

The very term 'short story' has a surprisingly brief history. The supplement to the *O.E.D.* defines it as 'a story with a fully worked-out motive but of much smaller compass and less elaborate in form than a novel'. This may imply that a short story is not as interesting as a novel, because it is shorter and more single-minded in its movement toward a climax. At any rate, the citations which document the age of the term do not go back much more than one hundred years.

The reasons for the delayed maturation of the genre are multiple. They include the development, after mid-century, of hot-metal composing machines that reduced costs spectacularly from those required by hand-labourers working with the screw-press, a technique that had dominated the printing industry for hundreds of years. The linotype and the autoplate multiplied production of sheets in a truly wondrous fashion. In turn, this revolution in technology (it cannot be called less) made possible the lowering of prices for mass-circulation periodicals specializing in fictions both long and short. By the 1890s *The Strand Magazine,* home of the Sherlock Holmes stories and publisher of short stories by Kipling, Wells, and the best practitioners in the field, was selling at the rate of half-a-million copies per month.

But of all the external factors affecting the explosion of short-story production during the Victorian Age, the broadening of the educational base for the general public must be accounted the most significant. It is worth a moment to consider the implications of the fact that in the 1830s, at the beginning of the Queen's reign, 41.6% of the population was illiterate (33.7% of the men, 49.5% of the women). Before 1845 there were no free public libraries. On Sunday, the only day of the week when ordinary Englishmen could find time to stroll in gardens or visit theatres or museums, they found these avenues of leisure and recreation closed. Methodists and Nonconformists fought bitterly against the reading of plays, romances, or books of humour on *any* day of the week. The wide-spread systems of Andrew Bell (1753–1832) and Joseph Lancaster (1778–1838), with their heavy emphasis upon student monitors and student teachers, weighed heavily on the children of the land. Set lessons, set questions, set answers: the only way to survive was to memorize blocks of information, facts, the approved wordings. (Dickens, in *Hard Times,* bitterly satirized this technique of pedagogy; but not all modern readers of Dickens's novel appreciate its factual basis.)

Not until W.E. Forster, a Quaker, pushed through the Forster Education Act in 1870 were substantial changes made in what was increasingly often interpreted as a situation seriously affecting England's ability to compete in world markets against such technologically progressive rivals as Germany. In the year that the Act passed, average school attendance was 1.5 million; within twenty years that figure had gone up to 4.5 million, and the amount of money spent on each child had doubled. Voluntary societies, organized into the National Education Union, were allowed six months to extend their financing of schools which had recognized deficiencies; after that time expired, Forster's Bill made it possible for the national government to 'fill the gaps' by means of School Boards elected by town councils or (in the case of rural areas) by the vestries. Thus, parents who could not pay the required fees of 9d. a week would be granted a free ticket for their children. By 1876 School Boards covered areas with 12.5 million people who could not have learned to read without the direct government intervention made possible by Forster's Education Act. A subsequent Act of 1876 made education compulsory for children up to the age of twelve (this became truly effective in 1880, and free education followed as a law in 1891). Under the Board of Trade the Science and Art Department provided grants to aid technical and art classes, a development that in turn made possible the rapid expansion of post-primary education and the founding of municipal technical colleges, as well as a number of new universities (Liverpool, Leeds, Sheffield, Bristol, and Reading); older universities (London, Durham, and Manchester) shifted to more stable financial bases; and the University Extension movement accelerated. The path was cleared for the great Education Bill of 1902, inspired by Sir Robert Morant, which abolished the School Boards because they had been using funds illegally for purposes other than elementary education, and because their administration left much to be desired. The new Bill redefined and reorganized both elementary and secondary education, and for the first time made it possible for County Councils to act through County Educational Committees. This, in brief, was the introduction of the 'ladder' concept, whereby poor but gifted students found themselves able, for the first time, to obtain places at universities, not only the new redbricks but Oxford and Cambridge as well.

By 1893 only 5% of men and 5.7% of women were unable to sign their names in the marriage register. But, of course, this improvement in the literacy rate was part of a larger pattern. The second half of the nineteenth century saw a slow but steady decrease in the number of hours worked during a day, and by 1900 a half-holiday on Saturday had become common. Free libraries proliferated. Cheap newspapers were everywhere, not just in London. Railways provided inexpensive excursions on Sunday. Art galleries and museums opened their doors at the weekend. City-dwellers understood the value of parks and open spaces, and fought for their preservation. Literary societies attracted a wide cross-section of the reading public.

It was understandable that those trained in an older and more exclusive tradition deplored the 'lower forms of literature and journalism' that seemed to cater to millions of 'half-educated and quarter-educated people'. But the inescapable conclusion is that from 1870 until the Great War of 1914–1918, the number of readers was multiplying at an unprecedented rate. The amount of leisure time available was also increasing in ways that none could have forseen at mid-century; reading-matter designed to divert and entertain was becoming far more important than literature meant to edify, and what's more, it was now readily available for pennies. The rapid growth of the short-story genre became a fact only because a market for the short story had suddenly, unexpectedly, and very dramatically materialized in the final decades of the Victorian Age.

Since this collection attempts to illustrate several kinds of short story, no definition, however gracefully worded, will account for all the techniques of story-telling, or for all the themes that attracted large numbers of readers. The narrative that exploited terror and the supernatural, for example, was as widely enjoyed a type of short story as any; it is represented here by J. Sheridan Le Fanu's 'Mr Justice Harbottle' and Robert Louis Stevenson's 'Thrawn Janet'. They demonstrate that tremendous effects can be compacted into a small space. The Gothic novel, by comparison, seems too sprawling and undisciplined to achieve the same intensity of horror that stuns a reader of Poe, Le Fanu, Stevenson, Machen, or M. R. James.

Although Dickens wrote some of the best such stories ('No. 1 Branch Line: The Signalman' is a classic, and has proved impressive as both a radio script and an opportunity for a stage monologue), it should be remembered that several women writing for Dickens's Christmas editions of *Household Words* – for example, Rosa Mulholland and Amelia Edwards – were particularly skilled in this sub-genre. Other fine writers of horror tales were Mrs Braddon, Mrs Riddell, and Mrs Oliphant.

At least part of the popularity of ghost stories may be attributed to the growing uneasiness caused by the claims of over-enthusiastic supporters of late nineteenth-century science. Many Victorians believed that there was something wrong with the argument that the mysteries of the universe were finite and ultimately solvable. These stories flourished in large part because of the very darkness of the phenomena they were dramatizing. Stories with rational endings, that sought to explain everything extraordinary that had happened, were – almost inevitably – less effective than those stories which left intact the magical or irrational element. The universe, in this view, is another name for chaos. We cannot fully understand it. Creatures within it can appal us before they overwhelm us.

A ghost story is, of course, not just about ghosts. The victim begins with comfortable and self-reassuring platitudes about the dailiness of his routine existence. When the unexpected materializes, he is stunned by its ferocity, seeming motivelessness, and its picking him out from all the human race. The author of the best ghost story refuses to comfort us with a final explanation. He is recounting a tale, after all, and a tale always connotes something of the marvellous.

A second highly visible type of story on the Victorian horizon is the one dealing with a detective hero. A fine example included here is Baroness Orczy's 'The Mysterious Death on the Underground Railway', which was influenced in its patterning by the success of Arthur Conan Doyle's stories about Sherlock Holmes's cases. But Doyle, who perfected the format of the detective story, was not its originator. That honour belongs to Edgar Allan Poe. His creation, C. Auguste Dupin, stressed the importance of logic in working out his solution to a grisly crime ('The Murders in the Rue Morgue'). He was our first true detective. Poe's emphasis on working backward from the *dénouement* was more carefully rationalized than anything Dickens had accomplished in *Barnaby Rudge* (Poe's admitted source, or inspiration). Poe wrote other stories of detection, including 'The Mystery of Marie Roget' and 'The Purloined Letter'; but the concept of the detective-hero became truly modern in Wilkie Collins's fiction. *The Moonstone* features the great Sergeant Cuff, and the process of detection is stressed in at least three of his novels (*The Law and the Lady, My Lady's Money,* and *'I Say No'*) and four of his short stories ('A Stolen Letter', 'The Biter Bit', 'Anne Rodway', and 'Mr Policeman and the Cook'). Collins benefited from the example of Dickens's Inspector Bucket in *Bleak House*, but that character had been very minor in a huge cast, and was at best a fine charcoal drawing compared to the water-colours of Sergeant Cuff. Sherlock Holmes continues this tradition, and extends it; his portrait is done in oils; and Doyle, as artist, became one of the best paid of all Victorian authors.

The distinguishing traits of the English detective-hero were all defined by the end of the Victorian Age. He (or she) knew a great deal of curious, extensive lore about the most arcane matters; loved detection as an amateur-enthusiast; cultivated unexpected hobbies (Sergeant Cuff grew roses, Holmes played the violin); and consistently acted on the assumption that crime was an aberration, and that the forces of civilization would ultimately triumph. All the 'rivals of Sherlock Holmes' (as they have sometimes been called) share these values; they appeared in such periodicals as *The Ludgate Monthly, The Harmsworth Magazine, The Strand Magazine, The Idler, The Windsor Magazine, Pearson's Magazine,* and *Cassell's Magazine;* and they included – in the years before the Queen died – Mrs Catherine Louisa Pirkis's Loveday Brooke ('Lady Detective'), Mrs Meade (who had two medical collaborators) and her 'Clifford Halifax and 'Robert Eustace', Arthur Morrison's Martin Hewitt, and Clarence Rook's Miss Van Snoop.

A third type of story, much loved during the entire sixty years of the Queen's reign, was the humorous sketch. It is true enough that the grim social and economic conditions of the nineteenth century led to the production of a literature specializing in high seriousness; but it is also true that the very best writers contributed to this light-hearted sub-genre: Thomas Hood, Charles Dickens, Robert Smith Surtees, Douglas William Jerrold, William Makepeace Thackeray, Charles Lutwidge Dodgson (Lewis Carroll), William Schwenk Gilbert – and the list can be extended. Victorians loved a free-wheeling, almost out-of-control sketch that many modern readers may find painfully violent, overdone, racist, or too strongly bound to topical issues that have long since faded from memory. But the best such sketches remain delightfully comic in the most modern sense.

Three examples are provided in this anthology: Douglas

Jerrold's 'Kind Cousin Tom', William Schwenk Gilbert's 'My Maiden Brief', and Oscar Wilde's 'The Sphinx without a Secret'. They are samplings from a truly vast literature. The market for such contributions – lighter-hearted interpretations of the problems that beset the Victorians – lay primarily in the comic journals that proliferated from the very beginning. *Punch* was founded in 1841, after Victoria had reigned for only four years; and there were *Punchinello, Figaro in London, Punch in London, Punch in Cambridge, The Penny Punch,* and *The Wag.* The most serious journals also made space for humorous sketches. Nor must we forget that the Victorian years constituted the Golden Age of light verse. Among the masters of this mode of expression: the Reverend Richard Harris Barham (Thomas Ingoldsby), William Edmonstoune Aytoun and Theodore Martin, Edward Lear, Frederick Locker (later Frederick Locker-Lampson), and Charles Stuart Calverley. The most serious poets of the second half of the nineteenth-century – Tennyson, Browning, Swinburne, and Wilde – wrote light verse, some of it very good indeed.

From the 1870s on most short stories were, however, marked by their strong interest in social, humanitarian, and political problems. The contributions made by realists and naturalists – painters like Courbet, novelists like Balzac, Flaubert, Champfleury, Tolstoy, and Zola, dramatists like Ibsen and Strindberg – revolutionized ways of thinking about human nature, social institutions, even the landscape. None of this escaped the notice of English writers of fiction. Much of what Thomas Hardy said in his essays 'Candour in English Fiction' (1890) and 'The Science of Fiction' (1891) was true: '. . . the magazine in particular and the circulating library in general do not foster the growth of the novel which reflects and reveals life.' But his bitter judgment on the impossibility of writing adult fiction for an immature, largely feminine reading public must be modified by our knowledge that the 1890s proved to be intellectually lively and experimental years. As Holbrook Jackson pointed out, there was a great deal of animated talk about 'new' things, and the possibility of making a fresh start in all the arts. The short story benefited – as did the novel, the drama, journalism, and some of the greatest works of Victorian scholarship.

I have tried to include examples of popular short-story types other than those dealing with horror, crime, and humorous subject-matter. For example, Victorians enjoyed interlinked stories which did not develop an over-all plot; individual stories might be read at leisure. Somerville and Ross's 'Great-Uncle McCarthy', first of the 'experiences' encountered by an Irish Resident Magistrate, is here reprinted. Then there are the action stories, perhaps the most popular of all the types: Arthur Conan Doyle's 'The Brazilian Cat' and H.G. Wells's 'The Cone' are among the finest in this category. The question of matrimonial arrangements, so important to us in this century, was no less vital to Victorian readers. Thomas Hardy's 'The Son's Veto', George Gissing's 'The Scrupulous Father', and 'Virgin Soil', by 'George Egerton' (Mary Chavelita Dunne), represent this grouping. The puzzling problem of failure (why do the unworthy succeed, while the talented go under?), which concerned many Victorian writers, is analysed in Charles Dickens's 'George Silverman's Explanation'. Social maladjustment is studied in Joseph Conrad's 'Amy Foster', while an inter-racial romance is at the heart of Rudyard Kipling's 'Without Benefit of Clergy'. An early form of the dialogue-story – with almost every important revelation coming as a speech that implies no less than it states directly – is here in Hubert Crackanthorpe's 'Modern Melodrama'.

In story after story we encounter the quality of restraint. Victorian writers, far more often than is commonly appreciated, refused to exploit easy expectations. If anything, the respect paid by short-story writers to the intelligence and good taste of their audience compares favourably with that paid by twentieth-century writers of fiction. Readers of this anthology will judge for themselves, but the understatement of Gissing's final sentence in 'The Scrupulous Father' – 'It was next morning that the father posted a formal, proper, self-respecting note of invitation, which bore results' – may profitably be studied if one is interested in the mysterious powers of relatively flat and unaccented diction to evoke the strongest sense of character. Even Oscar Wilde's story 'The Sphinx without a Secret', which deliberately sets up a fantastic situation (a woman of fashion, a 'Gioconda in sables', is unable to receive letters in her own house), reaches its surprising conclusion without the aid of editorial judgment. The reader of that tale's final line (' "I wonder?" he said at last') is invited, in modernist fashion, to collaborate in forming the story's full meaning.

A holding-back may not be the trait most of us associate with Victorian writers of fiction. Stevenson's 'Thrawn Janet', possibly the finest ghost story of the century, achieves a powerful impact, but not through the use of understatement. Wells's 'The Cone' is savage in its portrayal of a man's jealousy. Even so, stories such as these impress us by their economy of means. Stevenson and Wells seem to know more about their characters than they are telling; they provide no final explanation; the mysteries of human nature remain mysterious.

The Victorian short story can be, and frequently is, a subtle and sophisticated creation, capable of surprising those who think of the genre as essentially a twentieth-century creation. Dickens's 'George Silverman's Explanation' is a case in point. A miniature autobiography, it chronicles the life of a born loser, but one may reasonably inquire to whom the explanation is addressed, and for that matter what the narrative is intended to explain.

George Silverman's misery can be, and should be, affecting. As he himself notes after being orphaned and taken in hand by Hawkyard, an itinerant preacher, 'To that time I had never had the faintest impression of beauty.' (The need for knowledge of something lovely – Dickens believed – is nurtured deep in the bone even when a name for the need is lacking.) Unable to believe in himself (after all, those closest to him never express the slightest confidence in his abilities, whether real or potential), he stumbles through life continually surprised by reality and class arrogance. As a depiction of an inferiority complex, Charles Dickens's story can scarcely be bettered; and yet, rather unexpectedly, George's failure to do better than he does is not readily 'explained' by any reason or combination of reasons provided within the tale. George ends as he has begun, as one who endures: 'For years a cloud hung over me, and my name was tarnished. But my heart did not break, if a broken heart involved death; for I lived through it.' He fails to clarify the problems of character that prevent him from taking a more aggressive stance toward those wishing to exploit his gullibility, though he understands well the need to avoid appearing 'worldly'. In brief, he victimizes himself, but why he so willingly goes to the slaughter-block must puzzle the reader no less than it does George.

The primary emphasis here is on the workings of personality that cannot cope with more forceful wills, and a substantial fraction of the interest we have in the tale derives from our appreciation of its psychological truth. George Silverman's dilemma arises in large part from his failure to learn how to make a decent living wage, and Dickens, like most writers of fiction in the Victorian Age, was deeply absorbed by questions pertaining to money. Douglas Jerrold, in 'Kind Cousin Tom', treats the matter more wryly when he creates a Jack Martin who 'wants' a sense of poverty, and drives his prosperous, more ambitious cousin to distraction. Cousin Tom intends to rise even higher. To this end he cultivates the Honourable Alexander Mulington (who allows him, on one occasion, to grasp his two outstretched fingers as a sign of recognition); but Jack embarrasses him by insisting that he dine with him on 'a breast of veal hissing and bubbling on a bed of brown potatoes', and Tom, in despair, quits his club shortly thereafter. '. . . It was too much for the nerves of a stoic that his appearance should be the inevitable signal to divers members to commence an earnest inquiry of the waiters if there was in the house a breast of veal, with particular and most significant queries, touching – baked potatoes.' Tom has already failed in his attempt to persuade Jack to emigrate to New Zealand, where one can enjoy 'four harvests a-year and no taxes'. He seethes with resentment at the possibility – nay, the certainty – that his cousin Jack will materialize, at critical moments, with his wife ('as Jack himself would insist upon calling her, cousin Sally') and two children. One such moment comes on Derby Day, when Tom, keeping company with Dorothea Sybilwitz, 'a mere woman' with 'a very proper notion of the delightful privileges of worldly station' because she possesses a dowry of twenty-thousand pounds, is startled to behold his cousin, complete with family and neighbours in a low spring-cart drawn by a pony, and to be greeted in terms of easy familiarity. Tom's impending marriage is endangered by this vulgarity (cousin Sally, wearing 'a coarse straw bonnet and cotton shawl', is suckling her last-born); to avoid future meetings, he finances Jack's emigration to Wales, pays Jack forty pounds a year, and promises to place the boys 'very eligibly at sea' when they reach a suitable age. Every time he despatches a ten-pound note to Jack, paying his quarter's bribe to have him stay away from the city, he grinds his teeth and damns his cousin; while Jack, blissfully unaware of Tom's real feelings, toasts the health of his absent cousin: 'Here's cousin Tom's health! Yes, cousin Tom was always so fond of me!'

Money, Victorian story-tellers remind us more than once, determines social standing, and those who have it patronize those who do not; it defines who has a right to call himself a gentleman. The difficulties implicit in any effort to cross from one rank to another are always spelled out. Jerrold, aware that Tom has no high relations to satisfy Dorothea Sybilwitz's hunger for an alliance with nobility, must carefully anticipate the objection that Dorothea would sooner remain an old maid than marry beneath her station: '. . . upon his own showing, he had no poor, beggarly connections to cast a shadow on her golden fortunes. It was thus Dorothea compromised between her love of nobility and her love of cousin Tom. Rank was, after all, an abstract idea; whereas cousin Tom was really a tall, well-made young fellow, with very tantalising whiskers.' So she reasons before cousin Jack makes his unwelcome appearance.

Thomas Hardy, in 'The Son's Veto', makes it painfully clear that Randolph (the son) has become a snob because of 'his aristocratic school-knowledge, his grammars, and his aversions', and that he regards his mother as a woman 'whose mistakes and origin it was his painful lot as a gentleman to blush for'. He wants to belong to a higher social class than his mother is comfortable with; hers is a milieu of 'minor tradesmen and under-clerks', and Randolph cannot accommodate himself to the thought that she might marry a second time to anyone less than 'a gentleman'. In brief, he vetoes her choice with a searing speech of denunciation: 'I am ashamed of you! He will ruin me! A miserable boor! a churl! a clown! He will degrade me in the eyes of all the gentlemen of England!' The degrading manner in which he bends his mother to his will, depriving her forever of any chance for happiness, is best studied by a reading of the narrative; but Hardy, who began his fiction-writing career with a strong hatred of the linkages between money and class, and whose first manuscript *The Poor Man and the Lady* was rejected by George Meredith, the publisher's reader, as politically subversive, made plain his conviction that Randolph's education had 'ousted his humanity'.

Again, in George Gissing's 'The Scrupulous Father', Rose Whiston's opportunities to find the proper suitor are limited by her father's profound consciousness of social limits, which translates into a rigid concept of respectability; he works as a draughtsman in the office of a geographical publisher, and husbands his money carefully. Rose's 'kinfolk on both sides laid claim to the title of gentlefolk, but supported it on the narrowest margin of independence'. Gissing is rigorously honest in noting that, in such a household, the atmosphere is apt to be 'unfavourable to mental development', though Rose is naturally intelligent. Rose, an only child, lives in a suburb, in 'a house illumined with every domestic virtue; but scarcely a dozen persons crossed the threshold within a twelve-month'. The problem, clear from the very beginning, is how Rose can pursuade her father that the only male who ever displays an interest in her — an office-worker with red hair, 'anything but handsome', and on his first appearance at the little town to which the Whistons have gone for their holiday, 'flushed and perspiring from the sunny road', wearing an open jacket over 'a blue cotton shirt without waistcoat', carrying in his hand 'a shabby straw hat', and, to complete the picture, wearing boots covered by 'thick dust' — is really a gentleman. His manners are sufficiently energetic and cheerfully extraverted to disgust Mr Whiston. Rose herself does not know how to define the term 'gentleman'. Gissing, recording an early stage of the relationship between Rose and the office-worker, writes that Rose is agitated by the question: 'It involved so technical a definition, and she felt so doubtful as to the reply. Beyond doubt he had acted in a gentlemanly way; but his voice lacked something. Coarse? Gross? No, no, no!' Small wonder, then, that Rose suddenly feels 'very weary', discouraged, and dreary. Later still, after she has exchanged names and addresses with the young man during her father's absence, she is afflicted by pangs of conscience: 'She saw herself with the old eyes, and was shame-stricken to the very heart. Whose the fault? Towards dawn she argued it with the bitterness of misery. What a life was hers in this little world of choking respectabilities! Forbidden this, forbidden that; permitted – the pride of ladyhood. And she was not a lady, after all. What lady would have permitted herself to exchange names and addresses with a strange man in a railway carriage – furtively, too, escaping her father's observation? If not a lady, what *was* she? It meant the utter failure of her breeding and education. The sole end for which she had lived was frustrated. A common, vulgar young woman – well mated, doubtless, with an impudent clerk, whose noisy talk was of beer and tobacco!'

Ours is not so egalitarian a society that Rose's soul-wrenching battle between self-respect and a desire to find love has become hopelessly dated. Gissing may not have been as positive as Hardy about the need for including birth, breeding and formal education as elements in the making of a gentleman or lady, and Rose, as the preceding quotation makes clear, suffers from some confusion as to whether she herself has behaved in ladylike fashion; but both writers are sure that failure to come to terms with such questions will make for great unhappiness in late-Victorian England.

Another concern of several writers is loneliness. Lady Alroy, in Wilde's 'The Sphinx without a Secret', leads a private and deliberately mysterious existence. Perhaps the loneliest of all is Yanko Goorall, of Conrad's 'Amy Foster'. His name is twisted and misunderstood by the townspeople among whom this shipwrecked mariner – 'a poor emigrant from Central Europe bound to America and washed ashore here in a storm', for whom England is the same as 'an undiscovered country' where wild beasts or wild men might roam – lives for most of his wretched years. 'It is indeed hard upon a man,' muses Dr Kennedy, the narrator, 'to find himself a lost stranger, helpless, incomprehensible, and of a mysterious origin, in some obscure corner of the earth. Yet amongst all the adventurers shipwrecked in all the wild parts of the world, there is not one, it seems to me, that ever had to suffer a fate so simply tragic as the man I am speaking of. . . .'

But this generalization about the recurring motif of loneliness must be instantly modified, if only because most Victorian authors held strong views on the high value of society's rulings. The option of seceding from everyday affairs in order to cultivate one's private opinions is always open; but such withdrawal, one gathers, cannot be long-sustained, and ultimately the opinions must be shared. In Wilde's fable, the narrator's suspicion is strong, for example, that Lady Alroy – who does not want to share her secrets – has no opinions worth investigating. Conrad's foreigner remains permanently alien to English ways of thinking; his religion is Catholic, his walk unusual, his complexion 'swarthy', his way of tipping a hat over an ear and of wearing his coat over one shoulder somehow disagreeably exotic. When Yanko sings in his own language, or attempts to show tap-room customers how to dance, he meets hostility, and even, on one occasion, a black eye.

Published more often in Victorian periodicals are stories that dramatize a way of thinking shared by an entire community. Even if the judgments of the community are not presented as true and righteous altogether, they can never be dismissed summarily. Because Victorian writers depended on a shared frame of reference, their presentations of social attitudes took for granted the general validity of those attitudes, even though they often enough implied that some opinions were stifling, or behind the times.

Finally, a word about the extraordinary narrative drive of a typical Victorian short story, with particular reference to Arthur Conan Doyle's 'The Brazilian Cat'. It hardly matters that Doyle, with his interest in the exotic and the far-away, got his facts wrong about his big cat. (Pumas are often called cougars, mountain lions, or catamounts, and a number of Spanish names. Doyle gives Everard King the line, 'Some people call it a black puma, but really it is not a puma at all,' but scientists now agree that there is only a single species despite the proliferation of names. Moreover, as Ivan T. Sanderson, the distinguished zoologist, wrote in *Living Mammals of the World* (New York: 1958, p. 163), 'The Puma is the greatest coward of all the great or not so great cats. Despite voluminous fictional tales and innumerable accounts published as fact, the number of authenticated cases of deliberate attacks upon humans by these animals is so paltry as to be almost non-existent and most of these are open to some doubt.'). The story, without pausing for reflection on the implications of Everard's King's pathology, without much interest in symbolic overtones, without undue stress placed on verbal counters or signs, immediately attracts and holds our interest.

Doyle, whose short stories covered a much wider range of interests than those who know only his Sherlock Holmes stories can appreciate, was a highly successful writer, and – equally as important – a representative one. It would be a mistake to think of 'The Brazilian Cat' as a story so intent on final destination that it ignores – along the way – the finer touches of narrative art. This is a well-crafted tale. The first paragraph clearly sets down the relationship between the hero and his uncle, a wealthy relative who has taken no interest in the life and career of his heir; and it identifies the growing sense of panic of the narrator, who sees his financial ruin looming ever closer. The second paragraph tells us something about Everard King, the narrator's first cousin, who invites him to a country estate, and records the narrator's reaction: 'If I could only get on terms with this unknown relative of mine, I might pull through yet. For the family credit he would not let me go entirely to the wall.' More praises are sung to King's credit: he is charitable, he has travelled widely, he has made on his estate a zoo and an open-air aviary of Brazilian animals and birds. When King appears, he turns out to have a 'very homely and benevolent' appearance, with 'a round, good-humoured face'. But his wife is rude. She heartily wishes the narrator back in London (her speech, he decides, is insolent). All these details are given to us through a remarkably candid stream of consciousness, that of the young narrator, who writes in the first person (a favourite Victorian story-telling choice). Like the person who delivers a soliloquy in Elizabethan drama, the first-person narrator is under an obligation to tell his listener (or reader) the absolute truth about what he thinks, and what his opinions are. And Doyle, cleverly, with no waste motions, records the impressions of a young man seeking to get ahead in the world, without talents, without any visible determination to work for a living, and without any false modesty; the portrait is exact, and by implication an indictment of a class type; and, as the story proves, everything the narrator believes about Everard King is mistaken (dangerously so), and fatuous. The reader, retracing his impressions as they were shaped by Marshall King, the 'innocent eye' of the story, must marvel at how much essential information has been provided in the opening paragraphs, and how all of it, including the true villainy of Everard King, and the passionate outbursts of Mrs King, has been misinterpreted by the narrator. There are false trails, yes, and the narrator wanders down all of them; but Doyle has played fair with his reader. All the evidence is there, to be evaluated by the careful reader. The same technique enables Sherlock Holmes, working with the same data available to Dr Watson or Inspector Lestrade, to come up with the one *right* interpretation.

To the reader of Victorian stories (we all have read a larger number than perhaps we remember), narrative pace is a primary consideration. Even Henry James, who is deeply concerned with the alarming discrepancies between the outer looks of gracious living and 'the real thing', concerned himself first and foremost with human relationships and the subtle ways in which they change over time. But the art of story-telling is there, too, paring excess in description, number of characters, sub-plotting, and language; reminding us that the short-story genre is a respectable printed (rather than an oral) tradition, with conventions agreed upon by authors, editors, and reading-public, all of them firmly in place by the final quarter of the century; and producing fictions of excellence in prodigal number. Victorian story-tellers believed that their public wanted a shaped fiction with beginning, middle, and end. As the century waned, the emphasis of fiction writers on easy moral resolutions or happy endings correspondingly lightened; and the profoundly disturbing ethical questions raised by Kipling, Conrad, and James came dressed in more complex narrative forms. But the readers of short fiction in periodicals (which began as the major market for this genre, and remained so for more than a century) wanted – and got – a strong story-line, a pleasurable reading experience, and a heightened awareness of time and place. Only a very few genres, in the entire history of English literature, have been so popular, or earned the confidence of the reading public as successfully.

Moreover, the influence on modern short stories exerted by the thousands of short stories printed in *St James's, Belgravia, Household Words, All the Year Round, Blackwoods, Cornhill, Temple*

Bar, Tinsley's, The Strand, and literally hundreds of weeklies, monthlies, and quarterlies, as well as newspapers and literary annuals, has yet to be measured authoritatively. James Joyce's *Dubliners*, as one instance, is essentially a set of stories written to illustrate a single mood (the general paralysis of life in Ireland's capital), and in its moral earnestness as well as its structured form looks backward to the Victorian Age much more than practically all historians of the genre have understood. The sardonic wit of a typical story by 'Saki' (H.H. Monro) is not too far in its technique or its mood of disenchantment from the comic sketches of Jerrold, Hood, and Thackeray. The emphasis on the point of view of a disinterested bystander, attributed by many critics to Henry James (who himself lived by far the greater part of his life as a Victorian), has precedents in many of the short stories of Anthony Trollope and, for that matter, Charles Dickens in several of his late short stories. It is quite clear that the texturing of modern ghost stories – those written in this century – owes almost everything to the ghost stories written in the nineteenth century; those who praise Kipling's ghost stories of 'the mature period' need to be reminded of the splendid ghost stories he wrote between 1886 and 1901 (Kipling was born in 1865). The majority of English detective stories written since the Great War of 1914–18, and those which have the most enthusiastic following to this day, are basically Victorian in their temperament; that is to say, their model is Sherlock Holmes and they subscribe to the values of late nineteenth-century civilization. And one may reasonably ask whether modern short stories dealing with relationships between male and female sexes pose more shrewd questions than those raised in the narratives of Thomas Hardy, 'George Egerton', and George Gissing reprinted here. The Victorian short story has left us a marvellously rich legacy, and we may rejoice at the completeness of its triumph as a literary genre in the closing decades of the nineteenth century.

1986   Harold Orel

Douglas Jerrold

KIND COUSIN TOM

Poor Jack Martin! Nay, we do him grievous wrong – for he was not poor; but rich, imperial, in his simple honesty. He wanted – excellent want! – a sense of poverty. He wore a whole coat – had rarely a fracture in his shoe – slept under a roof of nights, and could sometime boast of five shillings in his pocket. Hence, Jack – ignorant Jack! – never dreamt of any worldly difference between himself and Tom Martin; his prosperous, and most ambitious cousin. 'God bless you! he didn't see me,' Jack would say to a companion, when having nodded, with a twinkling eye to Tom, the nod was unreturned, Tom quickening his pace, and looking into the sky, to avoid his pauper cousin. 'Depend on't he never saw me – bless you! – one of the best fellows in the world; always so pleased to see me.' And such was Jack's innocent belief: he could not understand that Tom – his old schoolfellow, his blood relation Tom – took any glory to himself from the seven hundred a-year, and the very genteel acquaintance acquired by the grace of such an income, to the disadvantage of cousin Jack – good-tempered, merry-hearted Jack; who, we may observe, defied fortune with seventy-five pounds per annum; terrible odds; the more especially, when increased by the addition of one wife and two children. Jack enjoyed – may we say as much – a small clerkship, and seemed one of the many whom fortune forgets either for good or evil. Years and years passed, and Jack Martin was only a poor clerk.

Tom Martin was not to be so overlooked. He attacked fortune with a boldness, a laughing confidence, which, when successful, is considered the certain evidence of genius: if it fail, it is rashness, ignorance, gross presumption. Jack and Tom started in life from the same point: Jack crept a step or two and then stuck fast: whilst Tom took ogre's strides into the pleasant places of the world. At times they met, or rather passed each other; nothing inducing Jack to suspect that there was the slightest distinction between them – that Tom, except from a growing defect of vision, could have failed to see him. 'Poor fellow! he always used to be dim-sighted,' Jack would say; 'but bless me! how very fast he walks. Capital fellow, cousin Tom – always very fond of me.'

It was, in truth, an annoyance to Tom, that his extraordinary position in the world – his increasing reputation in the market, was wholly unacknowledged by his vulgar cousin Jack; who saw cousin Tom – and would have seen only cousin Tom, had he been clothed in cloth of gold, and dubbed a knight. There was the same laugh – the same gripe of the hand – when Tom found impossible to avoid the grasp – the same kind salutation as in former years. Tom, when confronted by Jack, seemed humiliated by his very heartiness: his robust welcome awoke a recollection of former annoyance. Jack rose before the prosperous Tom the ghost of departed poverty.

'What an excellent fellow, is my cousin Tom!' said Jack, warm from one of these meetings, to a brother clerk – a fellow vassal – in the office of Smith and Smith.

'What's he done, Jack?' asked his friend.

'Oh, he's done nothing,' replied Jack; 'but he's a fine fellow! So anxious about me.'

'Well, I am happy to hear it. I suppose he promises something, then?'

'Not at all; but he has given me capital advice. Tom was always fond of me.'

'Advice? And shall you take it, eh, Jack?' asked his companion.

'I can't say I shall; but, poor fellow! he meant it well – a good-hearted creature! I'll tell you all about it. You see this morning, as I was going along Cheapside, I met Tom between Alderman Poger and Snarl the common-councilman. 'What! cousin Tom,' says I, and caught hold of his hand – 'how are you? How are you, cousin Tom?' "

'And what said the alderman and'——

'Oh, they nodded and laughed to Tom, and no doubt, thinking I'd something particular to say to my cousin, they dropped his arm, and walked on.'

'And was your cousin,' asked Jack's friend drily, 'very much pleased at the meeting?'

'To be sure he was – hav'n't I told you, Tom was always so fond of me?'

'Well, and his advice?'

'Why, he asked me to walk down Gutter-lane with him; and when we had gone a little way, he stopped, and looking at me in his kind, good way, he said, "Cousin John," ' —

'John!'

' "Say Jack," says I, ' "cousin Tom – no John between relations – Jack as always." – "Jack," says he, "what's your present salary?" – "Now ninety pounds a-year," says I. "It's very little," says he, and I couldn't deny it; "very little for a man of your talents." – "Why," says I, "not to say much about talents, I've known greater fools get a good deal more; but never mind that." – "And you've a wife and two children?" says he. "Ha! you've never come and taken a bit with us," says I, "as you promised: cousin Sally would be so happy" – "Well, I will come," says he; "but now to business. A wife and two children," says he. "Between you and me,' says I, "there's flannel wanted for a third." – "It's a great pity," says he. "Can't be helped," says I. "However," says Tom, "this makes the matter more urgent. Cousin Jack, you're wasting your abilities in England – you are, indeed," and, poor fellow, he seemed quite concerned as he spoke. "What would you have me do, then?" says I. "Do!" says he, "why, I wouldn't have you stop another week in London! If you want to be a man – they're the words of a friend, Jack," – and here he squeezed my hand quite like a brother, – "go to New Zealand: there's no place like it – four harvests a-year and no taxes – good-bye! but *do go* to New Zealand." '

Cousin Tom, in his benevolent condescension, had frequently promised to dine with cousin Jack, and, as Jack himself would insist upon calling her, cousin Sally. Twice had Tom named the day – twice had Jack mortgaged something of the comforts of the ensuing six days, that he might make the Sunday banquet more worthy of the patronage of Tom. Twice had cousin Sally – a plain, homely little woman – been thrown into a fluster by the promised advent of the important cousin Tom. More: Tom had been promised by Jack to the children as a most especial treat, and the little ones counted the days and then the hours for the arrival of

Douglas Jerrold

the mysterious, the wonderful cousin Tom.

'Bless, my heart, Sally!' cried cousin Jack, as the church clock, struck two, 'I hope nothing has happened to dear cousin Tom.'

'Happened to him,' cried cousin Sally, with lowering discontent, and an expressive look at a shoulder of mutton dished and soddening before the fire; whilst covered plates upon the hobs gave token of turnip-tops and dumplings – 'what should happen to him?'

'He couldn't have mistaken me – I'm sure I said one o'clock,' observed Jack, looking anxiously towards the window, where his two children, with noses flattened against the panes, were watching for cousin Tom.

'This is the third time he has made a fool of us,' exclaimed cousin Sally.

'Don't talk in that way, Sally; if he don't come now, something must have happened to him. He promised to come, and he's so fond of me! An excellent creature, cousin Tom.'

'The mutton's rags,' said cousin Sally, frowning on the seething joint.

'Always a man of his word,' said the husband.

'Turnip-tops not worth a farthing,' continued cousin Sally.

'Little forgetful, but has a heart of gold.'

'Dumplings like lead.'

'Here's cousin!' lisped one of the children, 'cousin Tom!'

'No, it isn't,' said the elder, ' 'tis only a funeral.'

For the third time, cousin Tom disappointed the hopes of the too sanguine Jack. In justice, however, to Tom, we must state that his promises to dine were rather inferred by Jack, than seriously made by the prosperous cousin.

'Tomorrow's Sunday,' Jack has cried, suddenly coming upon the unguarded Tom, at the time in high conversation with very genteel acquaintance; 'you must come – one o'clock – plain living you know – mutton and dumplings – you always liked dumplings – say you *will* come.'

On this, Tom, like Hotspur, 'all smarting' would make answer, he 'would', or 'would not', which answer Jack, in his gladness, immediately received as a serious pledge; and for this reason – a reason only discoverable by himself – 'Cousin Tom was so fond of him.'

Cousin Tom yearned for high connexions. Having fairly sweated to achieve the honour, cousin Tom was become a member of a small club. For many days he had hung upon the looks of the Honourable Alexander Mulington, a gentleman of somewhat confined means, and limited understanding. Happy moment! At precisely five minutes past one o'clock, on the first of April, 18 –, the hand of cousin Tom was for the first time suffered to grasp the two outstretched fingers of the Honourable Alexander Mulington. We are thus scrupulous as to the time, as it was the most important in Tom's existence. As the great Danish sculptor once called his birth-day, that day on which he first entered Rome, so did Tom only begin to live from the squeeze permitted to him by the benignant Mulington!

The day was Sunday – a May Sunday; and the friendship of Tom and his Honourable friend had become more glowing with the season. What could have brought the Honourable Alexander Mulington into the northern suburbs, we cannot guess; let it suffice, he was somewhere in Camden-town; and wandering in that unknown region was suddenly encountered by cousin Tom. We shall not chronicle all the discourse that ensued upon the meeting; however, we may state that Tom ventured to call his Honourable friend 'a devil of a fellow', Mulington smiling a mute confession to the charge. Moreover, an elderly spinster, passing, with a large Prayer-book, cast a withering look at the two friends, one of whom was at the time laughing very irreverently, whilst the other, as it seemed to the lady, incoherently exclaimed, 'D – d fine, – d – d fine, – quite an angel.'

Thus stood the friends, and thus, soul communing with soul, they laughed away the moments, when suddenly cousin Tom was roused to the gross events of wayfaring life by a most vehement slap on the shoulder. Quick as thought he turned, and – oh, shame! – oh, horror! – oh, death to his new-born friendship with the Honourable Alexander Mulington! – there stood cousin Jack, all his good-natured face melting with a smile, his right hand outstretched, while his left fore-finger pointed gracefully and significantly down to his feet, where in a red dish smoked a breast of veal, that moment from the baker's — a breast of veal hissing and bubbling on a bed of brown potatoes!

'I knew you'd come — I told Sally there must have been a mistake. She said it was pride — but la! I knew you'd drop in upon us and take pot-luck — come along — bring your friend with you — there'll be quite enough — and you'll be welcome, sir, as the flowers in May. Here, Tommy,' and cousin Jack turned to his eldest son, a plump urchin of seven years old, glistening in a white pinafore, and carrying in his two hands a mug of porter — 'Cousin Tom,' and Jacked smiled again as he displayed the boy, 'you know he's your namesake; I christened him after you, because I knew you were always so very fond of me. Here, Tommy, run to the Coach-and-Horses, and tell 'em to send home another pot of beer — in their own pot — mother won't mind the halfpenny — and, now, cousin Tom, if you and your friend will just follow me down that court'—

The despairing artist feeling that the passion of his heroine defied his skill, modestly yet cunningly hung a veil before her. A like difficulty suggests to us a like escape. We shall not attempt to describe the agony of cousin Tom — the tortures of the moment. Talk of the punishment of the brazen bull; what was it to the horrors of that breast of veal? We will not linger on the theme; but simply assure the reader that neither Tom, nor his friend, the Honourable Alexander Mulington, dined with cousin Jack. We have, however, to record another painful incident arising from this ill-timed hospitality. After many struggles, cousin Tom was compelled to quit the club; for a month he wrestled with his destiny; but it was too much for the nerves of a stoic that his appearance should be the inevitable signal to divers members to commence an earnest inquiry of the waiters if there was in the house a breast of veal, with particular and most significant queries, touching — baked potatoes.

How cousin Jack was anathematised by cousin Tom!

A year or two passed away, and cousin Tom fell in love; it was prudent in him to have an intense affection for Dorothea Sybil-witz, the only child of a German baron, who, philosophically regardless of the evanescent advantages of nobility, devoted his many days to the vending of a certain precious ointment made patent by the state. The daughter of the medicinal philosopher had a dowry of twenty thousand pounds; she had, moreover, a very proper notion of the delightful privileges of worldly station. She was a mere woman, and was not content to sink the nobility inherited from her father in her father's gallipots. Hence, Dorothea Sybilwitz, as the phrase runs, looked high. How it happened, let Cupid answer; but certain it is, that with all these aspirations, Dorothea fell in love with cousin Tom. It was true – she reasoned with herself – he had no high relations to recommend him; but then, upon his own showing, he had no poor, beggarly connexions to cast a shadow on her golden fortunes. It was thus Dorothea compromised between her love of nobility and her love of cousin Tom. Rank was, after all, an abstract idea; whereas cousin Tom was really a tall, well-made young fellow, with very tantalising whiskers. The match was settled – Dorothea Sybilwitz was the affianced bride of cousin Tom.

What a lovely day was the Derby day of —! Cousin Tom, within one month of his coming marriage with Dorothea Sybilwitz, with his bride and two female friends, took the road to Epsom. There never was such a delightful day: even the confusion that now and then occurred upon the way served to give a whet, a zest, to the pleasure of the scene. A thousand and a thousand vehicles lined the road. Cousin Tom was all attention, and Dorothea Sybilwitz was all bliss, when suddenly a voice roared above the hubbub, – 'Tom, Tom – cousin, Tom, I say,' and Tom casting his eyes down, beheld in a low spring-cart, drawn by a pony, something less than a Newfoundland dog, the smiling, happy cousin Jack! 'How are you, cousin Tom? – here we are, you see – here's Sally – and here's the two boys – and here's baby – couldn't leave baby behind, you know – and here's Mr and Mrs Simcox, all neighbours and friends – beautiful pony that – small; but I'll bet you a bottle of ginger beer that he keeps up with you all the way.'

Cousin Tom's face became yellow as his glove, and Miss Dorothea Sybilwitz with ashy lips, and terrible eyes, said mutteringly, 'Cousin! Cousin!' Cousin Tom said nothing; but cousin Jack was resolved to be seen, because he knew cousin Tom was so fond of him.

'Tom, cousin Tom,' he cried, 'here's Sarah! Don't you know your cousin Sarah?' and the husband with a look of triumph pulled the coat of cousin Tom, compelling him to glance at cousin Sarah, at the time in a coarse straw bonnet and cotton shawl, suckling her last-born. 'So you're going to be married, Tom are you? – I heard something of it – well, I wish you joy – and I wish you joy, ma'am, for I can see by your blushing and biting your lips, that' —

To the inexpressible relief of cousin Tom, the postillions cut out of the line and distanced the pony-chaise; hence, cousin Jack could see no more. Miss Dorothea Sybilwitz had, however, learned the existence of a horribly poor, and therefore horribly low cousin, and Dorothea smiled not again that day.

Early the next morning – even while cousin Jack was at his breakfast – cousin Tom, threading the intricacies of the Brill, Camden Town, presented himself at the humble dwelling of the poor lawyer's clerk. 'I knew some day you'd come to see me – I was sure you would,' cried joyous cousin Jack; 'because, though you are a little better off than I am, still I knew that could make no difference to you; no, no, I knew you were still very fond of me.'

In many words cousin Tom told the purpose of his errand. He thought the situation held by cousin Jack was far beneath his talents; and therefore, as he would not go abroad, if he would consent to retire into Wales, he and his family should be amply provided for by cousin Tom. This was the offer, recommended by all the arts of language at the command of the visitor.

'God bless you, Tom!' cried Jack, 'you have a heart indeed; you always were so kind to me. What I get is, to be sure, little enough for Sarah and – and – and they're nice little things, ar'n't they?' said Jack, in a tender voice, averting his head, and pointing to his children.

'Beautiful babes!' cried cousin Tom, taking one upon his knee, and trying to smile upon it. 'But what say you to my offer, Jack?'

'I say, God bless you – but I can't take it – no, I can't. Though as a poor clerk, I write my hand down to the stump, I can't eat the bread of obligation.'

And on this point cousin Jack was resolute; and cousin Tom, with a perplexed and angry face, quitted the house.

Misfortunes suddenly fell upon cousin Jack; for that day week he was discharged from his office. This was the more strange, as it was only two days before, that Smith and Smith, his employers, were splendidly entertained at the table of cousin Tom. Poor cousin Jack owed two or three debts; the creditors became clamorous – he could obtain no new employment; to make things worse, two of the children sickened, as it was thought, for the measles.

With an aching heart and a pale brow, cousin Jack knocked at the door of cousin Tom.

'God bless you, Tom,' he cried, 'it would be a long story to tell you what I've suffered for this fortnight past. Ha! you are a friend indeed – but I must take your offer – I will go, and for the sake of others, end my days in Wales. May God bless you,' and the tears ran down Jack's face, 'for your kindness to me!'

In six days cousin Jack and his family were buried amidst the mountains of North Wales; and Miss Dorothea Sybilwitz consented to bear the name of Cousin Tom; whose kindness for Jack was still further enhanced by an offer, that, when the boys should be old enough, he would place them very eligibly at sea.

Cousin Jack still lives in Wales; still enjoys his forty pounds a year from cousin Tom.

'That makes the fourth ten this year,' said cousin Tom, as he despatched the note, the last quarter's allowance to his cousin, 'the fourth ten —, d—n him!'

And all the world cries, 'How good is cousin Tom to cousin Jack – how kind is he to his poor relation!'

And the unsuspecting Jack, amidst the mountains quaffs his cup of small ale, and, to applauding neighbours, tells the virtues of his relative, and still the close of his eulogy is, 'Here's cousin Tom's health! Yes, cousin Tom was always so fond of me!'

MY MAIDEN BRIEF

Late on a certain May morning, as I was sitting at a modest breakfast in my 'residence chambers', Pump Court, Temple, my attention was claimed by a single knock at an outer door, common to the chambers of Felix Polter, and of myself, Horace Penditton, both barristers-at-law of the Inner Temple.

The outer door was not the only article common to Polter and myself. We also shared what Polter (who wrote farces) was pleased to term a 'property' clerk, who did nothing at all, and a 'practicable' laundress, who did everything. There existed also a communion of interest in tea-cups, razors, gridirons, candlesticks, etc.; for although neither of us was particularly well supplied with the necessities of domestic life, each happened to possess the very articles in which the other was deficient. So we got on uncommonly well together, each regarding his friend in the light of an indispensable other self. We had both embraced the 'higher walk' of the legal profession, and were patiently waiting for the legal profession to embrace us.

The single knock raised some well-founded apprehensions in both our minds.

'Walker!' said I to the property clerk.

'Sir!'

'If that knock is for me, I'm out, you know.'

'Of course, sir!'

'And Walker!' cried Polter.

'Sir!'

'If it's for me, I'm not at home!'

Polter always rejoiced if he could manage to make the conversation partake of a Maddisonian Mortonic character.

Mr Walker opened the door. 'Mr Penditton's a-breakfasting with the Master of the Rolls, if it's him you want; and if it isn't, Mr Polter's with the Attorney-General.'

'You don't say so!' remarked the visitor; 'then p'raps you'll give this to Mr Penditton, as soon as the Master can make up his mind to part with him.'

And so saying, he handed to Walker a lovely parcel of brief-paper, tied up neatly with a piece of red tape, and minuted –

'Central Criminal Court, May Sessions, 1860. – The Queen on the prosecution of Ann Back *v.* Elizabeth Briggs. Brief for the prisoner. Mr Penditton, one guinea. – Poddle and Shaddery, Hans Place.'

So it had come at last! Only an Old Bailey brief, it is true; but still a brief. We scarcely knew what to make of it. Polter looked at me, and I looked at Polter, and then we both looked at the brief.

It turned out to be a charge against Elizabeth Briggs, widow, of picking pockets in an omnibus. It appeared from my 'instructions' that my client was an elderly lady, and religious. On the 2nd April then last she entered an Islington omnibus, with the view of attending a tea and prayer meeting in Bell Court, Islington. A woman in the omnibus missed her purse, and accused Mrs Briggs, who sat on her right, of having stolen it. The poor soul, speechless with horror at the charge, was dragged out of the omnibus, and as the purse was found in a pocket on the left-hand side of her dress, she was given into custody. As it was stated by the police that she had been 'in trouble' before, the infatuated magistrate who examined her committed her for trial.

'There, my boy, your fortune's made!' said Polter.

'But I don't see the use of my taking it,' said I; 'there's nothing to be said for her.'

'Not take it? Won't you, though? I'll see about that. You *shall* take it, and you shall get her off, too! Highly respectable old lady – attentive member of well-known congregation – parson to speak to her character, no doubt. As honest as you are!'

'But the purse was found upon her!'

'Well, sir, and what of that? Poor woman left-handed, and pocket in left of dress. Robbed woman right-handed, and pocket in right of dress. Poor woman sat on right of robbed woman. Robbed woman, replacing her purse, slipped it accidentally into poor woman's pocket. Ample folds of dress, you know – crino-lines overlapping, and all that. Splendid defence for you!'

'Well, but she's an old hand, it seems. The police know her.'

'Police always do. "Always know everybody" – police maxim. Swear anything, they will.'

Polter really seemed so sanguine about it that I began to look at the case hopefully, and to think that something might be done with it. He talked to me to such effect that he not only convinced me that there was a good deal to be said in Mrs Briggs's favour, but I actually began to look upon her as an innocent victim of circumstantial evidence, and determined that no effort should be wanting on my part to procure her release from a degrading but unmerited confinement.

Of the firm of Poddle and Shaddery I knew nothing whatever, and how they came to entrust Mrs Briggs's case to me I can form no conception. As we (for Polter took so deep a personal interest in the success of Mrs Briggs's case that he completely identified himself, in my mind, with her fallen fortunes) resolved to go to work in a thoroughly businesslike manner, we determined to commence operations by searching for the firm of Poddle and Shaddery in the *Law List*. To our dismay the *Law List* of that year had no record of Poddle, neither did Shaddery find a place in its pages. This was serious, and Polter did not improve matters by suddenly recollecting that he had once heard an old Q.C. say that, as a rule, the farther west of Temple Bar, the shadier the attorney; so that assuming Polter's friend to have come to a correct conclusion on this point, a firm dating officially from Hans Place, and whose name did not appear in Mr Dalbiac's *Law List*, was a legitimate object of suspicion. But Polter, who took a hopeful view of anything which he thought might lead to good farce 'situations', and who probably imagined that my first appearance on any stage as counsel for the defence was likely to be rich in suggestions, remarked that they might possibly have been certificated since the publication of the last *Law List;* and as for the *dictum* about Temple Bar, why, the case of Poddle and Shaddery might be one of those very exceptions whose existence is necessary to the proof of every general rule. So Polter and I determined to treat the firm in a spirit of charity, and accept their brief.

As the May sessions of Oyer and Terminer did not commence until the 8th, I had four clear days in which to study my brief and prepare my defence. Besides, there was a murder case, and a desperate burglary or two, which would probably be taken first, so that it was unlikely that the case of the poor soul whose cause I had espoused would be tried before the 12th. So I had plenty of time to master what Polter and I agreed was one of the most painful cases of circumstantial evidence ever submitted to a British jury; and I really believe that, by the first day of the May sessions, I was intimately acquainted with the details of every case of pocket-picking reported in *Cox's Criminal Cases* and *Buckler's Short-hand Reports*.

On the night of the 11th I asked Bodger of Brazenose, Norton of Gray's Inn, Cadbury of the Lancers, and three or four other men, college chums principally, to drop in at Pump Court, and hear a rehearsal of my speech for the defence, in the forthcoming *cause célèbre* of the Queen on the prosecution of Ann Back *v*. Elizabeth Briggs. At nine o'clock they began to appear, and by ten all were assembled. Pipes and strong waters were produced, and Norton of Gray's was forthwith raised to the Bench by the style and dignity of Sir Joseph Norton, one of the barons of her Majesty's Court of Exchequer; Cadbury, Bodger, and another represented the jury; Wilkinson of Lincoln's Inn was counsel for the prosecution, Polter was clerk of arraigns, and Walker, my clerk, was the prosecutrix.

Everything went satisfactorily: Wilkinson broke down in his speech for the prosecution; his witness prevaricated and contradicted himself in a preposterous manner; and my speech for the defence was voted to be one of the most masterly specimens of forensic ingenuity that had ever come before the notice of the court; and the consequence was, that the prisoner (inadequately represented by a statuette of the Greek Slave) was discharged, and Norton (who would have looked more like a Baron of the Exchequer if he had looked less like a tipsy churchwarden) remarked that she left the court without a stain upon her character.

The court then adjourned for refreshment, and the conversation took a general turn, after canvassing the respective merits of 'May it please your ludship,' and 'May it please you, my lud,' as an introduction to a counsel's speech – a discussion which terminated in favour of the latter form, as being a trifle more independent in its character. I remember proposing that the health of Elizabeth Briggs should be drunk in a solemn and respectful bumper; and as the evening wore on, I am afraid I became exceedingly indignant with Cadbury because he had taken the liberty of holding up to public ridicule an imaginary (and highly undignified) *carte de visite* of my unfortunate client.

The 12th May, big with the fate of Penditton and of Briggs, dawned in the usual manner. At ten o'clock Polter and I drove up in wigs and gowns to the Old Bailey; as well because we kept those imposing garments at our chambers, not having any use for them elsewhere, as to impress passers-by, and the loungers below the court, with a conviction that we were not merely Old Bailey counsel, but had come down from our usual sphere of action at Westminster, to conduct a case of more than ordinary complication. Impressed with a sense of the propriety of presenting an accurate professional appearance, I had taken remarkable pains with my toilette. I had the previous morning shaved off a flourishing moustache, and sent Walker out for half-a-dozen serious collars, as substitutes for the unprofessional 'lay-downs' I usually wore. I was dressed in a correct evening suit, and wore a pair of thin gold spectacles, and Polter remarked, that I looked the sucking bencher to the life. Polter, whose interest in the accuracy of my 'get up' was almost fatherly, had totally neglected his own; and he made his appearance in the raggedest of beards and moustaches under his wig, and the sloppiest of cheap drab lounging-coats under his gown.

I modestly took my place in the back row of the seats allotted to the bar; Polter took his in the very front, in order to have an opportunity, at the close of the case, of telling the leading counsel in the hearing of the attorneys, the name and address of the young and rising barrister who had just electrified the court. In various parts of the building I detected Cadbury, Wilkinson, and others, who had represented judge, jury, and counsel, on the previous evening. They had been instructed by Polter (who had had some experience in 'packing' a house) to distribute themselves about the court, and, at the termination of the speech for the defence, to give vent to their feelings in that applause which is always so quickly suppressed by the officers of a court of justice. I was rather annoyed at this, as I did not consider it altogether legitimate; and my annoyance was immensely increased when I found that my three elderly maiden aunts, to whom I had been foolish enough to confide the fact of my having to appear on the 12th, were seated in state in that portion of the court allotted to friends of the bench and bar, and busied themselves by informing everybody within whisper-shot, that I was to defend Elizabeth Briggs, and that this was my first brief. It was some little consolation, however, to find that the unceremonious manner in which the facts of the cases that preceded mine were explained and commented upon by judge, jury, and counsel, caused those ladies great uneasiness, and indeed compelled them, on one or two occasions, to beat an unceremonious retreat.

At length the clerk of arraigns called the case of Briggs, and with my heart in my mouth I began to try to recollect the opening words of my speech for the defence, but I was interrupted in that hopeless task by the appearance of Elizabeth in the dock.

She was a pale, elderly widow, rather buxom, and remarkably neatly dressed, in slightly rusty mourning. Her hair was arranged in two sausage curls, one on each side of her head, and looped in two festoons over the forehead. She appeared to feel her position acutely, and although she did not weep, her red eyes showed evident traces of recent tears. She grasped the edge of the dock and rocked backwards and forwards, accompanying the motion with a low moaning sound, that was extremely touching. Polter looked back at me with an expression which plainly said, 'If ever an innocent woman appeared in that dock, that woman is Elizabeth Briggs!'

The clerk of arraigns now proceeded to charge the jury. 'Gentlemen of the jury, the prisoner at the bar, Elizabeth Briggs, is indicted for that she did, on the 2nd April last, steal from the person of Ann Back a purse containing ten shillings and four-pence, the moneys of the said Ann Back. There is another count to the indictment, charging her with having received the same, knowing it to have been stolen. To both of these counts the prisoner has pleaded "Not guilty", and it is your charge to try whether she is guilty or not guilty.' Then to the bar, 'Who appears in this case?'

Nobody replying in behalf of the crown, I rose and remarked that I appeared for the defence.

A counsel here said that he believed the brief for the prosecution was entrusted to Mr Porter, but that that gentleman was engaged at the Middlesex Sessions, in a case which was likely to occupy several hours, and that he (Mr Porter) did not expect that Briggs's case would come on that day.

A consulation then took place between the judge and the clerk of arraigns. At its termination, the latter functionary said, 'Who is the junior counsel present?'

To my horror, up jumped Polter, and said, 'I think it's very likely that I am the junior counsel in court. My name is Polter, and I was only called last term!'

A titter ran through the crowd, but Polter, whose least fault was bashfulness, only smiled benignly at those around him.

Another whispering between judge and clerk. At its conclusion, the clerk handed a bundle of papers to Polter, saying, at the same time.

'Mr Polter, his lordship wishes you to conduct the prosecution.'

'Certainly,' said Polter; and he opened the papers, glanced at them, and rose to address the court.

He began by requesting that the jury would take into consideration the fact that he had only that moment been placed in possession of the brief for the prosecution of the prisoner at the bar, who appeared, from what he could gather from a glance at his instructions, to have been guilty of as heartless a robbery as ever disgraced humanity. He would endeavour to do his duty, but he feared that, at so short a notice, he should scarcely be able to do justice to the brief with which he had been most unexpectedly entrusted. He then went on to state the case in masterly manner, appearing to gather the facts, with which, of course, he was perfectly intimate, from the papers in his hand. He commented on the growing frequency of omnibus robberies, and then went on to say: —

'Gentlemen, I am at no loss to anticipate the defence on which my learned friend will base his hope of inducing you to acquit that wretched woman. I don't know whether it has ever been your misfortune to try criminal cases before, but if it has, you will be able to anticipate his defence as certainly as I can. He will probably tell you, because the purse was found in the left-hand pocket of that miserable woman's dress, that she is left-handed, and on that account wears her pocket on the left side, and he will then, if I am not very much mistaken, ask the prosecutrix if she is not right-handed, and, lastly, he will ask you to believe that the prosecutrix, sitting on the prisoner's left, slipped the purse accidentally into the prisoner's pocket. But, gentlemen, I need not remind you that the facts of these omnibus robberies are always identical. The prisoner always *is* left-handed, the prosecutrix always *is* right-handed, and the prosecutrix always *does* slip the purse accidentally into the prisoner's pocket, instead of her own. My lord will tell you that this is so, and you will know how much faith to place upon such a defence, should my friend think proper to set it up.' He ended by entreating the jury to give the case their attentive consideration, and stated that he relied confidently on an immediate verdict of 'Guilty'. He then sat down, saying to the usher, 'Call Ann Back.'

Ann Back, who was in court, shuffled up into the witness-box and was duly sworn. Polter then drew out her evidence bit by bit, helping her with leading questions of the most flagrant description. I knew that I ought not to allow this, but I was too horrified at the turn matters had taken to interfere. At the conclusion of the examination in chief Polter sat down triumphantly, and I rose to cross-examine.

'You are right-handed, Mrs Back?' (*Laughter.*)

'Oh, yes, sir!'

'Very good. I've nothing else to ask you.'

So Mrs Back stood down, and the omnibus conductor took place. His evidence was not material, and I declined to cross-examine. The policeman who had charge of the case followed the conductor, and his evidence was to the effect that the purse was found in her pocket.

I felt that this witness ought to be cross-examined, but not having anything ready, I allowed him to stand down. A question, I am sorry to say, then occurred to me, and I requested his lordship to allow the witness to be recalled.

'You say you found the purse in her pocket, my man?'

'Yes, sir.'

'Did you find anything else?'

'Yes, sir.'

'What?'

'Two other purses, a watch with the bow broken, three hand-kerchiefs, two silver pencil-cases, and a hymn-book.' (*Roars of laughter.*)

'You may stand down.'

'That is the case, my lord,' said Polter.

It was now my turn to address the court. What could I say? I believe I observed that, undeterred by my learned friend's opening speech, I *did* intend to set up the defence he had anticipated. I set it up, but I don't think it did much good. The jury, who were perfectly well aware that this was Polter's first case, had no idea but that I was an old hand at it; and no doubt thought me an uncommonly clumsy one. They had made every allowance for Polter, who needed nothing of the kind, and they made none at all for me, who needed all they had at their disposal. I soon relin-quished my original line of defence, and endeavoured to influence the jury by vehement assertions of my personal conviction of the prisoner's innocence. I warmed with my subject, for Polter had not anticipated me here, and I believe I grew really eloquent. I think I staked my professional reputation on her innocence, and I sat down expressing my confidence in a verdict that would restore the unfortunate lady to a circle of private friends, several of whom were waiting in the court below to testify to her excellent charac-ter.

'Call witnesses to Mrs Briggs's character,' said I.

'Witness to the character of Briggs!' shouted the crier.

The cry was repeated three or four times outside the court; but there was no response.

'No witnesses to Briggs's character here, my lord!' said the crier.

Of course I knew this very well; but it sounded respectable to expect them.

'Dear, dear,' said I, 'this is really most unfortunate. They must have mistaken the day.'

'Shouldn't wonder,' observed Polter, rather drily.

I was not altogether sorry that I had no witnesses to adduce, as I am afraid that they would scarcely have borne the test of Polter's cross-examination. Besides, if I had examined witnesses for the defence, Polter would have been entitled to a reply, of which privilege he would, I was sure, avail himself.

Mr Baron Bounderby proceeded to sum up, grossly against the prisoner, as I then thought, but, as I have since had reason to believe, most impartially. He went carefully over the evidence, and told the jury that if they believed the witnesses for the prosecution, they should find the prisoner guilty, and if they did not – why, they should acquit her. The jury were then directed by the crier to 'consider their verdict', which they couldn't possibly have done, for they immediately returned a verdict of 'Guilty'. The prisoner not having anything to say in arrest of judgment, the learned judge proceeded to pronounce sentence – enquiring, first of all, whether anything was known about her?

A policeman stepped forward, and stated that she had been twice convicted at this court of felony, and once at the Middlesex Court.

Mr Baron Bounderby, addressing the prisoner, told her that she had been most properly convicted, on the clearest possible evidence; that she was an accomplished thief, and a most dangerous one; and that the sentence of the court was that she be imprisoned and kept to hard labour for the space of eighteen calendar months.

No sooner had the learned judge pronounced this sentence than the poor soul stooped down, and taking off a heavy boot, flung it at my head, as a reward for my eloquence on her behalf; accompanying the assault with a torrent of invective against my abilities as a counsel, and my line of defence. The language in which her oration was couched was perfectly shocking. The boot missed me, but hit a reporter on the head, and to this fact I am disposed to attribute the unfavourable light in which my speech for the defence was placed in two or three of the leading daily papers next morning. I hurried out of court as quickly as I could, and, hailing a Hansom, I dashed back to chambers, pitched my wig at a bust of Lord Brougham, bowled over Mrs Briggs's prototype with my gown, packed up, and started that evening for the west coast of Cornwall. Polter, on the other hand, remained in town, and got plenty of business in that and the ensuing session, and afterwards on circuit. He is now a flourishing Old Bailey counsel, while I am as briefless as ever.

Charles Dickens

GEORGE SILVERMAN'S EXPLANATION

FIRST CHAPTER

It happened in this wise:

– But, sitting with my pen in my hand looking at those words again, without descrying any hint in them of the words that should follow, it comes into my mind that they have an abrupt appearance. They may serve, however, if I let them remain, to suggest how very difficult I find it to begin to explain my Explanation. An uncouth phrase: and yet I do not see my way to a better.

SECOND CHAPTER

It happened in *this* wise:

– But, looking at those words, and comparing them with my former opening, I find they are the selfsame words repeated. This is the more surprising to me, because I employ them in quite a new connection. For indeed I declare that my intention was to discard the commencement I first had in my thoughts, and to give the preference to another of an entirely different nature, dating my explanation from an anterior period of my life. I will make a third trial, without erasing this second failure, protesting that it is not my design to conceal any of my infirmities, whether they be of head or heart.

THIRD CHAPTER

Not as yet directly aiming at how it came to pass, I will come upon it by degrees. The natural manner, after all, for God knows that is how it came upon me!

My parents were in a miserable condition of life, and my infant home was a cellar in Preston. I recollect the sound of Father's Lancashire clogs on the street pavement above, as being different in my young hearing from the sound of all other clogs; and I recollect that, when Mother came down the cellar-steps, I used tremblingly to speculate on her feet having a good or an ill-tempered look, – on her knees – on her waist, – until finally her face came into view and settled the question. From this it will be seen that I was timid, and that the cellar-steps were steep, and that the doorway was very low.

Mother had the gripe and clutch of Poverty upon her face, upon her figure, and not least of all upon her voice. Her sharp and high-pitched words were squeezed out of her, as by the compression of bony fingers on a leathern-bag; and she had a way of rolling her eyes about and about the cellar, as she scolded, that was gaunt and hungry. Father, with his shoulders rounded, would sit quiet on a three-legged stool, looking at the empty grate, until she would pluck the stool from under him, and bid him go bring some money home. Then he would dismally ascend the steps, and I, holding my ragged shirt and trousers together with a hand (my only braces), would feint and dodge from Mother's pursuing grasp at my hair.

A worldly little devil was Mother's usual name for me. Whether I cried for that I was in the dark, or for that it was cold, or for that I was hungry, or whether I squeezed myself into a warm corner when there was a fire, or ate voraciously when there was food, she would still say, 'O you worldly little devil!' And the sting of it was, that I quite well knew myself to be a worldly little devil. Worldly as to wanting to be housed and warmed, worldly as to wanting to be fed, worldly as to the greed with which I inwardly compared how much I got of those good things with how much Father and Mother got, when, rarely, those good things were going.

Sometimes they both went away seeking work, and then I would be locked up in the cellar for a day or two at a time. I was at my worldiest then. Left alone, I yielded myself up to a worldly yearning for enough of anything (except misery), and for the death of Mother's father, who was a machine-maker at Birmingham, and on whose decease, I had heard Mother say, she would come into a whole courtful of houses 'if she had her rights'. Worldly little devil, I would stand about, musingly fitting my cold bare feet into cracked bricks and crevices of the damp cellar floor, – walking over my grandfather's body, so to speak, into the courtful of houses, and selling them for meat and drink, and clothes to wear.

At last a change came down into our cellar. The universal change came down even as low as that, – so will it mount to any height on which a human creature can perch, – and brought other changes with it.

We had a heap of I don't know what foul litter in the darkest corner, which we called 'the bed'. For three days Mother lay upon it without getting up, and then began at times to laugh. If I had ever heard her laugh before, it had been so seldom that the strange sound frightened me. It frightened Father, too, and we took it by turns to give her water. Then she began to move her head from side to side, and sing. After that, she getting no better, Father fell a laughing and a singing, and then there was only I to give them both water, and they both died.

FOURTH CHAPTER

When I was lifted out of the cellar by two men, of whom one came peeping down alone first, and ran away and brought the other, I could hardly bear the light of the street. I was sitting in the roadway, blinking at it, and at a ring of people collected around me, but not close to me, when, true to my character of worldly little devil, I broke silence by saying, 'I am hungry and thirsty!'

'Does he know they are dead?' asked one of another.

'Do you know your father and mother are both dead of fever?' asked a third of me, severely.

'I don't know what it is to be dead. I supposed it meant that, when the cup rattled against their teeth and the water spilt over them. I am hungry and thirsty.' That was all I had to say about it.

The ring of people widened outward from the inner side as I looked around me; and I smelt vinegar, and what I now know to be camphor, thrown in towards where I sat. Presently some one put a great vessel of smoking vinegar on the ground near me, and then they all looked at me in silent horror as I ate and drank of what was brought for me. I knew at the time they had a horror of me, but I couldn't help it.

I was still eating and drinking, and a murmur of discussion had begun to arise respecting what was to be done with me next, when I heard a cracked voice somewhere in the ring say, 'My name is Hawkyard, Mr Verity Hawkyard, of West Bromwich.' Then the ring split in one place, and a yellow-faced, peak-nosed gentleman, clad all in iron-gray to his gaiters, pressed forward with a policeman and another official of some sort. He came forward close to the vessel of smoking vinegar; from which he sprinkled himself carefully, and me copiously.

'He had a grandfather at Birmingham, this young boy, who is just dead too,' said Mr Hawkyard.

I turned my eyes upon the speaker, and said in a ravening manner, 'Where's his houses?'

'Hah! Horrible worldliness on the edge of the grave,' said Mr Hawkyard, casting more of the vinegar over me, as if to get my devil out of me. 'I have undertaken a slight – a ve-ry slight – trust in behalf of this boy; quite a voluntary trust; a matter of mere honour, if not of mere sentiment; still I have taken it upon myself, and it shall be (O yes, it shall be!) discharged.'

The by-standers seemed to form an opinion of this gentleman much more favourable than their opinion of me.

'He shall be taught,' said Mr Hawkyard, '(O yes, he shall be taught!) but what is to be done with him for the present? He may be infected. He may disseminate infection.' The ring widened considerably. 'What is to be done with him?'

He held some talk with the two officials. I could distinguish no word save 'Farm-house'. There was another sound several times repeated, which was wholly meaningless in my ears then, but which I knew soon afterwards to be 'Hoghton Towers'.

'Yes,' said Mr Hawkyard, 'I think that sounds promising. I think that sounds hopeful. And he can be put by himself in a Ward, for a night or two, you say?'

It seemed to be the police-officer who had said so, for it was he who replied, Yes. It was he, too, who finally took me by the arm and walked me before him through the streets, into a whitewashed room in a bare building, where I had a chair to sit in, a table to sit at, an iron bedstead and good mattress to lie upon, and a rug and blanket to cover me. Where I had enough to eat too, and was shown how to clean the tin porringer in which it was conveyed to me, until it was as good as a looking-glass. Here, likewise, I was put in a bath, and had new clothes brought to me, and my old rags were burnt, and I was camphored and vinegared, and disinfected in a variety of ways.

When all this was done, – I don't know in how many days or how few, but it matters not, – Mr Hawkyard stepped in at the door, remaining close to it, and said: 'Go and stand against the opposite wall, George Silverman. As far off as you can. That'll do. How do you feel?

I told him that I didn't feel cold, and didn't feel hungry, and didn't feel thirsty. That was the whole round of human feelings, as far as I knew, except the pain of being beaten.

'Well,' said he, 'you are going, George, to a healthy farm-house to be purified. Keep in the air there, as much as you can. Live an out-of-door life there, until you are fetched away. You had better not say much – in fact, you had better be very careful not to say anything – about what your parents died of, or they might not like to take you in. Behave well, and I'll put you to school, (O yes, I'll put you to school!) though I am not obligated to do it. I am a servant of the Lord, George, and I have been a good servant to him (I have!) these five-and-thirty years. The Lord has had a good servant in me, and he knows it.'

What I then supposed him to mean by this, I cannot imagine. As little do I know when I began to comprehend that he was a prominent member of some obscure denomination or congregation, every member of which held forth to the rest when so inclined, and among whom he was called Brother Hawkyard. It was enough for me to know, on that day in the Ward, that the farmer's cart was waiting for me at the street corner. I was not slow to get into it, for it was the first ride I ever had in my life.

It made me sleepy, and I slept. First, I stared at Preston streets as long as they lasted, and meanwhile I may have had some small dumb wondering within me whereabouts our cellar was. But I doubt it. Such a worldly little devil was I, that I took no thought who would bury Father and Mother, or where they would be buried, or when. The question whether the eating and drinking by day, and the covering by night, would be as good at the farm-house as at the Ward superseded those questions.

The jolting of the cart on a loose stony road awoke me, and I found that we were mounting a steep hill, where the road was a rutty by-road through a field. And so, by fragments of an ancient terrace, and by some rugged out-buildings that had once been fortified, and passing under a ruined gateway, we came to the old farm-house in the thick stone wall outside the old quadrangle of Hoghton Towers. Which I looked at, like a stupid savage; seeing no specialty in; seeing no antiquity in; assuming all farm-houses to resemble it; assigning the decay I noticed to the one potent cause of all ruin that I knew, – Poverty; eyeing the pigeons in their flights, the cattle in their stalls, the ducks in the pond, and the fowls pecking about the yard, with a hungry hope that plenty of them might be killed for dinner while I stayed there; wondering whether the scrubbed dairy vessels drying in the sunlight could be the goodly porringers out of which the master ate his belly-filling food, and which he polished when he had done, according to my Ward experience; shrinkingly doubtful whether the shadows passing over that airy height on the bright spring day were not something in the nature of frowns; sordid, afraid, unadmiring, a small Brute to shudder at.

To that time I had never had the faintest impression of beauty. I had had no knowledge whatever that there was anything lovely in this life. When I had occasionally slunk up the cellar steps into the street, and glared in at shop-windows, I had done so with no higher feelings than we may suppose to animate a mangy young dog or wolf-cub. It is equally the fact that I had never been alone, in the sense of holding unselfish converse with myself. I had been solitary often enough, but nothing better.

Such was my condition when I sat down to my dinner that day, in the kitchen of the old farm-house. Such was my condition when I lay on my bed in the old farm-house that night, stretched out opposite the narrow mullioned window, in the cold light of the moon, like a young Vampire.

FIFTH CHAPTER

What do I know now of Hoghton Towers? Very little, for I have been gratefully unwilling to disturb my first impressions. A house, centuries old, on high ground a mile or so removed from the road between Preston and Blackburn, where the first James of England, in his hurry to make money by making Baronets, perhaps made some of those remunerative dignitaries. A house, centuries old, deserted and falling to pieces, its woods and gardens long since grass-land or ploughed up, the rivers Ribble and Darwen glancing below it, and a vague haze of smoke, against which not even the supernatural prescience of the first Stuart could foresee a Counterblast, hinting at Steam Power, powerful in two distances.

What did I know then of Hoghton Towers? When I first peeped in at the gate of the lifeless quadrangle, and started from the mouldering statue becoming visible to me like its Guardian Ghost; when I stole round by the back of the farm-house, and got in among the ancient rooms, many of them with their floors and ceilings falling, the beams and rafters hanging dangerously down, the plaster dropping as I trod, the oaken panels stripped away, the windows half walled up, half broken; when I discovered a gallery commanding the old kitchen, and looked down between balustrades upon a massive old table and benches, fearing to see I know not what dead-alive creatures come in and seat themselves, and look up with I know not what dreadful eyes, or lack of eyes, at me; when all over the house I was awed by gaps and chinks where the sky stared sorrowfully at me, where the birds passed, and the ivy rustled, and the stains of winter-weather blotched the rotten floors; when down at the bottom of dark pits of staircase, into which the stairs had sunk, green leaves trembled, butterflies fluttered, and bees hummed in and out through the broken doorways; when encircling the whole ruin were sweet scents and sights of fresh green growth and ever-renewing life, that I had never dreamed of, – I say, when I passed into such clouded perception of these things as my dark soul could compass, what did I know then of Hoghton Towers?

I have written that the sky stared sorrowfully at me. Therein have I anticipated the answer. I knew that all these things looked sorrowfully at me. That they seemed to sigh or whisper, not without pity for me: 'Alas! Poor wordly little devil!'

There were two or three rats at the bottom of one of the smaller pits of broken staircase when I craned over and looked in. They were scuffling for some prey that was there. And when they started and hid themselves, close together in the dark, I thought of the old life (it had grown old already) in the cellar.

How not to be this worldly little devil? How not to have a repugnance towards myself as I had towards the rats? I hid in a corner of one of the smaller chambers, frightened at myself, and crying (it was the first time I had ever cried for any cause not purely physical) and I tried to think about it. One of the farm-ploughs came into my range of view just then, and it seemed to help me as it went on with its two horses up and down the field so peacefully and quietly.

There was a girl of about my own age in the farm-house family, and she sat opposite to me at the narrow table at mealtimes. It had come into my mind at our first dinner that she might take the fever from me. The thought had not disquieted me then; I had only speculated how she would look under the altered circumstances, and whether she would die. But it came into my mind now, that I might try to prevent her taking the fever, by keeping away from her. I knew I should have but scrambling board if I did; so much the less worldly and less devilish the deed would be, I thought.

From that hour I withdrew myself at early morning into secret corners of the ruined house, and remained hidden there until she went to bed. At first, when meals were ready, I used to hear them calling me; and then my resolution weakened. But I strengthened it again, by going further off into the ruin, and getting out of hearing. I often watched for her at the dim windows; and, when I saw that she was fresh and rosy, felt much happier.

Out of this holding her in my thoughts, to the humanizing of myself, I suppose some childish love arose within me. I felt in some sort dignified by the pride of protecting her, by the pride of making the sacrifice for her. As my heart swelled with that new feeling, it insensibly softened about Mother and Father. It seemed to have been frozen before and now to be thawed. The old ruin and all the lovely things that haunted it were not sorrowful for me only, but sorrowful for Mother and Father as well. Therefore did I cry again, and often too.

The farm-house family conceived me to be of a morose temper, and were very short with me; though they never stinted me in such broken fare as was to be got out of regular hours. One night when I lifted the kitchen latch at my usual time, Sylvia (that was her pretty name) had but just gone out of the room. Seeing her ascending the opposite stairs, I stood still at the door. She had heard the clink of the latch, and looked round.

'George,' she called to me, in a pleased voice, 'tomorrow is my birthday, and we are to have a fiddler, and there's a party of boys and girls coming in a cart, and we shall dance. I invite you. Be sociable for once, George.'

'I am very sorry, miss,' I answered, 'but I – but no; I can't come.'

'You are a disagreeable, ill-humoured lad,' she returned, dis-dainfully, 'and I ought not to have asked you. I shall never speak to you again.'

As I stood with my eyes fixed on the fire after she was gone, I felt that the farmer bent his brows upon me.

'Eh, lad,' said he, 'Sylvy's right. You're as moody and broody a lad as never I set eyes on yet!'

I tried to assure him that I meant no harm; but he only said coldly: 'Maybe not, maybe not. There! Get thy supper, get thy supper, and then thou canst sulk to thy heart's content again.'

Ah! If they could have seen me next day in the ruin, watching for the arrival of the cart full of merry young guests; if they could have seen me at night, gliding out from behind the ghostly statue, listening to the music and the fall of dancing feet, and watching the lighted farm-house windows from the quadrangle when all the ruin was dark; if they could have read my heart as I crept up to bed by the back way, comforting myself with the reflection, 'They will take no hurt from me,' – they would not have thought mine a morose or an unsocial nature!

It was in these ways that I began to form a shy disposition; to be of a timidly silent character under misconstruction; to have an inexpressible, perhaps a morbid, dread of ever being sordid or worldly. It was in these ways that my nature came to shape itself to such a mould, even before it was affected by the influences of the studious and retired life of a poor scholar.

SIXTH CHAPTER

Brother Hawkyard (as he insisted on my calling him) put me to school, and told me to work my way. 'You are all right, George,' he said. 'I have been the best servant the Lord has had in his service for this five-and-thirty years, (O, I have!) and he knows the value of such a servant as I have been to him, (O yes, he does!) and he'll prosper your schooling as a part of my reward. That's what *he*'ll do, George. He'll do it for me.'

From the first I could not like this familiar knowledge of the ways of the sublime inscrutable Almighty, on Brother Hawkyard's part. As I grew a little wiser and still a little wiser, I liked it less and less. His manner, too, of confirming himself in a parenthesis, – as if, knowing himself, he doubted his own word, – I found distasteful. I cannot tell how much these dislikes cost me, for I had a dread that they were worldly.

As time went on, I became a Foundation-Boy on a good Foundation, and I cost Brother Hawkyard nothing. When I had worked my way so far, I worked yet harder, in the hope of ultimately getting a presentation to College and a Fellowship. My health has never been strong (some vapour from the Preston cellar cleaves to me I think), and what with much work and some weakness, I came again to be regarded – that is, by my fellow-students – as unsocial.

All through my time as a Foundation-Boy I was within a few miles of Brother Hawkyard's congregation, and whenever I was what we called a Leave-Boy on a Sunday, I went over there, at his desire. Before the knowledge became forced upon me that outside their place of meeting these Brothers and Sisters were no better than the rest of the human family, but on the whole were, to put the case mildly, as bad as most, in respect of giving short weight in their shops, and not speaking the truth, – I say, before this knowledge became forced upon me, their prolix addresses, their inordinate conceit, their daring ignorance, their investment of the Supreme Ruler of Heaven and Earth with their own miserable meannesses and littlenesses greatly shocked me. Still, as their term for the frame of mind that could not perceive them to be in an exalted state of Grace was the 'worldly' state, I did for a time suffer tortures under my inquiries of myself whether that young worldly-devilish spirit of mine could secretly be lingering at the bottom of my non-appreciation.

Brother Hawkyard was the popular expounder in this assembly, and generally occupied the platform (there was a little platform with a table on it, in lieu of a pulpit) first, on a Sunday afternoon. He was by trade a drysalter. Brother Gimblet, an elderly man with a crabbed face, a large dog's-eared shirt-collar, and a spotted blue neckerchief reaching up behind to the crown of his head, was also a drysalter, and an expounder. Brother Gimblet professed the greatest admiration for Brother Hawkyard, but (I had thought more than once) bore him a jealous grudge.

Let whosoever may peruse these lines kindly take the pains here to read twice my solemn pledge, that what I write of the language and customs of the congregation in question I write scrupulously, literally, exactly from the life and the truth.

On the first Sunday after I had won what I had so long tried for, and when it was certain that I was going up to college, Brother Hawkyard concluded a long exhortation thus:

'Well, my friends and fellow-sinners, now I told you, when I began, that I didn't know a word of what I was going to say to you, (and no, I did not!) but that it was all one to me, because I knew the Lord would put into my mouth the words I wanted.'

'(That's it!' From Brother Gimblet.)

'And he did put into my mouth the words I wanted.'

('So he did!' From Brother Gimblet.)

'And why?'

('Ah! Let's have that!' From Brother Gimblet.)

'Because I have been his faithful servant for five-and-thirty years, and because he knows it. For five-and-thirty years! And he knows it, mind you! I got those words that I wanted, on account of my wages. I got 'em from the Lord, my fellow-sinners. Down. I said, "Here's a heap of wages due; let us have something down on account." And I got it down, and I paid it over to you, and you won't wrap it up in a napkin, nor yet in a towel, nor yet pockethankercher, but you'll put it out at good interest. Very well. Now, my brothers and sisters and fellow-sinners, I am going to conclude with a question, and I'll make it so plain (with the help of the Lord, after five-and-thirty years, I should rather hope!) as that the Devil shall not be able to confuse it in your heads. Which he would be overjoyed to do.'

'(Just his way. Crafty old blackguard!' From Brother Gimblet.)

'And the question is this. Are the Angels learned?'

('Not they. Not a bit on it.' From Brother Gimblet, with the greatest confidence.)

'Not they. And where's the proof? Sent ready-made by the hand of the Lord. Why, there's one among us here now, that has got all the Learning that can be crammed into him. *I* got him all the Learning that could be crammed into him. His grandfather' (this I had never heard before) 'was a Brother of ours. He was Brother Parksop. That's what he was. Parksop. Brother Parksop. His worldly name was Parksop, and he was a Brother of this Brother-hood. Then wasn't he Brother Parksop?'

('Must be. Couldn't help hisself.' From Brother Gimblet.)

'Well. He left that one now here present among us to the care of a Brother-Sinner of his, (and that Brother-Sinner, mind you, was a sinner of a bigger size in his time than any of you, Praise the Lord!) Brother Hawkyard. Me *I* got him, without fee or reward, – without a morsel of myrrh, or frankincense, nor yet Amber, letting alone the honeycomb, – all the Learning that could be crammed into him. Has it brought him into our Temple, in the spirit? No. Have we had any ignorant Brothers and Sisters that didn't know round O from crooked S, come in among us mean-while? Many. Then the Angels are *not* learned. Then they don't so much as know their alphabet. And now, my friends and fellow-sinners, having brought it to that, perhaps some Brother present – perhaps you, Brother Gimblet – will pray a bit for us?'

Brother Gimblet undertook the sacred function, after having drawn his sleeve across his mouth, and muttered: 'Well! I don't know as I see my way to hitting any of you quite in the right place neither.' He said this with a dark smile, and then began to bellow. What we were specially to be preserved from, according to his solicitations, was despoilment of the orphan, suppression of testamentary intentions on the part of a Father or (say) Grand-father, appropriation of the orphan's house-property, feigning to give in charity to the wronged one from whom we withheld his due; and that class of sins. He ended with the petition, 'Give us peace!' Which, speaking for myself, was very much needed after twenty minutes of his bellowing.

Even though I had not seen him when he rose from his knees, steaming with perspiration, glance at Brother Hawkyard, and even though I had not heard Brother Hawkyard's tone of congratulating him on the vigour with which he had roared, I should have detected a malicious application in this prayer. Unformed suspicions to a similar effect had sometimes passed through my mind in my earlier schooldays, and had always caused me great distress; for they were worldly in their nature, and wide, very wide, of the spirit that had drawn me from Sylvia. They were sordid suspicions, without a shadow of proof. They were worthy to have originated in the unwholesome cellar. They were not only without proof, but against proof. For was I not myself a living proof of what Brother Hawkyard had done? And without him, how should I ever have seen the sky look sorrowfully down upon that wretched boy at Hoghton Towers?

Although the dread of a relapse into a state of savage selfishness was less strong upon me as I approached manhood, and could act in an increased degree for myself, yet I was always on my guard against any tendency to such relapse. After getting these suspicions under my feet, I had been troubled by not being able to like Brother Hawkyard's manner, or his professed religion. So it came about, that, as I walked back that Sunday evening, I thought it would be an act of reparation for any such injury my struggling thoughts had unwillingly done him, if I wrote, and placed in his hands, before going to College, a full acknowledgment of his goodness to me, and an ample tribute of thanks. It might serve as an implied vindication of him against any dark scandal from a rival Brother and Expounder, or from any other quarter.

Accordingly I wrote the document with much care. I may add with much feeling, too, for it affected me as I went on. Having no set studies to pursue, in the brief interval between leaving the Foundation and going to Cambridge, I determined to walk out to his place of business and give it into his own hands.

It was a winter afternoon when I tapped at the door of his little counting-house, which was at the farther end of his long, low shop. As I did so (having entered by the back yard, where casks and boxes were taken in, and where there was the inscription, 'Private Way to the Counting-house'), a shopman called to me from the counter that he was engaged.

'Brother Gimblet,' said the shopman (who was one of the Brotherhood), 'is with him.'

I thought this all the better for my purpose, and made bold to tap again. They were talking in a low tone, and money was passing, for I heard it being counted out.

'Who is it?' asked Brother Hawkyard, sharply.

'George Silverman,' I answered, holding the door open. 'May I come in?'

Both Brothers seemed so astounded to see me that I felt shier than usual. But they looked quite cadaverous in the early gaslight, and perhaps that accidental circumstance exaggerated the expression of their faces.

'What is the matter?' asked Brother Hawkyard.

'Ay! What is the matter?' asked Brother Gimblet.

'Nothing at all,' I said, diffidently producing my document. 'I am only the bearer of a letter from myself.'

'From yourself, George?' cried Brother Hawkyard.

'And to you,' said I

'And to me, George?'

He turned paler, and opened it hurriedly; but looking over it, and seeing generally what it was, became less hurried, recovered his colour, and said, 'Praise the Lord!'

'That's it!' cried Brother Gimblet. 'Well put! Amen.'

Brother Hawkyard then said, in a livelier strain: 'You must know, George, that Brother Gimblet and I are going to make our two businesses one. We are going into partnership. We are settling it now. Brother Gimblet is to take one clear half of the profits. (O yes! And he shall have it, he shall have it to the last farthing!)'

'D.V.!' said Brother Gimblet, with his right fist firmly clenched on his right leg.

'There is no objection,' pursued Brother Hawkyard, 'to my reading this aloud, George?'

As it was what I expressly desired should be done, after yesterday's prayer, I more than readily begged him to read it aloud. He did so, and Brother Gimblet listened with a crabbed smile.

'It was in a good hour that I came here,' he said, wrinkling up his eyes. 'It was in a good hour, likewise, that I was moved yesterday to depict for the terror of evil-doers a character the direct opposite of Brother Hawkyard's. But it was the Lord that done it. I felt him at it, while I was perspiring.'

After that, it was proposed by both of them that I should attend the congregation once more, before my final departure. What my shy reserve would undergo, from being expressly preached at and prayed at, I knew beforehand. But I reflected that it would be for the last time, and that it might add to the weight of my letter. It was well known to the Brothers and Sisters that there was no place taken for me in *their* Paradise; and if I showed this last token of deference to Brother Hawkyard, notoriously in despite of my own sinful inclinations, it might go some little way in aid of my statement that he had been good to me, and that I was grateful to him. Merely stipulating, therefore, that no express endeavour should be made for my conversion, – which would involve the rolling of several Brothers and Sisters on the floor, declaring that they felt all their sins in a heap on their left side, weighing so many pounds avoirdupois, as I knew from what I had seen of those repulsive mysteries, – I promised.

Since the reading of my letter, Brother Gimblet had been at intervals wiping one eye with an end of his spotted blue necker-chief, and grinning to himself. It was, however, a habit that Brother had, to grin in an ugly manner even while expounding. I call to mind a delighted snarl with which he used to detail from the platform the torments reserved for the wicked (meaning all human creation except the Brotherhood), as being remarkably hideous.

I left the two to settle their articles of partnership, and count money; and I never saw them again but on the following Sunday. Brother Hawkyard died within two or three years, leaving all he possessed to Brother Gimblet, in virtue of a will dated (as I have been told) that very day.

Now, I was so far at rest with myself when Sunday came, knowing that I had conquered my own mistrust, and righted

Brother Hawkyard in the jaundiced vision of a rival, that I went, even to that coarse chapel, in a less sensitive state than usual. How could I foresee that the delicate, perhaps the diseased, corner of my mind, where I winced and shrunk when it was touched, or was even approached, would be handled as the theme of the whole proceedings?

On this occasion it was assigned to Brother Hawkyard to pray, and to Brother Gimblet to preach. The prayer was to open the ceremonies; the discourse was to come next. Brothers Hawkyard and Gimblet were both on the platform; Brother Hawkyard on his knees at the table, unmusically ready to pray; Brother Gimblet sitting against the wall, grinningly ready to preach.

'Let us offer up the sacrifice of prayer, my brothers and sisters and fellow-sinners.' Yes. But it was I who was the sacrifice. It was our poor sinful worldly-minded Brother here present who was wrestled for. The now-opening career of this our unawakened Brother might lead to his becoming a minister of what was called The Church. That was what *he* looked to. The Church. Not the chapel, Lord. The Church. No rectors, no vicars, no archdeacons, no bishops, no archbishops in the chapel, but, O Lord, many such in the Church! Protect our sinful Brother from his love of lucre. Cleanse from our unawakened Brother's breast his sin of worldly-mindedness. The prayer said infinitely more in words, but nothing more to any intelligble effect.

Then Brother Gimblet came forward, and took (as I knew he would) the text, My kingdom is not of this world. Ah! But whose was, my fellow-sinners? Whose? Why, our Brother's here present was. The only kingdom he had an idea of was of this world ('That's it!' from several of the congregation). What did the woman do when she lost the piece of money? Went and looked for it. What should our Brother do when he lost his way? ('Go and look for it,' from a Sister.) Go and look for it. True. But must he look for it in the right direction or in the wrong? ('In the right,' from a Brother.) There spake the prophets! He must look for it in the right direction, or he couldn't find it. But he had turned his back upon the right direction, and he wouldn't find it. Now, my fellow-sinners, to show you the difference betwixt worldly-mindedness and unworldly-mindedness, betwixt kingdoms not of this world and kingdoms *of* this world, here was a letter wrote by even our worldly-minded Brother unto Brother Hawkyard. Judge, from hearing of it read, whether Brother Hawkyard was the faithful steward that the Lord had in his mind only t' other day, when, in this very place, he drew you the picter of the unfaithful one. For it was him that done it, not me. Don't doubt that!

Brother Gimblet then grinned and bellowed his way through my composition, and subsequently through an hour. The service closed with a hymn, in which the Brothers unanimously roared, and the Sisters unanimously shrieked, at me, that I by wiles of worldly gain was mocked, and they on waters of sweet love were rocked; that I was Mammon struggled in the dark, while they were floating in a second Ark.

I went out from all this with an aching heart and a weary spirit; not because I was quite so weak as to consider these narrow creatures interpreters of the Divine majesty and wisdom; but because I was weak enough to feel as though it were my hard fortune to be misrepresented and misunderstood, when I most tried to subdue any risings of mere worldliness within me, and when I most hoped, that, by dint of trying earnestly, I had succeeded.

SEVENTH CHAPTER

My timidity and my obscurity occasioned me to live a secluded life at College, and to be little known. No relative ever came to visit me, for I had no relative. No intimate friends broke in upon my studies, for I made no intimate friends. I supported myself on my scholarship, and read much. My College time was otherwise not so very different from my time at Hoghton Towers.

Knowing myself to be unfit for the noisier stir of social existence, but believing myself qualified to do my duty in a moderate though earnest way if I could obtain some small preferment in the Church, I applied my mind to the clerical profession. In due sequence I took orders, was ordained, and began to look about me for employment. I must observe that I had taken a good degree, that I had succeeded in winning a good fellowship, and that my means were ample for my retired way of life. By this time I had read with several young men, and the occupation increased my income, while it was highly interesting to me. I once accidentally overheard our greatest Don say, to my boundless joy, 'That he heard it reported of Silverman that his gift of quiet explanation, his patience, his amiable temper, and his conscientiousness, made him the best of Coaches'. May my 'gift of quiet explanation' come more seasonably and powerfully to my aid in this present explanation than I think it will!

It may be, in a certain degree, owing to the situation of my College rooms (in a corner where the daylight was sobered), but it is in a much larger degree referable to the state of my own mind, that I seem to myself, on looking back to this time of my life, to have been always in the peaceful shade. I can see others in the sunlight; I can see our boats' crews and our athletic young men on the glistening water, or speckled with the moving lights of sunlit leaves; but I myself am always in the shadow looking on. Not unsympathetically, – God forbid! – but looking on, alone, much as I looked at Sylvia from the shadows of the ruined house, or looked at the red gleam shining through the farmer's windows, and listened to the fall of dancing feet, when all the ruin was dark that night in the quadrangle.

I now come to the reason of my quoting that laudation of myself above given. Without such reason, to repeat it would have been mere boastfulness.

Among those who had read with me was Mr Fareway, second son of Lady Fareway, widow of Sir Gaston Fareway, Baronet. This young gentleman's abilities were much above the average, but he came of a rich family, and was idle and luxurious. He presented himself to me too late, and afterwards came to me too irregularly, to admit of my being of much service to him. In the end I considered it my duty to dissuade him from going up for an examination which he could never pass, and he left College without taking a degree. After his departure, Lady Fareway wrote to me representing the justice of my returning half my fee, as I had been of so little use to her son. Within my knowledge a similar demand had not been made in any other case, and I most freely admit that the justice of it had not occurred to me until it was pointed out. But I at once perceived it, yielded to it, and returned the money.

Mr Fareway had been gone two years or more and I had forgotten him, when he one day walked into my rooms as I was sitting at my books.

Said he, after the usual salutations had passed: 'Mr Silverman, my mother is in town here, at the hotel, and wishes me to present you to her.'

I was not comfortable with strangers, and I dare say I betrayed that I was a little nervous or unwilling. For, said he, without my having spoken, 'I think the interview may tend to the advancement of your prospects.'

It put me to the blush to think that I should be tempted by a worldly reason, and I rose immediately.

Said Mr Fareway, as we went along, 'Are you a good hand at business?'

'I think not,' said I.

Said Mr Fareway then, 'My mother is.'

'Truly?' said I.

'Yes. My mother is what is usually called a managing woman. Doesn't make a bad thing, for instance, even out of the spendthrift habits of my eldest brother abroad. In short, a managing woman. This is in confidence.'

He had never spoken to me in confidence, and I was surprised by his doing so. I said I should respect his confidence, of course, and said no more on the delicate subject. We had but a little way to walk, and I was soon in his mother's company. He presented me, shook hands with me, and left us two (as he said) to business.

I saw in my Lady Fareway a handsome, well-preserved lady of somewhat large stature, with a steady glare in her great round dark eyes that embarrassed me.

Said my Lady: 'I have heard from my son, Mr Silverman, that you would be glad of some preferment in the Church?'

I gave my Lady to understand that was so.

'I don't know whether you are aware,' my Lady proceeded, 'that we have a presentation to a living? I say *we* have, but in point of fact *I* have.'

I gave my Lady to understand that I had not been aware of this.

Said my Lady: 'So it is. Indeed, I have two presentations: one, to two hundred a year; one, to six. Both livings are in our county –

North Devonshire, as you probably know. The first is vacant. Would you like it?'

What with my Lady's eyes, and what with the suddenness of this proposed gift, I was much confused.

'I am sorry it is not the larger presentation,' said my Lady, rather coldly, 'though I will not, Mr Silverman, pay you the bad compliment of supposing that *you* are, because that would be mercenary, – and mercenary I am persuaded you are not.'

Said I, with my utmost earnestness: 'Thank you, Lady Fareway, thank you, thank you! I should be deeply hurt if I thought I bore the character.'

'Naturally,' said my Lady. 'Always detestable, but particularly in a clergyman. You have not said whether you will like the Living?'

With apologies for my remissness or indistinctness, I assured my Lady that I accepted it most readily and gratefully. I added that I hoped she would not estimate my appreciation of the generosity of her choice by my flow of words, for I was not a ready man in that respect when taken by surprise or touched at heart.

'The affair is concluded,' said my Lady. 'Concluded. You will find the duties very light, Mr Silverman. Charming house; charming little garden, orchard, and all that. You will be able to take pupils. By the by! No. I will return to the word afterwards. What was I going to mention, when it put me out?'

My Lady stared at me, as if I knew. And I didn't know. And that perplexed me afresh.

Said my Lady, after some consideration: 'Oh! Of course. How very dull of me! The last incumbent, – least mercenary man I ever saw, – in consideration of the duties being so light and the house so delicious, couldn't rest, he said, unless I permitted him to help me with my correspondence, accounts, and various little things of that kind; nothing in themselves, but which it worries a lady to cope with. Would Mr Silverman also like to –? Or shall I –?'

I hastened to say that my poor help would be always at her ladyship's service.

'I am absolutely blessed,' said my Lady, casting up her eyes (and so taking them off of me for one moment), 'in having to do with gentlemen who cannot endure an approach to the idea of being mercenary!' She shivered at the word. 'And now as to the pupil.'

'The –?' I was quite at a loss.

'Mr Silverman, you have no idea what she is. She is,' said my Lady, laying her touch upon my coat-sleeve, 'I do verily believe, the most extraordinary girl in this world. Already knows more Greek and Latin than Lady Jane Grey. And taught herself! Has not yet, remember, derived a moment's advantage from Mr Silverman's classical acquirements. To say nothing of mathematics, which she is bent upon becoming versed in, and in which (as I hear from my son and others) Mr Silverman's reputation is so deservedly high!'

Under my Lady's eyes, I must have lost the clew, I felt persuaded; and yet I did not know where I could have dropped it.

'Adelina,' said my Lady, 'is my only daughter. If I did not feel quite convinced that I am not blinded by a mother's partiality; unless I was absolutely sure that when you know her, Mr Silverman, you will esteem it a high and unusual privilege to direct her studies, – I should introduce a mercenary element into this conversation, and ask you on what terms –'

I entreated my Lady to go no further. My Lady saw that I was troubled, and did me the honour to comply with my request.

EIGHTH CHAPTER

Everything in mental acquisition that her brother might have been, if he would, and everything in all gracious charms and admirable qualities that no one but herself could be, – this was Adelina.

I will not expatiate upon her beauty. I will not expatiate upon her intelligence, her quickness of perception, her powers of memory, her sweet consideration from the first moment for the slow-paced tutor who ministered to her wonderful gifts. I was thirty then; I am over sixty now; she is ever present to me in these hours as she was in those, bright and beautiful and young, wise and fanciful and good.

When I discovered that I loved her, how can I say? In the first day? In the first week? In the first month? Impossible to trace. If I be (as I am) unable to represent to myself any previous period of my life as quite separable from her attracting power, how can I answer for this one detail?

Whensoever I made the discovery, it laid a heavy burden on me. And yet, comparing it with the far heavier burden that I afterwards took up, it does not seem to me now to have been very hard to bear. In the knowledge that I did love her, and that I should love her while my life lasted, and that I was ever to hide my secret deep in my own breast, and she was never to find it, there was a kind of sustaining joy or pride or comfort mingled with my pain.

But later on — say a year later on — when I made another discovery, then indeed my suffering and my struggle were strong. That other discovery was —?

These words will never see the light, if ever, until my heart is dust; until her bright spirit has returned to the regions of which, when imprisoned here, it surely retained some unusual glimpse of remembrance; until all the pulses that ever beat around us shall have long been quiet; until all the fruits of all the tiny victories and defeats achieved in our little breasts shall have withered away. That discovery was, that she loved me.

She may have enhanced my knowledge, and loved me for that; she may have overvalued my discharge of duty to her, and loved me for that; she may have refined upon a playful compassion which she would sometimes show for what she called my want of wisdom according to the light of the world's dark lanterns, and loved me for that; she may — she must — have confused the borrowed light of what I had only learned, with its brightness in its pure original rays; but she loved me at that time, and she made me know it.

Pride of family and pride of wealth put me as far off from her in my Lady's eyes as if I had been some domesticated creature of another kind. But they could not put me farther from her than I put myself when I set my merits against hers. More than that. They could not put me, by millions of fathoms, half so low beneath her as I put myself when in imagination I took advantage of her noble trustfulness, took the fortune that I knew she must possess in her own right, and left her to find herself, in the zenith of her beauty and genius, bound to poor rusty plodding Me.

No. Worldliness should not enter here, at any cost. If I had tried to keep it out of other ground, how much harder was I bound to try to keep it from this sacred place.

But there was something daring in her broad generous character that demanded at so delicate a crisis to be delicately and patiently addressed. After many and many a bitter night (O, I found I could cry for reasons not purely physical, at this pass of my life!) I took my course.

My Lady had in our first interview unconsciously overstated the accommodation of my pretty house. There was room in it for only one pupil. He was a young gentleman near coming of age, very well connected, but what is called a poor relation. His parents were dead. The charges of his living and reading with me were defrayed by an uncle, and he and I were to do our utmost together for three years towards qualifying him to make his way. At this time he had entered into his second year with me. He was well-looking, clever, energetic, enthusiastic, bold; in the best sense of the term, a thorough young Anglo-Saxon.

I resolved to bring these two together.

NINTH CHAPTER

Said I, one night when I had conquered myself: 'Mr Granville,' – Mr Granville Wharton his name was, – 'I doubt if you have ever yet so much as seen Miss Fareway.'

'Well, sir,' returned he, laughing, 'you see her so much yourself, that you hardly leave another fellow a chance of seeing her.'

'I am her tutor, you know,' said I.

And there the subject dropped for that time. But I so contrived as that they should come together shortly afterwards. I had previously so contrived as to keep them asunder, for while I loved her – I mean before I had determined on my sacrifice – a lurking jealousy of Mr Granville lay within my unworthy breast.

It was quite an ordinary interview in the Fareway Park; but they talked easily together for some time; like takes to like, and they had many points of resemblance. Said Mr Granville to me, when he and I sat at our supper that night: 'Miss Fareway is remarkably beautiful, sir, and remarkably engaging. Don't you think so?' 'I think so,' said I. And I stole a glance at him, and saw that he had reddened and was thoughtful. I remember it most vividly, because the mixed feeling of grave pleasure and acute pain that the slight circumstance caused me was the first of a long, long series of such mixed impressions under which my hair turned slowly gray.

I had not much need to feign to be subdued, but I counterfeited to be older than I was in all respects, (Heaven knows, my heart being all too young the while!) and feigned to be more of a recluse and bookworm than I had really become, and gradually set up more and more of a fatherly manner towards Adelina. Likewise, I made my tuition less imaginative than before; separated myself from my poets and philosophers; was careful to present them in their own light, and me, their lowly servant, in my own shade. Moreover, in the matter of apparel I was equally mindful. Not that I had ever been dapper that way, but that I was slovenly now.

As I depressed myself with one hand, so did I labour to raise Mr Granville with the other; directing his attention to such subjects as I too well knew most interested her, and fashioning him (do not deride or misconstrue the expression, unknown reader of this writing, for I have suffered!) into a greater resemblance to myself in my solitary one strong aspect. And gradually, gradually, as I saw him take more and more to these thrown-out lures of mine, then did I come to know better and better that love was drawing him on, and was drawing Her from me.

So passed more than another year; every day a year in its number of my mixed impressions of grave pleasure and acute pain; and then, these two being of age and free to act legally for themselves, came before me, hand in hand (my hair being now quite white), and entreated me that I would unite them together. 'And indeed, dear Tutor,' said Adelina, 'it is but consistent in you that you should do this thing for us, seeing that we should never have spoken together that first time but for you, and that but for you we could never have met so often afterwards.' The whole of which was literally true, for I had availed myself on my many business attendances on, and conferences with, my Lady, to take Mr Granville to the house, and leave him in the outer room with Adelina.

I knew that my Lady would object to such a marriage for her

daughter, or to any marriage that was other than an exchange of her for stipulated lands, goods, and moneys. But, looking on the two, and seeing with full eyes that they were both young and beautiful; and knowing that they were alike in the tastes and acquirements that will outlive youth and beauty; and considering that Adelina had a fortune now, in her own keeping; and considering further that Mr Granville, though for the present poor, was of a good family that had never lived in a cellar in Preston; and believing that their love would endure, neither having any great discrepancy to find out in the other, – I told them of my readiness to do this thing which Adelina asked of her dear Tutor, and to send them forth, Husband and Wife, into the shining world with golden gates that awaited them.

It was on a summer morning that I rose before the sun, to compose myself for the crowning of my work with this end. And my dwelling being near to the sea, I walked down to the rocks on the shore, in order that I might behold the sun rise in his majesty.

The tranquillity upon the Deep and on the firmament, the orderly withdrawal of the stars, the calm promise of coming day, the rosy suffusion of the sky and waters, the ineffable splendour that then burst forth, attuned my mind afresh after the discords of the night. Methought that all I looked on said to me, and that all I heard in the sea and in the air said to me, 'Be comforted, mortal, that thy life is so short. Our preparation for what is to follow has endured, and shall endure, for unimaginable ages.'

I married them. I knew that my hand was cold when I placed it on their hands clasped together; but the words with which I had to accompany the action I could say without faltering, and I was at peace.

They being well away from my house and from the place, after our simple breakfast, the time was come when I must do what I had pledged myself to them that I would do, – break the intelligence to my Lady.

I went up to the house, and found my Lady in her ordinary business room. She happened to have an unusual amount of commissions to intrust to me that day, and she had filled my hands with papers before I could originate a word.

'My Lady,' – I then began, as I stood beside her table.

'Why, what's the matter?' she said, quickly, looking up.

'Not much, I would fain hope, after you shall have prepared yourself, and considered a little.'

'Prepared myself! And considered a little! You appear to have prepared *yourself* but indifferently, anyhow, Mr Silverman.' This, mighty scornfully, as I experienced my usual embarrassment under her stare.

Said I, in self-extenuation, once for all: 'Lady Fareway, I have but to say for myself that I have tried to do my duty.'

'For yourself?' repeated my Lady. 'Then there are others concerned, I see. Who are they?'

I was about to answer, when she made towards the bell with a dart that stopped me, and said, 'Why, where is Adelina?'

'Forbear. Be calm, my Lady. I married her this morning to Mr Granville Wharton.'

She set her lips, looked more intently at me than ever, raised her right hand and smote me hard upon the cheek.

'Give me back those papers, give me back those papers!' She tore them out of my hands and tossed them on her table. Then seating herself defiantly in her great chair, and folding her arms, she stabbed me to the heart with the unlooked-for reproach: 'You worldly wretch!'

'Worldly?' I cried. 'Worldly!'

'This, if you please,' she went on with supreme scorn, pointing me out as if there were someone there to see, – 'this, if you please, is the disinterested scholar, with not a design beyond his books! This, if you please, is the simple creature whom any one could overreach in a bargain! This, if you please, is Mr Silverman! Not of this world, not he! He has too much simplicity for this world's cunning. He has too much singleness of purpose to be a match for this world's double-dealing. What did he give you for it?'

'For what? And who?'

'How much,' she asked, bending forward in her great chair, and insultingly tapping the fingers of her right hand on the palm of her left – 'how much does Mr Granville Wharton pay you for getting him Adelina's money? What is the amount of your percentage upon Adelina's fortune? What were the terms of the agreement that you proposed to this boy when you, the Reverend George Silverman, licensed to marry, engaged to put him in possession of this girl? You made good terms for yourself, whatever they were. He would stand a poor chance against your keenness.'

Bewildered, horrified, stunned by this cruel perversion, I could not speak. But I trust that I looked innocent, being so.

'Listen to me, shrewd hypocrite,' said my Lady, whose anger increased as she gave it utterance. 'Attend to my words, you cunning schemer who have carried this plot through with such a practised double face that I have never suspected you. I had my projects for my daughter; projects for family connection; projects for fortune. You have thwarted them, and overreached me; but I am not one to be thwarted and overreached without retaliation. Do you mean to hold this Living another month?'

'Do you deem it possible, Lady Fareway, that I can hold it another hour, under your injurious words?'

'Is it resigned, then?'

'It was mentally resigned, my Lady, some minutes ago.'

'Don't equivocate, sir. *Is* it resigned?'

'Unconditionally and entirely. And I would that I had never, never come near it!'

'A cordial response from me to *that* wish, Mr Silverman! But take this with you, sir. If you had not resigned it, I would have had you deprived of it. And though you have resigned it, you will not get quit of me as easily as you think for. I will pursue you with this story. I will make this nefarious conspiracy of yours, for money, known. You have made money by it, but you have at the same time made an enemy by it. *You* will take good care that the money sticks to you; *I* will take good care that the enemy sticks to you.'

Then said I, finally: 'Lady Fareway, I think my heart is broken. Until I came into this room just now, the possibility of such mean wickedness as you have imputed to me never dawned upon my thoughts. Your suspicions –'

'Suspicions! Pah!' said she, indignantly. 'Certainties.'

'Your certainties, my Lady, as you call them, your suspicions, as I call them, are cruel, unjust, wholly devoid of foundation in fact. I can declare no more, except that I have not acted for my own profit or my own pleasure. I have not in this proceeding considered myself. Once again, I think my heart is broken. If I have unwittingly done any wrong with a righteous motive, that is some penalty to pay.'

She received this with another and a more indignant 'Pah!' and I made my way out of her room (I think I felt my way out with my hands, although my eyes were open), almost suspecting that my voice had a repulsive sound, and that I was a repulsive object.

There was a great stir made, the Bishop was appealed to, I received a severe reprimand, and narrowly escaped suspension. For years a cloud hung over me, and my name was tarnished. But my heart did not break, if a broken heart involves death; for I lived through it.

They stood by me, Adelina and her husband, through it all. Those who had known me at College, and even most of those who had only known me there by reputation, stood by me too. Little by little, the belief widened that I was not capable of what was laid to my charge. At length I was presented to a College-Living in a sequestered place, and there I now pen my Explanation. I pen it at my open window in the summer-time; before me, lying the churchyard, equal resting-place for sound hearts, wounded hearts, and broken hearts. I pen it for the relief of my own mind, not foreseeing whether or no it will ever have a reader.

Joseph Sheridan Le Fanu

MR JUSTICE HARBOTTLE

PROLOGUE

On this case Doctor Hesselius has inscribed nothing more than the words, 'Harman's Report', and a simple reference to his own extraordinary Essay on 'The Interior Sense, and the Conditions of the Opening thereof'.

The reference is to Vol. I., Section 317, Note Z[a]. The note to which reference is thus made, simply says: 'There are two accounts of the remarkable case of the Honourable Mr Justice Harbottle, one furnished to me by Mrs Trimmer, of Tunbridge Wells (June, 1805); the other at a much later date, by Anthony Harman, Esq. I much prefer the former; in the first place, because it is minute and detailed, and written, it seems to me, with more caution and knowledge; and in the next, because the letters from Dr Hedstone, which are embodied in it, furnish matter of the highest value to a right apprehension of the nature of the case. It was one of the best declared cases of an opening of the interior sense, which I have met with. It was affected too, by the phenomenon, which occurs so frequently as to indicate a law of these eccentric conditions; that is to say, it exhibited what I may term, the contagious character of this sort of intrusion of the spirit-world upon the proper domain of matter. So soon as the spirit-action has established itself in the case of one patient, its developed energy begins to radiate, more or less effectually, upon others. The interior vision of the child was opened; as was, also, that of its mother, Mrs Pyneweck; and both the interior vision and hearing of the scullery-maid, were opened on the same occasion. After-appearances are the result of the law explained in Vol. II., Section 17 to 49. The common centre of association, simultaneously recalled, unites, or *re*unites, as the case may be, for a period measured, as we see, in Section 37. The *maximum* will extend to days, the *minimum* is little more than a second. We see the operation of this principle perfectly displayed, in certain cases of lunacy, of epilepsy, of catalepsy, and of mania, of a peculiar and painful character, though unattended by incapacity of business.'

The memorandum of the case of Judge Harbottle, which was written by Mrs Trimmer, of Tunbridge Wells, which Doctor Hesselius thought the better of the two, I have been unable to discover among his papers. I found in his escritoire a note to the effect that he had lent the Report of Judge Harbottle's case, written by Mrs Trimmer, to Dr F. Heyne. To that learned and able gentleman accordingly I wrote, and received from him, in his reply, which was full of alarms and regrets, on account of the uncertain safety of that 'valuable MS', a line written long since by Dr Hesselius, which completely exonerated him, inasmuch as it acknowledged the safe return of the papers. The narrative of Mr Harman, is therefore, the only one available for this collection. The late Dr Hesselius, in another passage of the note that I have cited, says, 'As to the facts (non-medical) of the case, the narrative of Mr Harman exactly tallies with that furnished by Mrs Trimmer.' The strictly scientific view of the case would scarcely interest the popular reader; and, possibly, for the purposes of this selection, I should, even had I both papers to choose between, have preferred that of Mr Harman, which is given, in full, in the following pages.

I *The Judge's House*

Thirty years ago, an elderly man, to whom I paid quarterly a small annuity charged on some property of mine, came on the quarter-day to receive it. He was a dry, sad, quiet man, who had known better days, and had always maintained an unexceptionable character. No better authority could be imagined for a ghost story.

He told me one, though with a manifest reluctance; he was drawn into the narration by his choosing to explain what I should not have remarked, that he had called two days earlier than that week after the strict day of payment, which he had usually allowed to elapse. His reason was a sudden determination to change his lodgings, and the consequent necessity of paying his rent a little before it was due.

He lodged in a dark street in Westminster, in a spacious old house, very warm, being wainscoted from top to bottom, and furnished with no undue abundance of windows, and those fitted with thick sashes and small panes.

This house was, as the bills upon the window testified, offered to be sold or let. But no one seemed to care to look at it.

A thin matron, in rusty black silk, very taciturn, with large, steady, alarmed eyes, that seemed to look in your face, to read what you might have seen in the dark room and passages through which you had passed, was in charge of it, with a solitary 'maid-of-all-work' under her command. My poor friend had taken lodgings in this house, on account of their extraordinary cheapness. He had occupied them for nearly a year without the slightest disturbance, and was the only tenant, under rent, in the house. He had two rooms; a sitting-room and a bedroom with a closet opening from it, in which he kept his books and papers locked up. He had gone to his bed, having also locked the outer door. Unable to sleep, he had lighted a candle, and after having read for a time, had laid the book beside him. He heard the old clock at the stairhead strike one; and very shortly after, to his alarm, he saw the closet door, which he thought he had locked, open stealthily, and a slight dark man, particularly sinister, and somewhere about fifty, dressed in mourning of a very antique fashion, such a suit as we see in Hogarth, entered the room on tip-toe. He was followed by an elder man, stout, and blotched with scurvy, and whose features, fixed as a corpse's, were stamped with dreadful force with a character of sensuality and villainy.

This old man wore a flowered silk dressing-gown and ruffles, and he remarked a gold ring on his finger, and on his head a cap of velvet, such as, in the days of perukes, gentlemen wore in undress.

This direful old man carried in his ringed and ruffled hand a coil of rope; and these two figures crossed the floor diagonally, passing the foot of his bed, from the closet door at the farther end of the room, at the left, near the window, to the door opening upon the lobby, close to the bed's head, at his right.

He did not attempt to describe his sensations as these figures passed so near him. He merely said, that so far from sleeping in that room again, no consideration the world could offer would induce him so much as to enter it again alone, even in the daylight. He found both doors, that of the closet, and that of the room opening upon the lobby, in the morning fast locked as he had left them before going to bed.

In answer to a question of mine, he said that neither appeared the least conscious of his presence. They did not seem to glide, but walked as living men do, but without any sound, and he felt a vibration on the floor as they crossed it. He so obviously suffered from speaking about the apparitions, that I asked him no more questions.

There were in his description, however, certain coincidences so very singular, as to induce me, by that very post, to write to a friend much my senior, then living in a remote part of England, for the information which I knew he could give me. He had himself more than once pointed out that old house to my attention, and told me, though very briefly, the strange story which I now asked him to give me in greater detail.

His answer satisfied me; and the following pages convey its substance.

Your letter (he wrote) tells me you desire some particulars about the closing years of the life of Mr Justice Harbottle, one of the judges of the Court of Common Pleas. You refer, of course, to the extraordinary occurrences that made that period of his life long after a theme for 'winter tales' and metaphysical speculation. I happen to know perhaps more than any other man living of those mysterious particulars.

The old family mansion, when I revisited London, more than thirty years ago, I examined for the last time. During the years that have passed since then, I hear that improvement, with its pre-liminary demolitions, has been doing wonders for the quarter of Westminster in which it stood. If I were quite certain that the house had been taken down, I should have no difficulty about naming the street in which it stood. As what I have to tell, how-ever, is not likely to improve its letting value, and as I should not care to get into trouble, I prefer being silent on that particular point.

How old the house was, I can't tell. People said it was built by Roger Harbottle, a Turkey merchant, in the reign of King James I. I am not a good opinion upon such questions; but having been in it, though in its forlorn and deserted state, I can tell you in a general way what it was like. It was built of dark-red brick, and the door and windows were faced with stone that had turned yellow by time. It receded some feet from the line of the other houses in the street; and it had a florid and fanciful rail of iron about the broad steps that invited your ascent to the hall-door, in which were fixed, under a file of lamps among scrolls and twisted leaves, two immense 'extinguishers', like the conical caps of fairies, into which, in old times, the footmen used to thrust their flambeaux when their chairs or coaches had set down their great people, in the hall or at the steps, as the case might be. That hall is panelled up to the ceiling, and has a large fireplace. Two or three stately old rooms open from it at each side. The windows of these are tall, with many small panes. Passing through the arch at the back of the hall, you come upon the wide and heavy well-staircase. There is a back staircase also. The mansion is large, and has not as much light, by any means, in proportion to its extent, as modern houses enjoy. When I saw it, it had long been untenanted, and had the gloomy reputation beside of a haunted house. Cobwebs floated from the ceilings or spanned the corners of the cornices, and dust lay thick over everything. The windows were stained with the dust and rain of fifty years, and darkness had thus grown darker.

When I made it my first visit, it was in company with my father, when I was still a boy, in the year 1808. I was about twelve years old, and my imagination impressible, as it always is at that age. I looked about me with great awe. I was here in the very centre and scene of those occurrences which I had heard recounted at the fireside at home, with so delightful a horror.

My father was an old bachelor of nearly sixty when he married. He had, when a child, seen Judge Harbottle on the bench in his robes and wig a dozen times at least before his death, which took place in 1748, and his appearance made a powerful and unpleasant impression, not only on his imagination, but upon his nerves.

The Judge was at that time a man of some sixty-seven years. He had a great mulberry-coloured face, a big, carbuncled nose, fierce eyes, and a grim and brutal mouth. My father, who was young at the time, thought it the most formidable face he had ever seen; for there were evidences of intellectual power in the formation and lines of the forehead. His voice was loud and harsh, and gave effect to the sarcasm which was his habitual weapon on the bench.

This old gentleman had the reputation of being about the wickedest man in England. Even on the bench he now and then showed his scorn of opinion. He had carried cases his own way, it was said, in spite of counsel, authorities, and even of juries, by a sort of cajolery, violence, and bamboozling, that somehow confused and overpowered resistance. He had never actually committed himself; he was too cunning to do that. He had the character of being, however, a dangerous and unscrupulous judge; but his character did not trouble him. The associates he chose for his hours of relaxation cared as little as he did about it.

II *Mr Peters*

One night during the session of 1746 this old Judge went down in his chair to wait in one of the rooms of the House of Lords for the result of a division in which he and his order were interested.

This over, he was about to return to his house close by, in his chair; but the night had become so soft and fine that he changed his mind, sent it home empty, and with two footmen, each with a flambeau, set out on foot in preference. Gout had made him rather a slow pedestrian. It took him some time to get through the two or three streets he had to pass before reaching his house.

In one of those narrow streets of tall houses, perfectly silent at that hour, he overtook, slowly as he was walking, a very singular-looking old gentleman.

He had a bottle-green coat on, with a cape to it, and large stone buttons, a broad-leafed low-crowned hat, from under which a big powdered wig escaped; he stooped very much, and supported his bending knees with the aid of a crutch-handled cane, and so shuffled and tottered along painfully.

'I ask your pardon, sir,' said this old man, in a very quavering voice, as the burly Judge came up with him, and he extended his hand feebly towards his arm.

Mr Justice Harbottle saw that the man was by no means poorly dressed, and his manner that of a gentleman.

The Judge stopped short, and said, in his harsh peremptory tones, 'Well, sir, how can I serve you?'

'Can you direct me to Judge Harbottle's house? I have some intelligence of the very last importance to communicate to him.'

'Can you tell it before witnesses?' asked the Judge.

'By no means; it must reach *his* ear only,' quavered the old man earnestly.

'If that be so, sir, you have only to accompany me a few steps farther to reach my house, and obtain a private audience; for I am Judge Harbottle.'

With this invitation the infirm gentleman in the white wig complied very readily; and in another minute the stranger stood in what was then termed the front parlour of the Judge's house, *tête-à-tête* with that shrewd and dangerous functionary.

He had to sit down, being very much exhausted, and unable for a little time to speak; and then he had a fit of coughing, and after that a fit of gasping; and thus two or three minutes passed, during which the Judge dropped his roquelaure on an armchair, and threw his cocked-hat over that.

The venerable pedestrian in the white wig quickly recovered his voice. With closed doors they remained together for some time.

There were guests waiting in the drawing-rooms, and the sound of men's voices laughing, and then of a female voice singing to a harpsichord, were heard distinctly in the hall over the stairs; for old Judge Harbottle had arranged one of his dubious jollifications, such as might well make the hair of godly men's heads stand upright for that night.

This old gentleman in the powdered white wig, that rested on his stooped shoulders, must have had something to say that interested the Judge very much; for he would not have parted on easy terms with the ten minutes and upwards which that conference filched from the sort of revelry in which he most delighted, and in which he was the roaring king, and in some sort the tyrant also, of his company.

The footman who showed the aged gentleman out observed that the Judge's mulberry-coloured face, pimples and all, were bleached to a dingy yellow, and there was the abstraction of agitated thought in his manner, as he bid the stranger goodnight. The servant saw that the conversation had been of serious import, and that the Judge was frightened.

Instead of stumping upstairs forthwith to his scandalous hilarities, his profane company, and his great china bowl of punch – the identical bowl from which a bygone Bishop of London, good easy man, had baptised this Judge's grandfather, now clinking round the rim with silver ladles, and hung with scrolls of lemon-peel – instead, I say, of stumping and clambering up the great staircase to the cavern of his Circean enchantment, he stood with his big nose flattened against the window-pane, watching the progress of the feeble old man, who clung stiffly to the iron rail as he got down, step by step, to the pavement.

The hall-door had hardly closed, when the old Judge was in the hall bawling hasty orders, with such stimulating expletives as old colonels under excitement sometimes indulge in now-a-days, with a stamp or two of his big foot, and a waving of his clenched fist in the air. He commanded the footman to overtake the old gentleman in the white wig, to offer him his protection on his way home, and in no case to show his face again without having ascertained where he lodged, and who he was, and all about him.

'By —, sirrah! if you fail me in this, you doff my livery tonight!'

Forth bounced the stalwart footman, with his heavy cane under his arm, and skipped down the steps, and looked up and down the street after the singular figure, so easy to recognize.

What were his adventures I shall not tell you just now.

The old man, in the conference to which he had been admitted in that stately panelled room, had just told the Judge a very strange story. He might be himself a conspirator; he might possibly be crazed; or possibly his whole story was straight and true.

The aged gentleman in the bottle-green coat, in finding himself alone with Mr Justice Harbottle, had become agitated. He said,

'There is, perhaps you are not aware, my lord, a prisoner in Shrewsbury jail, charged with having forged a bill of exchange for a hundred and twenty pounds, and his name is Lewis Pyneweck, a grocer of that town.'

'Is there?' says the Judge, who knew well that there was.

'Yes, my lord,' says the old man.

'Then you had better say nothing to affect this case. If you do, by –, I'll commit you! for I'm to try it,' says the judge, with his terrible look and tone.

'I am not going to do anything of the kind, my lord; of him or his case I know nothing, and care nothing. But a fact has come to my knowledge which it behoves you to well consider.'

'And what may that fact be?' inquired the Judge; 'I'm in haste, sir, and beg you will use dispatch.'

'It has come to my knowledge, my lord, that a secret tribunal is in process of formation, the object of which is to take cognisance of the conduct of the judges; and first, of *your* conduct, my lord; it is a wicked conspiracy.'

'Who are of it?' demands the Judge.

'I know not a single name as yet. I know but the fact, my lord; it is most certainly true.'

'I'll have you before the Privy Council, sir,' says the Judge.

'That is what I most desire; but not for a day or two, my lord.'

'And why so?'

'I have not as yet a single name, as I told your lordship; but I expect to have a list of the most forward men in it, and some other papers connected with the plot, in two or three days.'

'You said one or two just now.'

'About that time, my lord.'

'Is this a Jacobite plot?'

'In the main I think it is, my lord.'

'Why, then, it is political. I have tried no State prisoners, nor am like to try any such. How, then, doth it concern me?'

'From what I can gather, my lord, there are those in it who desire private revenges upon certain judges.'

'What do they call their cabal?'

'The High Court of Appeal, my lord.'

'Who are you, sir? What is your name?'

'Hugh Peters, my lord.'

'That should be a Whig name?'

'It is, my lord.'

'Where do you lodge, Mr Peters?'

'In Thames Street, my lord, over against the sign of the "Three Kings".'

' "Three Kings?" Take care one be not too many for you, Mr Peters! How come you, an honest Whig, as you say, to be privy to a Jacobite plot? Answer me that.'

'My lord, a person in whom I take an interest has been seduced to take a part in it; and being frightened at the unexpected wickedness of their plans, he is resolved to become an informer for the Crown.'

'He resolves like a wise man, sir. What does he say of the persons? Who are in the plot? Doth he know them?'

'Only two, my lord; but he will be introduced to the club in a few days, and he will then have a list, and more exact information of their plans, and above all of their oaths, and their hours and places of meeting, with which he wishes to be aquainted before they can have any suspicions of his intentions. And being so informed, to whom, think you, my lord, had he best go then?'

'To the king's attorney-general straight. But you say this concerns me, sir, in particular? How about this prisoner, Lewis Pyneweck? Is he one of them?'

'I can't tell, my lord; but for some reason, it is thought your lordship will be well advised if you try him not. For if you do, it is feared 'twill shorten your days.'

'So far as I can learn, Mr Peters, this business smells pretty strong of blood and treason. The king's attorney-general will know how to deal with it. When shall I see you again, sir?'

'If you give me leave, my lord, either before your lordship's court sits, or after it rises, tomorrow. I should like to come and tell your lordship what has passed.'

'Do so, Mr Peters, at nine o'clock tomorrow morning. And see you play me no trick, sir, in this matter; if you do, by –, sir, I'll lay you by the heels!'

'You need fear no trick from me, my lord; had I not wished to serve you, and acquit my own conscience, I never would have come all this way to talk with your lordship.'

'I'm willing to believe you, Mr Peters; I'm willing to believe you, sir.'

And upon this they parted.

'He has either painted his face, or he is consumedly sick,' thought the old Judge.

The light had shown more effectually upon his features, as he turned to leave the room with a low bow, and they looked, he fancied, unnaturally chalky.

'D– him!' said the Judge ungraciously, as he began to scale the stairs: 'he has half-spoiled my supper.'

But if he had, no one but the Judge himself perceived it, and the evidence was all, as any one might perceive, the other way.

III *Lewis Pyneweck*

In the meantime the footman dispatched in pursuit of Mr Peters speedily overtook that feeble gentleman. The old man stopped when he heard the sound of pursuing steps, but any alarms that may have crossed his mind seemed to disappear on his recognizing the livery. He very gratefully accepted the proffered assistance, and placed his tremulous arm within the servant's for support. They had not gone far, however, when the old man stopped suddenly, saying,

'Dear me! as I live, I have dropped it. You heard it fall. My eyes, I fear, won't serve me, and I'm unable to stoop low enough; but if *you* will look, you shall have half the find. It is a guinea; I carried it in my glove.'

The street was silent and deserted. The footman had hardly descended to what he termed his 'hunkers', and begun to search the pavement about the spot which the old man indicated, when Mr Peters, who seemed very much exhausted, and breathed with difficulty, struck him a violent blow, from above, over the back of the head with a heavy instrument, and then another; and leaving him bleeding and senseless in the gutter, ran like a lamplighter down a lane to the right, and was gone.

When an hour later, the watchman brought the man in livery home, still stupid and covered with blood, Judge Harbottle cursed his servant roundly, swore he was drunk, threatened him with an indictment for taking bribes to betray his master, and cheered him with a perspective of the broad street leading from the Old Bailey to Tyburn, the cart's tail, and the hangman's lash.

Notwithstanding this demonstration, the Judge was pleased. It was a disguised 'affidavit man', or footpad, no doubt, who had been employed to frighten him. The trick had fallen through.

A 'court of appeal', such as the false Hugh Peters had indicated, with assassination for its sanction, would be an uncomfortable institution for a 'hanging judge' like the Honourable Justice Harbottle. That sarcastic and ferocious administrator of the criminal code of England, at that time a rather pharisaical, bloody and heinous system of justice, had reasons of his own for choosing to try that very Lewis Pyneweck, on whose behalf this audacious trick was devised. Try him he would. No man living should take that morsel out of his mouth.

Of Lewis Pyneweck, of course, so far as the outer world could see, he knew nothing. He would try him after his fasion, without fear, favour, or affection.

But did he not remember a certain thin man, dressed in mourning, in whose house, in Shrewsbury, the Judge's lodgings used to be, until a scandal of ill-treating his wife came suddenly to light? A grocer with a demure look, a soft step, and a lean face as dark as mahogany, with a nose sharp and long, standing ever so little awry, and a pair of dark steady brown eyes under thinly traced black brows – a man whose thin lips wore always a faint unpleasant smile.

Had not that scoundrel an account to settle with the Judge? had he not been troublesome lately? and was not his name Lewis Pyneweck, some time grocer in Shrewsbury, and now prisoner in the jail of that town?

The reader may take it, if he pleases, as a sign that Judge Harbottle was a good Christian, that he suffered nothing ever from remorse. That was undoubtedly true. He had, nevertheless, done this grocer, forger, what you will, some five or six years before, a grievous wrong; but it was not that, but a possible scandal, and possible complications, that troubled the learned Judge now.

Did he not, as a lawyer, know, that to bring a man from his

shop to the dock, the chances must be at least ninety-nine out of a hundred that he is guilty?

A weak man like his learned brother Withershins was not a judge to keep the high-roads safe, and make crime tremble. Old Judge Harbottle was the man to make the evil-disposed quiver, and to refresh the world with showers of wicked blood, and thus save the innocent, to the refrain of the ancient saw he loved to quote:

> Foolish pity
> Ruins a city.

In hanging that fellow he could not be wrong. The eye of a man accustomed to look upon the dock could not fail to read 'villain' written sharp and clear in his plotting face. Of course he would try him, and no one else should.

A saucy-looking woman, still handsome, in a mob-cap gay with blue ribbons, in a saque of flowered silk, with lace and rings on, much too fine for the Judge's housekeeper, which nevertheless she was, peeped into his study next morning, and, seeing the Judge alone, stepped in.

'Here's another letter from him, come by the post this morning. Can't you do nothing for him?' she said wheedlingly, with her arm over his neck, and her delicate finger and thumb fiddling with the lobe of his purple ear.

'I'll try,' said Judge Harbottle, not raising his eyes from the paper he was reading.

'I knew you'd do what I asked you,' she said.

The Judge clapt his gouty claw over his heart, and made her an ironical bow.

'What,' she asked, 'will you do?'

'Hang him,' said the Judge with a chuckle.

'You don't mean to; no, you don't, my little man,' said she, surveying herself in a mirror on the wall.

'I'm d – d but I think you're falling in love with your husband at last!' said Judge Harbottle.

'I'm blest but I think you're growing jealous of him,' replied the lady with a laugh. 'But no; he was always a bad one to me; I've done with him long ago.'

'And he with you, by George! When he took your fortune, and your spoons, and your earrings, he had all he wanted of you. He drove you from his house; and when he discovered you had made yourself comfortable, and found a good situation, he'd have taken your guineas, and your silver, and your earrings over again, and then allowed you half-a-dozen years more to make a new harvest for his mill. You don't wish him good; if you say you do, you lie.'

She laughed a wicked, saucy laugh, and gave the terrible Rhadamanthus a playful tap on the chops.

'He wants me to send him money to fee a counsellor,' she said, while her eyes wandered over the pictures on the wall, and back again to the looking-glass; and certainly she did not look as if his jeopardy troubled her very much.

'Confound his impudence, the *scoundrel!*' thundered the old Judge, throwing himself back in his chair, as he used to do *in furore* on the bench, and the lines of his mouth looked brutal, and his eyes ready to leap from their sockets. 'If you answer his letter from my house to please yourself, you'll write your next from somebody else's to please me. You understand, my pretty witch, I'll not be pestered. Come, no pouting; whimpering won't do. You don't care a brass farthing for the villain, body or soul. You came here but to make a row. You are one of Mother Carey's chickens; and where you come, the storm is up. Get you gone, baggage! get you *gone!*' he repeated, with a stamp; for a knock at the hall-door made her instantaneous disappearance indispensable.

I need hardly say that the venerable Hugh Peters did not appear again. The Judge never mentioned him. But oddly enough, considering how he laughed to scorn the weak invention which he had blown into dust at the very first puff, his white-wigged visitor and the conference in the dark front parlour were often in his memory.

His shrewd eye told him that allowing for change of tints and such disguises as the playhouse affords every night, the features of this false old man, who had turned out too hard for his tall footman, were identical with those of Lewis Pyneweck.

Judge Harbottle made his registrar call upon the crown solicitor, and tell him that there was a man in town who bore a wonderful resemblance to a prisoner in Shrewsbury jail named Lewis Pyneweck, and to make inquiry through the post forthwith whether any one was personating Pyneweck in prison and whether he had thus or otherwise made his escape.

The prisoner was safe, however, and no question as to his identity.

IV *Interruption in Court*

In due time Judge Harbottle went circuit; and in due time the judges were in Shrewsbury. News travelled slowly in those days, and newspapers, like the wagons and stage coaches, took matters easily. Mrs Pyneweck, in the Judge's house, with a diminished household – the greater part of the Judge's servants having gone with him, for he had given up riding circuit, and travelled in his coach in state – kept house rather solitarily at home.

In spite of quarrels, in spite of mutual injuries – some of them, inflicted by herself, enormous – in spite of a married life of spited bickerings – a life in which there seemed no love or liking or forbearance, for years – now that Pyneweck stood in near danger of death, something like remorse came suddenly upon her. She knew that in Shrewsbury were transacting the scenes which were to determine his fate. She knew she did not love him; but she could not have supposed, even a fortnight before, that the hour of suspense could have affected her so powerfully.

She knew the day on which the trial was expected to take place. She could not get it out of her head for a minute; she felt faint as it drew towards evening.

Two or three days passed; and then she knew that the trial must be over by this time. There were floods between London and Shrewsbury, and news was long delayed. She wished the floods would last forever. It was dreadful waiting to hear; dreadful to know that the event was over, and that she could not hear till self-willed rivers subsided; dreadful to know that they must subside and the news come at last.

She had some vague trust in the Judge's good nature, and much in the resources of chance and accident. She had contrived to send the money he wanted. He would not be without legal advice and energetic and skilled support.

At last the news did come – a long arrear all in a gush: a letter from a female friend in Shrewsbury; a return of the sentences, sent up for the Judge; and most important, because most easily got at, being told with great aplomb and brevity, the long-deferred intelligence of the Shrewsbury Assizes in the *Morning Advertiser*. Like an impatient reader of a novel, who reads the last page first, she read with dizzy eyes the list of the executions.

Two were respited, seven were hanged; and in that capital catalogue was this line:

'Lewis Pyneweck – forgery.'

She had to read it a half-a-dozen times over before she was sure she understood it. Here was the paragraph:

> *Sentence, Death – 7.*
> Executed accordingly, on Friday the 13th instant, to wit:
> Thomas Primer, *alias* Duck – highway robbery.
> Flora Guy – stealing to the value of 11s. 6d.
> Arthur Pounden – burglary.
> Matilda Mummery – riot.
> Lewis Pyneweck – forgery, bill of exchange.

And when she reached this, she read it over and over, feeling very cold and sick.

This buxom housekeeper was known in the house as Mrs Carwell – Carwell being her maiden name, which she had re-sumed.

No one in the house except its master knew her history. Her introduction had been managed craftily. No one suspected that it had been concerted between her and the old reprobate in scarlet and ermine.

Flora Carwell ran up the stairs now, and snatched her little girl, hardly seven years of age, whom she met on the lobby, hurriedly up in her arms, and carried her into her bedroom, without well knowing what she was doing, and sat down, placing the child before her. She was not able to speak. She held the child before her, and looked in the little girl's wondering face, and burst into tears of horror.

She thought the Judge could have saved him. I daresay he could. For a time she was furious with him, and hugged and kissed her bewildered little girl, who returned her gaze with large round eyes.

That little girl had lost her father, and knew nothing of the matter. She had always been told that her father was dead long ago.

A woman, coarse, uneducated, vain, and violent, does not reason, or even feel, very distinctly; but in these tears of consternation were mingling a self-upbraiding. She felt afraid of that little child.

But Mrs Carwell was a person who lived not upon sentiment, but upon beef and pudding; she consoled herself with punch; she did not trouble herself long even with resentments; she was a gross and material person, and could not mourn over the irrevocable for more than a limited number of hours, even if she would.

Judge Harbottle was soon in London again. Except the gout, this savage old epicurean never knew a day's sickness. He laughed, and coaxed, and bullied away the young woman's faint upbraidings, and in a little time Lewis Pyneweck troubled her no more; and the Judge secretly chuckled over the perfectly fair removal of a bore, who might have grown little by little into something very like a tyrant.

It was the lot of the Judge whose adventures I am now recounting to try criminal cases at the Old Bailey shortly after his return. He had commenced his charge to the jury in a case of forgery, and was, after his wont, thundering dead against the prisoner, with many a hard aggravation and cynical gibe, when suddenly all died away in silence, and, instead of looking at the jury, the eloquent Judge was gaping at some person in the body of the court.

Among the persons of small importance who stand and listen at the sides was one tall enough to show with a little prominence; a slight mean figure, dressed in seedy black, lean and dark of visage. He had just handed a letter to the crier, before he caught the Judge's eye.

That Judge descried, to his amazement, the features of Lewis Pyneweck. He had the usual faint thin-lipped smile; and with his blue chin raised in air, and as it seemed quite unconscious of the distinguished notice he has attracted, he was stretching his low cravat with his crooked fingers, while he slowly turned his head from side to side – a process which enabled the Judge to see distinctly a stripe of swollen blue round his neck, which indicated, he thought, the grip of the rope.

This man, with a few others, had got a footing on a step, from which he could better see the court. He now stepped down, and the Judge lost sight of him.

His lordship signed energetically with his hand in the direction in which this man had vanished. He turned to the tipstaff. His first effort to speak ended in a gasp. He cleared his throat, and told the astounded official to arrest that man who had interrupted the court.

'He's but this moment gone down *there*. Bring him in custody before me, within ten minutes' time, or I'll strip your gown from your shoulders and fine the sheriff!' he thundered, while his eyes flashed round the court in search of the functionary.

Attorneys, counsellors, idle spectators, gazed in the direction in which Mr Justice Harbottle had shaken his gnarled old hand. They compared notes. Not one had seen any one making a disturbance. They asked one another if the Judge was losing his head.

Nothing came of the search. His lordship concluded his charge a great deal more tamely; and when the jury retired, he stared round the court with a wandering mind, and looked as if he would not have given sixpence to see the prisoner hanged.

V *Caleb Searcher*

The Judge had received the letter; had he known from whom it came, he would no doubt have read it instantaneously. As it was he simply read the direction:

> *To the Honourable*
> *The Lord Justice*
> *Elijah Harbottle,*
> *One of his Majesty's Justices of*
> *the Honourable Court of Common Pleas.*

It remained forgotten in his pocket till he reached home.

When he pulled out that and others from the capacious pocket of his coat, it had its turn, as he sat in his library in his thick silk dressing-gown; and then he found its contents to be a closely written letter, in a clerk's hand, and an enclosure in 'secretary hand', as I believe the angular scrivinary of law-writings in those days was termed, engrossed on a bit of parchment about the size of this page. The letter said:

MR JUSTICE HARBOTTLE, – MY LORD,

I am ordered by the High Court of Appeal to acquaint your lordship, in order to your better preparing yourself for your trial, that a true bill hath been sent down, and the indictment lieth against your lordship for the murder of one Lewis Pyneweck of Shrewsbury, citizen, wrongfully executed for the forgery of a bill of exchange, on the –th day of — last, by reason of the wilful perversion of the evidence, and the undue pressure put upon the jury, together with the illegal admission of evidence by your lordship, well knowing the same to be illegal, by all which the promoter of the prosecution of the said indictment, before the High Court of Appeal, hath lost his life.

And the trial of the said indictment, I am farther ordered to acquaint your lordship, is fixed for the 10th day of — next ensuing, by the right honourable the Lord Chief Justice Twofold, of the court aforesaid, to wit, the High Court of Appeal, on which day it will most certainly take place. And I am farther to acquaint your lordship, to prevent any surprise or miscarriage, that your case stands first for the said day, and that the said High Court of Appeal sits day and night, and never rises; and herewith, by order of the said court, I furnish your lordship with a copy (extract) of the record in this case, except of the indictment, whereof, notwithstanding, the substance and effect is supplied to your lordship in this Notice. And farther I am to inform you, that in case the jury then to try your lordship should find you guilty, the right honourable the Lord Chief Justice will, in passing sentence of death upon you, fix the day of execution for the 10th day of —, being one calendar month from the day of your trial.

It was signed by

CALEB SEARCHER,
Officer of the Crown Solicitor in the
Kingdom of Life and Death.

The Judge glanced through the parchment.

' 'Sblood! Do they think a man like me is to be bamboozled by their buffoonery?'

The Judge's coarse features were wrung into one of his sneers; but he was pale. Possibly, after all, there was a conspiracy on foot. It was queer. Did they mean to pistol him in his carriage? or did they only aim at frightening him?

Judge Harbottle had more than enough of animal courage. He was not afraid of highwaymen, and he had fought more than his share of duels, being a foul-mouthed advocate while he held briefs at the bar. No one questioned his fighting qualities. But with respect to this particular case of Pyneweck, he lived in a house of glass. Was there not his pretty, dark-eyed, over-dressed housekeeper, Mrs Flora Carwell? Very easy for people who knew Shrewsbury to identify Mrs Pyneweck, if once put upon the scent; and had he not stormed and worked hard in that case? Had he not made it hard sailing for the prisoner? Did he not know very well what the bar thought of it? It would be the worst scandal that ever blasted Judge.

So much there was intimidating in the matter but nothing more. The Judge was a little bit gloomy for a day or two after, and more testy with every one than usual.

He locked up the papers; and about a week after he asked his housekeeper, one day, in the library:

'Had your husband never a brother?'

Mrs Carwell squalled on this sudden introduction of the funereal topic, and cried exemplary 'piggins full', as the Judge used pleasantly to say. But he was in no mood for trifling now, and he said sternly:

'Come, madam! this wearies me. Do it another time; and give me an answer to my question.' So she did.

Pyneweck had no brother living. He once had one; but he died in Jamaica.

'How do you know he is dead?' asked the Judge.

'Because he told me so.'

'Not the dead man.'

'Pyneweck told me so.'

'Is that all?' sneered the Judge.

He pondered this matter; and time went on. The Judge was growing a little morose, and less enjoying. The subject struck nearer to his thoughts than he fancied it could have done. But so it is with most undivulged vexations, and there was no one to whom he could tell this one.

It was now the ninth; and Mr Justice Harbottle was glad. He knew nothing would come of it. Still it bothered him; and tomorrow would see it well over.

[What of the paper I have cited? No one saw it during his life; no one, after his death. He spoke of it to Dr Hedstone; and what purported to be 'a copy', in the old Judge's handwriting, was found. The original was nowhere. Was it a copy of an illusion, incident to brain disease? Such is my belief.]

VI *Arrested*

Judge Harbottle went this night to the play at Drury Lane. He was one of the old fellows who care nothing for late hours, and occasional knocking about in pursuit of pleasure. He had appointed with two cronies of Lincoln's Inn to come home in his coach with him to sup after the play.

They were not in his box, but were to meet him near the entrance, and get into his carriage there; and Mr Justice Harbottle, who hated waiting, was looking a little impatiently from the window.

The Judge yawned.

He told the footman to watch for Counsellor Thavies and Counsellor Beller, who were coming; and, with another yawn, he laid his cocked hat on his knees, closed his eyes, leaned back in his corner, wrapped his mantle closer about him, and began to think of pretty Mrs Abington.

And being a man who could sleep like a sailor, at a moment's notice, he was thinking of taking a nap. Those fellows had no business to keep a judge waiting.

He heard their voices now. Those rake-hell counsellors were laughing, and bantering, and sparring after their wont. The carriage swayed and jerked, as one got in, and then again as the other followed. The door clapped, and the coach was now jogging and rumbling over the pavement. The Judge was a little bit sulky. He did not care to sit up and open his eyes. Let them suppose he was asleep. He heard them laugh with more malice than good-humour, he thought, as they observed it. He would give them a d – d hard knock or two when they got to his door, and till then he would counterfeit his nap.

The clocks were chiming twelve. Beller and Thavies were silent as tombstones. They were generally loquacious and merry rascals.

The Judge suddenly felt himself roughly seized and thrust from his corner into the middle of the seat, and opening his eyes, instantly he found himself between his two companions.

Before he could blurt out the oath that was at his lips, he saw that they were two strangers – evil-looking fellows, each with a pistol in his hand, and dressed like Bow Street officers.

The Judge clutched at the check-string. The coach pulled up. He stared about him. They were not among houses; but through the windows, under a broad moonlight, he saw a black moor stretching lifelessly from right to left, with rotting trees, pointing fantastic branches in the air, standing here and there in groups, as if they held up their arms and twigs like fingers, in horrible glee at the Judge's coming.

A footman came to the window. He knew his long face and sunken eyes. He knew it was Dingly Chuff, fifteen years ago a footman in his service, whom he had turned off at a moment's notice, in a burst of jealousy, and indicted for a missing spoon. The man had died in prison of the jail-fever.

The Judge drew back in utter amazement. His armed companions signed mutely; and they were again gliding over this unknown moor.

The bloated and gouty old man, in his horror considered the question of resistance. But his athletic days were long over. This moor was a desert. There was no help to be had. He was in the hands of strange servants, even if his recognition turned out to be a delusion, and they were under the command of his captors. There was nothing for it but submission, for the present.

Suddenly the coach was brought nearly to a standstill, so that the prisoner saw an ominous sight from the window.

It was a gigantic gallows beside the road; it stood three-sided, and from each of its three broad beams at top depended in chains some eight or ten bodies, from several of which the cere-clothes had dropped away, leaving the skeletons swinging lightly by their chains. A tall ladder reached to the summit of the structure, and on the peat beneath lay bones.

On top of the dark transverse beam facing the road, from which, as from the other two completing the triangle of death, dangled a row of these unfortunates in chains, a hangman, with a pipe in his mouth, much as we see him in the famous print of the 'Idle Apprentice', though here his perch was ever so much higher, was reclining at his ease and listlessly shying bones, from a little heap at his elbow, at the skeletons that hung round, bringing down now a rib or two, now a hand, now half a leg. A long-sighted man could have discerned that he was a dark fellow, lean; and from continually looking down on the earth from the elevation over which, in another sense, he always hung, his nose, his lips, his chin were pendulous and loose, and drawn down into a monstrous grotesque.

This fellow took his pipe from his mouth on seeing the coach, stood up, and cut some solemn capers high on his beam, and shook a new rope in the air, crying with a voice high and distant as the caw of a raven hovering over a gibbet, 'A robe for Judge Harbottle!'

The coach was now driving on at its old swift pace.

So high a gallows as that, the Judge had never, even in his most hilarious moments, dreamed of. He thought he must be raving. And the dead footman! He shook his ears and strained his eyelids; but if he was dreaming, he was unable to awake himself.

There was no good in threatening these scoundrels. A *brutum fulmen* might bring a real one on his head.

Any submission to get out of their hands; and then heaven and earth he would move to unearth and hunt them down.

Suddenly they drove round a corner of a vast white building, and under a *porte-cochère*.

VII   *Chief-Justice Twofold*

The Judge found himself in a corridor lighted with dingy oil lamps, the walls of bare stone; it looked like a passage in a prison.

His guards placed him in the hands of other people. Here and there he saw bony and gigantic soldiers passing to and fro, with muskets over their shoulders. They looked straight before them, grinding their teeth, in bleak fury, with no noise but the clank of their shoes. He saw these by glimpses, round corners, and at the ends of passages, but he did not actually pass them by.

And now, passing under a narrow doorway, he found himself in the dock, confronting a judge in his scarlet robes, in a large courthouse. There was nothing to elevate this Temple of Themis above its vulgar kind elsewhere. Dingy enough it looked, in spite of candles lighted in decent abundance. A case had just closed, and the last juror's back was seen escaping through the door in the wall of the jury-box. There were some dozen barristers, some fiddling with pen and ink, others buried in briefs, some beckoning, with the plumes of their pens, to their attorneys, of whom there were no lack; there were clerks to-ing and fro-ing, and the officers of the court, and the registrar, who was handing up a paper to the judge; and the tipstaff, who was presenting a note at the end of his wand to a king's counsel over the heads of the crowd between. If this was the High Court of Appeal, which never rose day or night, it might account for the pale and jaded aspect of everybody in it. An air of indescribable gloom hung upon the pallid features of all the people here; no one ever smiled; all looked more or less secretly suffering.

'The King against Elijah Harbottle!' shouted the officer.

'Is the appellant Lewis Pyneweck in court?' asked Chief-Justice Twofold, in a voice of thunder, that shook the woodwork of the court, and boomed down the corridors.

Up stood Pyneweck from his place at the table.

'Arraign the prisoner!' roared the Chief: and Judge Harbottle felt the panels of the dock round him, and the floor, and the rails quiver in the vibrations of that tremendous voice.

The prisoner, *in limine*, objected to this pretended court, as being a sham, and non-existent in point of law; and then, that even if it were a court constituted by law (the Judge was growing dazed), it had not and could not have any jurisdiction to try him for his conduct on the bench.

Whereupon the chief-justice laughed suddenly, and every one

in court, turning round upon the prisoner, laughed also, till the laugh grew and roared all round like a deafening acclamation; he saw nothing but glittering eyes and teeth, a universal stare and grin; but though all the voices laughed, not a single face of all those that concentrated their gaze upon him looked like a laughing face. The mirth subsided as suddenly as it began.

The indictment was read. Judge Harbottle actually pleaded! He pleaded 'Not Guilty'. A jury were sworn. The trial proceeded. Judge Harbottle was bewildered. This could not be real. He must be either mad, or *going* mad, he thought.

One thing could not fail to strike even him. This Chief-Justice Twofold, who was knocking him about at every turn with sneer and gibe, and roaring him down with his tremendous voice, was a dilated effigy of himself; an image of Mr Justice Harbottle, at least double his size, and with all his fierce colouring, and his ferocity of eye and visage, enhanced awfully.

Nothing the prisoner could argue, cite, or state, was permitted to retard for a moment the march of the case towards its catastrophe.

The chief-justice seemed to feel his power over the jury, and to exult and riot in the display of it. He glared at them, he nodded to them; he seemed to have established an understanding with them. The lights were faint in that part of the court. The jurors were mere shadows, sitting in rows; the prisoner could see a dozen pair of white eyes shining, coldly, out of the darkness; and whenever the judge in his charge, which was contemptuously brief, nodded and grinned and gibed, the prisoner could see, in the obscurity, by the dip of all these rows of eyes together, that the jury nodded in acquiescence.

And now the charge was over, the huge chief-justice leaned back panting and gloating on the prisoner. Everyone in the court turned about, and gazed with steadfast hatred on the man in the dock. From the jury box where the twelve sworn brethren were whispering together, a sound in the general stillness like a prolonged 'hiss-s-s!' was heard; and then, in answer to the challenge of the officer, 'How say you, gentlemen of the jury, guilty or not guilty?' came in a melancholy voice the finding, 'Guilty'.

The place seemed to the eyes of the prisoner to grow gradually darker and darker, till he could discern nothing distinctly but the lumen of the eyes that were turned upon him from every bench and side and corner and gallery of the building. The prisoner doubtless thought that he had quite enough to say, and conclusive, why sentence of death should not be pronounced upon him; but the lord chief-justice puffed it contemptuously away, like so much smoke, and proceeded to pass sentence of death upon the prisoner, having named the tenth of the ensuing month for his execution.

Before he had recovered the stun of this ominous farce, in obedience to the mandate, 'Remove the prisoner', he was led from the dock. The lamps seemed all to have gone out, and there were stoves and charcoal-fires here and there, that threw a faint crimson light on the walls of the corridors through which he passed. The stones that composed them looked now enormous, cracked and unhewn.

He came into a vaulted smithy, where two men, naked to the waist, with heads like bulls, round shoulders, and the arms of giants, were welding red-hot chains together with hammers that pelted like thunderbolts.

They looked on the prisoner with fierce red eyes, and rested on their hammers for a minute; and said the elder to his companion, 'Take out Elijah Harbottle's gyves'; and with a pincers he plucked the end which lay dazzling in the fire from the furnace.

'One end locks,' said he, taking the cool end of the iron in one hand, while with the grip of a vice he seized the leg of the Judge, and locked the ring round his ankle. 'The other,' he said with a grin, 'is welded.'

The iron band that was to form the ring for the other leg lay still red hot upon the stone floor, with brilliant sparks sporting up and down its surface.

His companion, in his gigantic hands, seized the old Judge's other leg, and pressed his foot immovably to the stone floor; while his senior, in a twinkling, with a masterly application of pincers and hammer, sped the glowing bar around his ankle so tight that the skin and sinews smoked and bubbled again, and old Judge Harbottle uttered a yell that seemed to chill the very stones, and make the iron chains quiver on the wall.

Chains, vaults, smiths, and smithy all vanished in a moment; but the pain continued. Mr Justice Harbottle was suffering torture all round the ankle on which the infernal smiths had just been operating.

His friends, Thavies and Beller, were startled by the Judge's roar in the midst of their elegant trifling about a marriage *à-la-mode* case which was going on. The Judge was in panic as well as pain. The street lamps and the light of his own hall door restored him.

'I'm very bad,' growled he between his set teeth; 'my foot's blazing. Who was he that hurt my foot? 'Tis the gout – 'tis the gout!' he said, awaking completely. 'How many hours have we been coming from the playhouse? 'Sblood, what has happened on the way? I've slept half the night!'

There had been no hitch or delay, and they had driven home at a good pace.

The Judge, however, was in gout; he was feverish too; and the attack, though very short, was sharp; and when, in about a fortnight, it subsided, his ferocious joviality did not return. He could not get this dream, as he chose to call it, out of his head.

VIII   *Somebody Has Got Into the House*

People remarked that the Judge was in the vapours. His doctor said he should go for a fortnight to Buxton.

Whenever the Judge fell into a brown study, he was always conning over the terms of the sentence pronounced upon him in his vision – 'in one calendar month from the date of this day'; and then the usual form, 'and you shall be hanged by the neck till you are dead', etc. 'That will be the 10th – I'm not much in the way of being hanged. I know what stuff dreams are, and I laugh at them; but this is continually in my thoughts, as if it forecast misfortune of some sort. I wish the day my dream gave me were passed and over. I wish I were well purged of my gout. I wish I were as I used to be. 'Tis nothing but vapours, nothing but a maggot.' The copy of the parchment and letter which had announced his trial with many a snort and sneer he would read over and over again, and the scenery and people of his dream would rise about him in places the most unlikely, and steal him in a moment from all that surrounded him into a world of shadows.

The Judge had lost his iron energy and banter. He was growing taciturn and morose. The Bar remarked the change, as well they might. His friends thought him ill. The doctor said he was troubled with hypochondria, and that his gout was still lurking in his system, and ordered him to that ancient haunt of crutches and chalk-stones, Buxton.

The Judge's spirits were very low; he was frightened about himself; and he described to his housekeeper, having sent for her to his study to drink a dish of tea, his strange dream in his drive home from Drury Lane Playhouse. He was sinking into the state of nervous dejection in which men lose their faith in orthodox advice, and in despair consult quacks, astrologers, and nursery story-tellers. Could such a dream mean that he was to have a fit, and so die on the 10th? She did not think so. On the contrary, it was certain some good luck must happen on that day.

The Judge kindled; and for the first time for many days, he looked for a minute or two like himself, and he tapped her on the cheek with the hand that was not in flannel.

'Odsbud! odsheart! you dear rogue! I had forgot. There is young Tom – yellow Tom, my nephew, you know, lies sick at Harrogate; why shouldn't he go that day as well as another, and if he does, I get an estate by it? Why, lookee, I asked Doctor Hedstone yesterday if I was like to take a fit any time, and he laughed, and swore I was the last man in town to go off that way.'

The Judge sent most of his servants down to Buxton to make his lodgings and all things comfortable for him. He was to follow in a day or two.

It was now the 9th; and the next day well over, he might laugh at his visions and auguries.

On the evening of the 9th, Dr Hedstone's footman knocked at the Judge's door. The Doctor ran up the dusky stairs to the drawing-room. It was a March evening, near the hour of sunset, with an east wind whistling sharply through the chimney-stacks. A wood fire blazed cheerily on the hearth. And Judge Harbottle, in what was then called a brigadier-wig, with his red roquelaure on, helped the glowing effect of the darkened chamber, which looked red all over like a room on fire.

The Judge had his feet on a stool, and his huge grim purple face confronted the fire, and seemed to pant and swell, as the blaze alternately spread upward and collapsed. He had fallen again among his blue devils, and was thinking of retiring from the Bench, and of fifty other gloomy things.

But the doctor, who was an energetic son of Aesculapius, would listen to no croaking, told the Judge he was full of gout, and in his present condition no judge even of his own case, but promised him leave to pronounce on all those melancholy questions, a fortnight later.

In the meantime the Judge must be very careful. He was over-charged with gout, and he must not provoke an attack, till the waters of Buxton should do that office for him, in their own salutary way.

The Doctor did not think him perhaps quite so well as he pretended, for he told him he wanted rest, and would be better if he went forthwith to his bed.

Mr Gerningham, his valet, assisted him, and gave him his drops; and the Judge told him to wait in his bedroom till he should go to sleep.

Three persons that night had specially odd stories to tell.

The housekeeper had got rid of the trouble of amusing her little girl at this anxious time, by giving her leave to run about the sitting-rooms and look at the pictures and china, on the usual condition of touching nothing. It was not until the last gleam of sunset had for some time faded, and the twilight had so deepened that she could no longer discern the colours on the china figures on the chimneypiece or in the cabinets, that the child returned to the housekeeper's room to find her mother.

To her she related, after some prattle about the china, and the pictures, and the Judge's two grand wigs in the dressing-room off the library, an adventure of an extraordinary kind.

In the hall was placed, as was customary in those times, the sedan-chair which the master of the house occasionally used, covered with stamped leather, and studded with gilt nails, and with its red silk blinds down. In this case, the doors of this old-fashioned conveyance were locked, the windows up, and, as I said, the blinds down, but not so closely that the curious child could not peep underneath one of them, and see into the interior.

A parting beam from the setting sun, admitted through the window of a back room, shot obliquely through the open door, and lighting on the chair, shone with a dull transparency through the crimson blind.

To her surprise, the child saw in the shadow a thin man, dressed in black, seated in it; he had sharp dark features; his nose, she fancied, a little awry, and his brown eyes were looking straight before him; his hand was on his thigh, and he stirred no more than the waxen figure she had seen at Southwark fair.

A child is so often lectured for asking questions, and on the propriety of silence, and the superior wisdom of its elders, that it accepts most things at last in good faith; and the little girl acquiesced respectfully in the occupation of the chair by this mahogany-faced person as being all right and proper.

It was not until she asked her mother who this man was, and observed her scared face as she questioned her more minutely upon the appearance of the stranger, that she began to understand that she had seen something unaccountable.

Mrs Carwell took the key of the chair from its nail over the footman's shelf, and led the child by the hand up to the hall, having a lighted candle in her other hand. She stopped at a distance from the chair, and placed the candlestick in the child's hand.

'Peep in, Margery, again, and try if there's anything there,' she whispered; 'hold the candle near the blind so as to throw its light through the curtain.'

The child peeped, this time with a very solemn face, and intimated at once that he was gone.

'Look again, and be sure,' urged her mother.

The little girl was quite certain; and Mrs Carwell, with her mob-cap of lace and cherry-coloured ribbons, and her dark brown hair, not yet powdered, over a very pale face, unlocked the door, looked in, and beheld emptiness.

'All a mistake, child, you see.'

'*There!* ma'am! see there! He's gone round the corner,' said the child.

'Where?' said Mrs Carwell, stepping backward a step.

'Into that room.'

'Tut, child! 'twas the shadow,' cried Mrs Carwell, angrily, because she was frightened. 'I moved the candle.' But she clutched one of the poles of the chair, which leant against the wall in the corner, and pounded the floor furiously with one end of it, being afraid to pass the open door the child had pointed to.

The cook and two kitchen-maids came running upstairs, not knowing what to make of this unwonted alarm.

They all searched the room; but it was still and empty, and no sign of anyone's having been there.

Some people may suppose that the direction given to her thoughts by this odd little incident will account for a very strange illusion which Mrs Carwell herself experienced about two hours later.

IX   *The Judge Leaves His House*

Mrs Flora Carwell was going up the great staircase with a posset for the Judge in a china bowl, on a little silver tray.

Across the top of the well-staircase there runs a massive oak rail; and, raising her eyes accidentally, she saw an extremely odd-looking stranger, slim and long, leaning carelessly over with a pipe between his finger and thumb. Nose, lips, and chin seemed all to droop downward into extraordinary length, as he leant his odd peering face over the banister. In his other hand he held a coil of rope, one end of which escaped from under his elbow and hung over the rail.

Mrs Carwell, who had no suspicion at the moment, that he was not a real person, and fancied that he was some one employed in cording the Judge's luggage, called to know what he was doing there.

Instead of answering, he turned about, and walked across the lobby, at about the same leisurely pace at which she was ascending, and entered a room, into which she followed him. It was an uncarpeted and unfurnished chamber. An open trunk lay upon the floor empty, and beside it the coil of rope; but except herself there was no one in the room.

Mrs Carwell was very much frightened, and now concluded that the child must have seen the same ghost that had just appeared to her. Perhaps, when she was able to think it over, it was a relief to believe so; for the face, figure, and dress described by the child were awfully like Pyneweck; and this certainly was not he.

Very much scared and very hysterical, Mrs Carwell ran down to her room, afraid to look over her shoulder, and got some companions about her, and wept, and talked, and drank more than one cordial, and talked and wept again, and so on, until, in those early days, it was ten o'clock, and time to go to bed.

A scullery maid remained up finishing some of her scouring and 'scalding' for some time after the other servants – who, as I said, were few in number – that night had got to their beds. This was a low-browed, broad-faced, intrepid wench with black hair, who did not "vally a ghost not a button", and treated the house-keeper's hysterics with measureless scorn.

The old house was quiet now. It was near twelve o'clock, no sounds were audible except the muffled wailing of the wintry winds, piping high among the roofs and chimneys, or rumbling at intervals, in under gusts, through the narrow channels of the street.

The spacious solitudes of the kitchen level were awfully dark, and this sceptical kitchen-wench was the only person now up and about the house. She hummed tunes to herself, for a time; and then stopped and listened; and then resumed her work again. At last, she was destined to be more terrified than even was the housekeeper.

There was a back kitchen in this house, and from this she heard, as if coming from below its foundatons, a sound like heavy strokes, that seemed to shake the earth beneath her feet. Sometimes a dozen in sequence, at regular intervals; sometimes fewer. She walked out softly into the passage, and was surprised to see a dusky glow issuing from this room, as if from a charcoal fire. The room seemed thick with smoke.

Looking in she very dimly beheld a monstrous figure, over a furnace, beating with a mighty hammer the rings and rivets of a chain.

The strokes, swift and heavy as they looked, sounded hollow and distant. The man stopped, and pointed to something on the floor, that, through the smoky haze, looked, she thought, like a dead body. She remarked no more; but the servants in the room close by, startled from their sleep by a hideous scream, found her in a swoon on the flags, close to the door, where she had just witnessed this ghastly vision.

Startled by the girl's incoherent asseverations that she had seen the Judge's corpse on the floor, two servants having first searched the lower part of the house, went rather frightened upstairs to inquire whether their master was well. They found him, not in his bed, but in his room. He had a table with candles burning at his bedside, and was getting on his clothes again; and he swore and cursed at them roundly in his old style, telling them that he had business, and that he would discharge on the spot any scoundrel who should dare to disturb him again.

So the invalid was left to his quietude.

In the morning it was rumoured here and there in the street that the Judge was dead. A servant was sent from the house three doors away, by Counsellor Traverse, to inquire at Judge Harbottle's hall door.

The servant who opened it was pale and reserved, and would only say that the Judge was ill. He had had a dangerous accident; Doctor Hedstone had been with him at seven o'clock in the morning.

There were averted looks, short answers, pale and frowning faces, and all the usual signs that there was a secret that sat heavily upon their minds and the time for disclosing which had not yet come. That time would arrive when the coroner had arrived, and the mortal scandal that had befallen the house could be no longer hidden. For that morning Mr Justice Harbottle had been found hanging by the neck from the banister at the top of the great staircase, and quite dead.

There was not the smallest sign of any struggle or resistance. There had not been heard a cry or any other noise in the slightest degree indicative of violence. There was medical evidence to show that, in his atrabilious state, it was quite on the cards that he might have made away with himself. The jury found accordingly that it was a case of suicide. But to those who were acquainted with the strange story which Judge Harbottle had related to at least two persons, the fact that the catastrophe occurred on the morning of March 10th seemed a startling coincidence.

A few days after, the pomp of a great funeral attended him to the grave; and so, in the language of Scripture, 'the rich man died, and was buried'.

THRAWN JANET

The Reverend Murdoch Soulis was long minister of the moorland parish of Balweary, in the vale of Dule. A severe, bleak-faced old man, dreadful to his hearers, he dwelt in the last years of his life, without relative or servant or any human company, in the small and lonely manse under the Hanging Shaw. In spite of the iron composure of his features, his eye was wild, scared, and uncertain; and when he dwelt, in private admonitions, on the future of the impenitent, it seemed as if his eye pierced through the storms of time to the terrors of eternity. Many young persons, coming to prepare themselves against the season of the Holy Communion, were dreadfully affected by his talk. He had a sermon on 1st Peter, v. and 8th, "The devil as a roaring lion", on the Sunday after every seventeenth of August, and he was accustomed to surpass himself upon that text both by the appalling nature of the matter and the terror of his bearing in the pulpit. The children were frightened into fits, and the old looked more than usually oracular, and were, all that day, full of those hints that Hamlet deprecated. The manse itself, where it stood by the water of Dule among some thick trees, with the Shaw overhanging it on the one side, and on the other many cold, moorish hilltops rising towards the sky, had begun, at a very early period of Mr Soulis's ministry, to be avoided in the dusk hours by all who valued themselves upon their prudence; and guidmen sitting at the clachan alehouse shook their heads together at the thought of passing late by that uncanny neighbourhood. There was one spot, to be more particular, which was regarded with especial awe. The manse stood between the high road and the water of Dule, with a gable to each; its back was towards the kirktown of Balweary, nearly half a mile away; in front of it, a bare garden, hedged with thorn, occupied the land between the river and the road. The house was two stories high, with two large rooms on each. It opened not directly on the garden, but on a causewayed path, or passage, giving on the road on the one hand, and closed on the other by the tall willows and elders that bordered on the stream. And it was this strip of causeway that enjoyed among the young parishioners of Balweary so infamous a reputation. The minister walked there often after dark, sometimes groaning aloud in the instancy of his unspoken prayers; and when he was from home, and the manse door was locked, the more daring schoolboys ventured, with beating hearts, to "follow my leader" across that legendary spot.

This atmosphere of terror, surrounding, as it did, a man of God of spotless character and orthodoxy, was a common cause of wonder and subject of inquiry among the few strangers who were led by chance or business into that unknown, outlying country. But many even of the people of the parish were ignorant of the strange events which had marked the first year of Mr Soulis's ministrations; and among those who were better informed, some were naturally reticent, and others shy of that particular topic. Now and again, only, one of the older folk would warm into courage over his third tumbler, and recount the cause of the minister's strange looks and solitary life.

Fifty years syne, when Mr Soulis cam first into Ba'weary, he was still a young man – a callant, the folk said – fu' o' book learnin' and grand at the exposition, but, as was natural in sae young a man, wi' nae leevin' experience in religion. The younger sort were greatly taken wi' his gifts and his gab; but auld, concerned, serious men and women were moved even to prayer for the young man, whom they took to be a self-deceiver, and the parish that was like to be sae ill-supplied. It was before the days o' the moderates – weary fa' them; but ill things are like guid – they baith come bit by bit, a pickle at a time; and there were folk even then that said the Lord had left the college professors to their ain devices, an' the lads that went to study wi' them wad hae done mair and better sittin' in a peat-bog, like their forbears of the persecution, wi' a Bible under their oxter and a speerit o' prayer in their heart. There was nae doubt, onyway, but that Mr Soulis had been ower lang at the college. He was careful and troubled for mony things besides the ae thing needful. He had a feck o' books wi' him – mair than had ever been seen before in a' that presbytery;

and a sair wark the carrier had wi' them, for they were a'like to have smoored in the Deil's Hag between this and Kilmackerlie. They were books o' divinity, to be sure, or so they ca'd them; but the serious were o' opinion there was little service for sae mony, when the hail o' God's Word would gang in the neuk of a plaid. Then he wad sit half the day and half the nicht forbye, which was scant decent – writin', nae less; and first, they were feared he wad read his sermons; and syne it proved he was writin' a book himsel', which was surely no fittin' for ane of his years an' sma' experience.

Onyway it behoved him to get an auld, decent wife to keep the manse for him an' see to his bit denners; and he was recommended to an auld limmer – Janet M'Clour, they ca'd her – and sae far left to himsel' as to be ower persuaded. There was mony advised him to the contrar, for Janet was mair than suspeckit by the best folk in Ba'weary. Lang or that, she had had a wean to a dragoon; she hadnae come forrit* for maybe thretty year; and bairns had seen her mumblin' to hersel' up on Key's Loan in the gloamin', whilk was an unco time an' place for a God-fearin' woman. Howsoever, it was the laird himsel' that had first tauld the minister o' Janet; and in thae days he wad have gane a far gate to pleesure the laird. When folk tauld him that Janet was sib to the deil, it was a' superstition by his way of it; an' when they cast up the Bible to him an' the witch of Endor, he wad threep it doun their thrapples that thir days were a'gane by, and the deil was mercifully restrained.

Weel, when it got about the clachan that Janet M'Clour was to be servant at the manse, the folk were fair mad wi'her an' him thegether; and some o' the guidwives had nae better to dae than get round her door cheeks and chairge her wi' a'that was ken't again her, frae the sodger's bairn to John Tamson's twa kye. She was nae great speaker; folk usually let her gang her ain gate, an' she let them gang theirs, wi' neither Fair-guid-een nor Fair-guid-day; but when she buckled to, she had a tongue to deave the miller. Up she got, an' there wasnae an auld story in Ba'weary but she gart somebody lowp for it that day; they couldnae say ae thing

* To come forrit – to offer oneself as a communicant.

but she could say twa to it; till, at the hinder end, the guidwives up and claucht haud of her, and clawed the coats aff her back, and pu'd her doun the clachan to the water o'Dule, to see if she were a witch or no, soum or droun. The carline skirled till ye could hear her at the Hangin' Shaw, and she focht like ten; there was mony a guidwife bure the mark of her neist day an' mony a lang day after; and just in the hettest o' the collieshangie, wha suld come up (for his sins) but the new minister.

"Women," said he (and he had a grand voice), "I charge you in the Lord's name to let her go."

Janet ran to him – she was fair wud wi' terror – an' clang to him, an' prayed him, for Christ's sake, save her frae the cummers; an' they, for their pairt, tauld him a' that was ken't, and maybe mair.

"Woman," says he to Janet, "is this true?"

"As the Lord sees me," says she, "as the Lord made me, no a word o't. Forbye the bairn," says she, "I've been a decent woman a' my days."

"Will you," says Mr Soulis, "in the name of God, and before me, His unworthy minister, renounce the devil and his works?"

Weel, it wad appear that when he askit that, she gave a girn that fairly frichtit them that saw her, an' they could hear her teeth play dirl thegether in her chafts; but there was naething for it but the ae way or the ither; an' Janet lifted up her hand and renounced the deil before them a'.

"And now," says Mr Soulis to the guidwives, "home with ye, one and all, and pray to God for His forgiveness."

And he gied Janet his arm, though she had little on her but a sark, and took her up the clachan to her ain door like a leddy of the land; an' her scrieghin' and laughin' as was a scandal to be heard.

There were mony grave folk lang ower their prayers that nicht; but when the morn cam' there was sic a fear fell upon a' Ba'weary that the bairns hid theirsels, and even the men folk stood and keekit frae their doors. For there was Janet comin' doun the clachan – her or her likeness, nane could tell – wi' her neck thrawn, and her heid on ae side, like a body that has been hangit, and a girn on her face like an unstreakit corp. By an' by they got used wi' it, and even speered at her to ken what was wrang; but frae that day forth she couldnae speak like a Christian woman, but slavered and played click wi' her teeth like a pair o' shears; and frae that day forth the name o' God cam never on her lips. Whiles she wad try to say it, but it michtnae be. Them that kenned best said least; but they never gied that Thing the name o' Janet M'Clour; for the auld Janet, by their way o't, was in muckle hell that day. But the minister was neither to haud nor to bind; he preached about naething but the folk's cruelty that had gi'en her a stroke of the palsy; he skelpt the bairns that meddled her; and he had her up to the manse that same nicht, and dwalled there a' his lane wi' her under the Hangin' Shaw.

Weel, time gaed by: and the idler sort commenced to think mair lichtly o' that black business. The minister was weel thocht o'; he was aye late at the writing, folk wad see his can'le doon by the Dule water after twal'at e'en; and he seemed pleased wi himsel' and upsitten as at first, though a' body could see that he was dwining. As for Janet she cam an' she gaed; if she didnae speak muckle afore, it was reason she should speak less then; she meddled naebody; but she was an eldritch thing to see, an' nane wad hae mistrysted wi' her for Ba'weary glebe.

About the end o' July there cam' a spell o' weather, the like o't never was in that country side; it was lown an' het an' heartless; the herds couldnae win up the Black Hill, the bairns were ower weariet to play; an' yet it was gousty too, wi' claps o'het wund that rumm'led in the glens, and bits o' shouers that slockened naething. We aye thocht it but to thun'er on the morn; but the morn cam, an' the morn's morning, and it was aye the same uncanny weather, sair on folks and bestial. Of a' that were the waur, nane suffered like Mr Soulis; he could neither sleep nor eat, he tauld his elders; an' when he wasnae writin' at his weary book, he wad be stravaguin' ower a' the countryside like a man possessed, when a' body else was blythe to keep caller ben the house.

Abune Hangin' Shaw, in the bield o' the Black Hill, there's a bit enclosed grund wi' an iron yett; and it seems, in the auld days, that was the kirdyaird o' Ba'weary, and consecrated by the Papists before the blessed licht shone upon the kingdom. It was a great howff, o' Mr Soulis's onyway; there he would sit an' consider his sermons; and inded it's a bieldy bit. Weel, as he came ower the wast end o' the Black Hill, ae day, he saw first twa, an syne fower, an' syne seeven corbie craws fleein' round an' round abune the auld kirkyaird. They flew laigh and heavy, an' squawked to ither as they gaed; and it was clear to Mr Soulis that something had put them frae their ordinar. He wasnae easy fleyed, an' gaed straucht up to the wa's; and what suld he find there but a man, or the appearance of a man, sittin' in the inside upon a grave. He was of a great stature, an' black as hell, and his e'en were singular to see.* Mr Soulis had heard tell of o' black men, mony's the time; but there was something unco about this black man that daunted him. Het as he was, he took a kind o' cauld grue in the marrow o' his banes; but up he spak for a' that; an' says he: "My friend, are you a stranger in this place?" The black man answered never a word; he got upon his feet, an' begude to hirsle to the wa' on the far side; but he aye lookit at the minister; an' the minister stood an' lookit back; till a' in a meenute the black man was ower the wa' an' rinnin' for the bield o' the trees. Mr Soulis, he hardly kenned why, ran after him; but he was sair forjaskit wi' his walk an' the het, unhalesome weather; and rin as he likit, he got nae mair than a glisk o' the black man amang the birks, till he won doun to the foot o' the hill-side, an' there he saw him ance mair, gaun, hap, step, an lowp, ower Dule water to the manse.

Mr Soulis wasnae weel pleased that this fearsome gangrel suld mak' sae free wi' Ba'weary manse; an' he ran the harder, an' wet shoon, ower the burn, an' up the walk; but the deil a black man was there to see. He stepped out upon the road, but there was naebody there; he gae a' ower the gairden, but na, nae black man. At the hinder end, and a bit feared as was but natural, he lifted the hasp and into the manse; and there was Janet M'Clour before his een, wi' her thrawn craig, and nane sae pleased to see him. And he aye minded sinsyne, when first he set his een upon her, he had the same cauld and deidly grue.

"Janet," says he, "have you seen a black man?"

"A black man?" quo' she. "Save us a'! Ye're no wise, minister. There's nae black man in a' Ba-weary."

* It was a common belief in Scotland that the devil appeared as a black man. This appears in several witch trials and I think in Law's *Memorials*, that delightful store-house of the quaint and grisly.

But she didnae speak plain, ye maun understand; but yam-yammered, like a powny wi' the bit in its moo.

"Weel," says he, "Janet, if there was nae black man, I have spoken with the Accuser of the Brethren."

And he sat down like ane wi' a fever, an' his teeth chittered in his heid.

"Hoots," says she, "think shame to yoursel', minister;" an' gied him a drap brandy that she keept aye by her.

Syne Mr Soulis gaed into his study amang a' his books. It's a lang, laigh, mirk chalmer, perishin' cauld in winter, an' no very dry even in the top o' the simmer, for the manse stands near the burn. Sae doun he sat, and thocht of a' that had come an' gane since he was in Ba-weary, an' his hame, an' the days when he was a bairn an' ran daffin' on the braes; and that black man aye ran in his heid like the ower-come of a sang. Aye the mair he thocht, the mair he thocht o' the black man. He tried the prayer, an' the words wouldnae come to him; an' he tried, they say, to write at his book, but he could nae mak' nae mair o' that. There was whiles he thocht the black man was at his oxter, an' the swat stood upon him cauld as well-water; and there was other whiles, when he cam to himsel' like a christened bairn and minded naething.

The upshot was that he gaed to the window an' stood glowrin' at Dule water. The trees are unco thick, an' the water lies deep an' black under the manse; and there was Janet washin' the cla'es wi' her coats kilted. She had her back to the minister, an' he, for his pairt, hardly kenned what he was lookin' at. Syne she turned round, an' shawed her face; Mr Soulis had the same cauld grue as twice that day afore, an' it was borne in upon him what folk said, that Janet was deid lang syne, an' this was a bogle in her clay-cauld flesh. He drew back a pickle and he scanned her narrowly. She was tramp-trampin' in the cla'es, croonin' to hersel'; and eh! Gude guide us, but it was a fearsome face. Whiles she sang louder, but there was nae man born o' woman that could tell the words o' her sang; an' whiles she lookit side-lang doun, but there was naething there for her to look at. There gaed a scunner through the flesh upon his banes; and that was Heeven's advertisement. But Mr Soulis just blamed himsel', he said, to think sae ill of a puir, auld afflicted wife that hadnae a freend forbye himsel'; an' he put up a bit prayer for him an' her, an' drank a little caller water – for his heart rose again the meat – an' gaed up to his naked bed in the gloaming.

That was a nicht that has never been forgotten in Ba'weary, the nicht o' the seeventeenth of August, seventeen hun'er' and twal'. It had been het afore, as I hae said, but that nicht it was hetter than ever. The sun gaed doun among unco-lookin' clouds; it fell as mirk as the pit; no a star, no a breath o' wund; ye couldnae see your han' afore your face, and even the auld folk cuist the covers frae their beds and lay pechin' for their breath. Wi' a' that he had upon his mind, it was gey and unlikely Mr Soulis wad get muckle sleep. He lay an' he tummled; the gude, caller bed that he got into brunt his very banes; whiles he slept, and whiles he waukened; whiles he heard the time o' nicht, and whiles a tyke yowlin' up the muir, as if somebody was deid; whiles he thocht he heard bogles claverin' in his lug, an' whiles he saw spunkies in the room. He behoved, he judged, to be sick; an' sick he was – little he jaloosed the sickness.

At the hinder end, he got a clearness in his mind, sat up in his sark on the bedside, and fell thinkin' ance mair o' the black man an' Janet. He couldnae weel tell how – maybe it was the cauld to his feet – but it cam' in upon him wi' a spate that there was some connection between thir twa, an' that either or baith o' them were bogles. And just at that moment, in Janet's room, which was neist to his, there cam' a stramp o' feet as if men were wars'lin', an' then a wund gaed reishling round the fower quarters of the house; an' then a' was aince mair as seelent as the grave.

Mr Soulis was feared for neither man nor deevil. He got his tinder-box, an' lit a can'le, an' made three steps o't ower to Janet's door. It was on the hasp, an' he pushed it open, an' keeked bauldly in. It was a big room, as big as the minister's ain, an' plenished wi' grand, auld, solid gear, for he had naething else. There was a fower-posted bed wi' auld tapestry; and a braw cabinet of aik, that was fu' o' the minister's divinity books, an' put there to be out o' the gate; an' a wheen duds o' Janet's lying here and there about the floor. But nae Janet could Mr Soulis see; nor ony sign of a contention. In he gaed (an' there's few that wad ha'e followed him) an' lookit a' round, an' listened. But there was was naethin' to be heard, neither inside the manse nor in a' Ba'weary parish, an' naethin' to be seen but the muckle shadows turnin' round the can'le. An' then a' at aince, the minister's heart played dunt an' stood stock-still; an' a cauld wund blew amang the hairs o' his heid. Whaten a weary sicht was that for the puir man's een! For there was Janet hangin' frae a nail beside the auld aik cabinet: her heid aye lay on her shoother, her een were steeked, the tongue projekit frae her mouth, and her heels were twa feet clear abune the floor.

"God forgive us all!" thocht Mr Soulis, "poor Janet's dead."

He cam' a step nearer to the corp; an' then his heart fair whammled in his inside. For by what cantrip it wad ill-beseem a man to judge, she was hingin' frae a single nail an' by a single wursted thread for darnin' hose.

It's an awfu' thing to be your lane at nicht wi' siccan prodigies o' darkness; but Mr Soulis was strong in the Lord. He turned an' gaed his ways oot o' that room, and lockit the door ahint him; and set doon the can'le on the table at the stairfoot. He couldnae pray, he couldnae think, he was dreepin' wi' caul' swat, an' naething could he hear but the dunt-dunt-duntin' o' his ain heart. He micht maybe have stood there an hour, or maybe twa, he minded sae little; when a' o' a sudden, he heard a laigh, uncanny steer upstairs; a foot gaed to an' fro in the cham'er whaur the corp was hingin'; syne the door was opened, though he minded weel that he had lockit it; an' syne there was a step upon the landin', an' it seemed to him as if the corp was lookin' ower the rail and doun upon him whaur he stood.

He took up the can'le again (for he couldnae want the licht), and as saftly as ever he could, gaed straucht out o' the manse an to the far end o' the causeway. It was aye pit-mirk; the flame o' the can'le, when he set it on the grund, brunt steedy and clear as in a room; naething moved, but the Dule water seepin' and sabbin' doon the glen, an' yon unhaly footstep that cam' ploddin doun the stairs inside the manse. He kenned the foot over weel, for it was Janet's; and at ilka step that cam' a wee thing nearer, the cauld got deeper in his vitals. He commended his soul to Him that made an' keepit him; "and O Lord," said he, "give me strength this night to war against the powers of evil."

By this time the foot was comin' through the passage for the door; he could hear a hand skirt alang the wa', as if the fearsome thing was feelin' for its way. The saughs tossed an' maned thegether, a long sigh cam' ower the hills, the flame o' the candle was blawn aboot; an' there stood the corp of Thrawn Janet, wi' her grogram goun an' her black mutch, wi' the heid aye upon the shouther, an' the girn still upon the face o't – leevin', ye wad hae said – deid, as Mr Soulis weel kenned – upon the threshold o' the manse.

It's a strange thing that the saul of man should be that thirled into his perishable body; but the minister saw that, an' his heart didnae break.

She didnae stand there lang; she began to move again an' cam' slowly towards Mr Soulis whaur he stood under the saughs. A' the life o' his body, a' the strength o' his speerit, were glowerin' frae his een. It seemed she was gaun to speak, but wanted words, an' made a sign wi' the left hand. There cam' a clap o' wund, like a cat's fuff; oot gaed the can'le, the saughs skrieghed like folk; an' Mr Soulis kenned that, live or die, this was the end o't.

"Witch, beldame, devil!" he cried, "I charge you, by the power of God, begone – if you be dead, to the grave – if you be damned, to hell."

An' at that moment the Lord's ain hand out o' the Heevens struck the Horror whaur it stood; the auld, deid, desecrated corp o' the witch-wife, sae lang keepit frae the grave and hirsled round by deils, lowed up like a brunstane spunk and fell in ashes to the grund; the thunder followed, peal on dirling peal, the rairing rain upon the back o' that; and Mr Soulis lowped through the garden hedge, and ran, wi' skelloch upon skelloch, for the clachan.

That same mornin', John Christie saw the Black Man pass the Muckle Cairn as it was chappin' six; before eicht, he gaed by the change-house at Knockdow; an' no lang after, Sandy M'Lellan saw him gaun linkin' doun the braes frae Kilmackerlie. There's little doubt but it was him that dwalled sae lang in Janet's body; but he was awa' at last; and sinsyne the deil has never fashed us in Ba'weary.

But it was a sair dispensation for the minister; lang, lang he lay ravin' in his bed; and frae that hour to this, he was the man ye ken the day.

Oscar Wilde

THE SPHINX WITHOUT A SECRET

An etching

One afternoon I was sitting outside the Café de la Paix, watching the splendour and shabbiness of Parisian life, and wondering over my vermouth at the strange panorama of pride and poverty that was passing before me, when I heard some one call my name. I turned round, and saw Lord Murchison. We had not met since we had been at college together, nearly ten years before, so I was delighted to come across him again, and we shook hands warmly. At Oxford we had been great friends. I had liked him immensely, he was so handsome, so high-spirited, and so honourable. We used to say of him that he would be the best of fellows, if he did not always speak the truth, but I think we really admired him all the more for his frankness. I found him a good deal changed. He looked anxious and puzzled, and seemed to be in doubt about something. I felt it could not be modern scepticism, for Murchison was the stoutest of Tories, and believed in the Pentateuch as firmly as he believed in the House of Peers; so I concluded that it was a woman, and asked him if he was married yet.

'I don't understand women well enough,' he answered.

'My dear Gerald,' I said, 'women are meant to be loved, not to be understood.'

'I cannot love where I cannot trust,' he replied.

'I believe you have a mystery in your life, Gerald,' I exclaimed; 'tell me about it.'

'Let us go for a drive,' he answered, 'it is too crowded here. No, not a yellow carriage, any other colour – there, that dark-green one will do;' and in a few moments we were trotting down the boulevard in the direction of the Madeleine.

'Where shall we go to?' I said.

'Oh, anywhere you like!' he answered – 'to the restaurant in the Bois; we will dine there, and you shall tell me all about yourself.'

'I want to hear about you first,' I said. 'Tell me your mystery.'

He took from his pocket a little silver-clasped morocco case, and handed it to me. I opened it. Inside there was the photograph of a woman. She was tall and slight, and strangely picturesque with her large vague eyes and loosened hair. She looked like a *clairvoyante*, and was wrapped in rich furs.

'What do you think of that face?' he said; 'is it truthful?'

I examined it carefully. It seemed to me the face of some one who had a secret, but whether that secret was good or evil I could not say. Its beauty was a beauty moulded out of many mysteries – the beauty, in fact, which is psychological, not plastic – and the faint smile that just played across the lips was far too subtle to be really sweet.

'Well,' he cried impatiently, 'what do you say?'

'She is the Gioconda in sables,' I answered. 'Let me know all about her.'

'Not now,' he said; 'after dinner;' and began to talk of other things.

When the waiter brought us our coffee and cigarettes I reminded Gerald of his promise. He rose from his seat, walked two or three times up and down the room, and, sinking into an armchair, told me the following story:-

'One evening', he said, 'I was walking down Bond Street about five o'clock. There was a terrific crush of carriages, and the traffic was almost stopped. Close to the pavement was standing a little yellow brougham, which, for some reason or other, attracted my attention. As I passed by there looked out from it the face I showed you this afternoon. It fascinated me immediately. All that night I kept thinking of it, and all the next day. I wandered up and down that wretched Row, peering into every carriage, and waiting for the yellow brougham; but I could not find *ma belle inconnue*, and at last I began to think she was merely a dream. About a week afterwards I was dining with Madame de Rastail. Dinner was for eight o'clock; but at half-past eight we were still waiting in the drawing-room. Finally the servant threw open the door, and announced Lady Alroy. It was the woman I had been looking for. She came in very slowly, looking like a moonbeam in grey lace, and, to my intense delight, I was asked to take her in to dinner. After we had sat down I remarked quite innocently, "I think I caught sight of you in Bond Street some time ago, Lady Alroy." She grew very pale, and said to me in a low voice, 'Pray do not talk so loud; you may be overheard.' I felt miserable at having made such a bad beginning, and plunged recklessly into the subject of the French plays. She spoke very little, always in the same low musical voice, and seemed as if she was afraid of some one listening. I fell passionately, stupidly in love, and the indefinable atmosphere of mystery that surrounded her excited my most ardent curiosity. When she was going away, which she did very soon after dinner, I asked her if I might call and see her. She hesitated for a moment, glanced round to see if any one was near us, and then said, "Yes; tomorrow at a quarter to five." I begged Madame de Rastail to tell me about her; but all that I could learn was that she was a widow with a beautiful house in Park Lane, and as some scientific bore began a dissertation on widows, as exemplifying the survival of the matrimonially fittest, I left and went home.

'The next day I arrived at Park Lane punctual to the moment, but was told by the butler that Lady Alroy had just gone out. I went down to the club quite unhappy and very much puzzled, and after long consideration wrote her a letter, asking if I might be allowed to try my chance some other afternoon. I had no answer for several days, but at last I got a little note saying she would be at home on Sunday at four, and with this extraordinary postscript: "Please do not write to me here again; I will explain when I see you." On Sunday she received me, and was perfectly charming; but when I was going away she begged of me if I ever had occasion to write to her again, to address my letter to "Mrs Knox, care of Whittaker's Library, Green Street." "There are reasons", she said, "why I cannot receive letters in my own house."

'All through the season I saw a great deal of her, and the atmosphere of mystery never left her. Sometimes I thought that she was in the power of some man, but she looked so unapproachable that I could not believe it. It was really very difficult for me to come to any conclusion, for she was like one of those strange crystals that one sees in museums, which are at one moment clear, and at another clouded. At last I determined to ask her to be my wife: I was sick and tired of the incessant secrecy that she imposed on all my visits, and on the few letters I sent her. I wrote to her at the library to ask her if she could see me the following Monday at six. She answered yes, and I was in the seventh heaven of delight. I was infatuated with her: in spite of the mystery, I thought then – in consequence of it, I see now. No; it was the woman herself I loved. The mystery troubled me, maddened me. Why did chance put me in its track?'

'You discovered it, then?' I cried.

'I fear so,' he answered. 'You can judge for yourself.'

'When Monday came round I went to lunch with my uncle, and about four o'clock found myself in the Marylebone Road. My uncle, you know, lives in Regent's Park. I wanted to get to Piccadilly, and took a short cut through a lot of shabby little streets. Suddenly I saw in front of me Lady Alroy, deeply veiled and walking very fast. On coming to the last house in the street, she went up the steps, took out a latch-key, and let herself in. "Here is the mystery," I said to myself; and I hurried on and examined the house. It seemed a sort of place for letting lodgings. On the doorstep lay her handkerchief, which she had dropped. I picked it up and put it in my pocket. Then I began to consider what I should do. I came to the conclusion that I had no right to spy on her, and I drove down to the club. At six I called to see her. She was lying on a sofa, in a tea-gown of silver tissue looped up by some strange moonstones that she always wore. She was looking quite lovely. "I am so glad to see you," she said; "I have not been out all day." I stared at her in amazement, and pulling the handkerchief out of my pocket, handed it to her. "You dropped this in Cumnor Street this afternoon, Lady Alroy," I said very calmly. She looked at me in terror, but made no attempt to take the handkerchief. "What were you doing there?" I asked. "What right have you to question me?" she answered. "The right of a man who loves you," I replied; "I came here to ask you to be my wife." She hid her face in her hands, and burst into floods of tears. "You must tell me," I continued. She stood up, and, looking me straight in the face, said, "Lord Murchison, there is nothing to tell you." – "You went to meet some one," I cried; "this is your mystery." She grew dreadfully white, and said, "I went to meet no one." – "Can't you tell the truth?" I exclaimed. "I have told it," she replied. I was mad, frantic; I don't know what I said, but I said terrible things to her. Finally I rushed out of the house. She wrote me a letter the next day; I sent it back unopened, and started for Norway with Alan Colville. After a month I came back, and the first thing I saw in the *Morning Post* was the death of Lady Alroy. She had caught a chill at the Opera, and had died in five days of congestion of the lungs. I shut myself up and saw no one. I had loved her so much, I had loved her so madly. Good God! how I had loved that woman!'

'You went to the street, to the house in it?' I said.

'Yes,' he answered.

'One day I went to Cumnor Street. I could not help it; I was tortured with doubt. I knocked at the door, and a respectable-looking woman opened it to me. I asked her if she had any rooms to let. "Well, sir," she replied, "the drawing-rooms are supposed to be let; but I have not seen the lady for three months, and as rent is owing on them, you can have them." – "Is this the lady?" I said, showing the photograph. "That's her, sure enough," she exclaimed; "and when is she coming back, sir?" – "The lady is dead," I replied. "Oh, sir, I hope not!" said the woman; "she was my best lodger. She paid me three guineas a week merely to sit in my drawing-rooms now and then." – "She met some one here?" I said; but the woman assured me that it was not so, that she always came alone, and saw no one. "What on earth did she do here?" I cried. "She simply sat in the drawing-room, sir, reading books, and sometimes had tea," the woman answered. I did not know what to say, so I gave her a sovereign and went away. Now, what do you think it all meant? You don't believe the woman was telling the truth?'

'I do.'

'Then why did Lady Alroy go there?'

'My dear Gerald,' I answered, 'Lady Alroy was simply a woman with a mania for mystery. She took these rooms for the pleasure of going there with her veil down, and imagining she was a heroine. She had a passion for secrecy, but she herself was merely a Sphinx without a secret.'

'Do you really think so?'

'I am sure of it,' I replied.

He took out the morocco case, opened it, and looked at the photograph. 'I wonder?' he said at last.

Rudyard Kipling

WITHOUT
BENEFIT OF CLERGY

Before my Spring I garnered Autumn's gain,
Out of her time my field was white with grain,
   The year gave up her secrets to my woe.
Forced and deflowered each sick season lay,
In mystery of increase and decay;
I saw the sunset ere men saw the day,
   Who am too wise in that I should not know.
                              Bitter Waters.

I

'But if it be a girl?'

'Lord of my life, it cannot be. I have prayed for so many nights, and sent gifts to Sheikh Badl's shrine so often, that I know God will give us a son – a man-child that shall grow into a man. Think of this and be glad. My mother shall be his mother till I can take him again, and the mullah of the Pattan mosque shall cast his nativity – God send he be born in an auspicious hour! – and then, and then thou wilt never weary of me, thy slave.'

'Since when has thou been a slave, my queen?'

'Since the beginning – till this mercy came to me. How could I be sure of thy love when I knew that I had been bought with silver?'

'Nay, that was the dowry. I paid it to thy mother.'

'And she has buried it, and sits upon it all day long like a hen. What talk is yours of dower! I was bought as though I had been a Lucknow dancing-girl instead of a child.'

'Art thou sorry for the sale?'

'I have sorrowed; but to-day I am glad. Thou wilt never cease to love me now? – answer, my king.'

'Never – never. No.'

'Not even though the *mem-log* – the white women of thy own

blood – love thee? And remember, I have watched them driving in the evening; they are very fair.'

'I have seen fire-balloons by the hundred. I have seen the moon, and – then I saw no more fire-balloons.'

Ameera clapped her hands and laughed. 'Very good talk,' she said. Then with an assumption of great stateliness, 'It is enough. Thou hast my permission to depart, – if thou wilt.'

The man did not move. He was sitting on a low red-lacquered couch in a room furnished only with a blue and white floor-cloth, some rugs, and a very complete collection of native cushions. At his feet sat a woman of sixteen, and she was all but all the world in his eyes. By every rule and law she should have been otherwise, for he was an Englishman, and she a Mussulman's daughter bought two years before from her mother, who, being left without money, would have sold Ameera shrieking to the Prince of Darkness if the price had been sufficient.

It was a contract entered into with a light heart; but even before the girl had reached her bloom she came to fill the greater portion of John Holden's life. For her, and the withered hag her mother, he had taken a little house overlooking the great red-walled city, and found, – when the marigolds had sprung up by the well in the courtyard and Ameera had established herself according to her own ideas of comfort, and her mother had ceased grumbling at the inadequacy of the cooking-places, the distance from the daily market, and at matters of housekeeping in general, – that the house was to him his home. Any one could enter his bachelor's bungalow by day or night, and the life that he led there was an unlovely one. In the house in the city his feet only could pass beyond the outer courtyard to the women's rooms; and when the big wooden gate was bolted behind him he was king in his own territory, with Ameera for queen. And there was going to be added to this kingdom a third person whose arrival Holden felt inclined to resent. It interfered with his perfect happiness. It disarranged the orderly peace of the house that was his own. But Ameera was wild with delight at the thought of it, and her mother not less so. The love of a man, and particularly a white man, was at the best an inconstant affair, but it might, both women argued, be held fast by a baby's hands. 'And then,' Ameera would always

say, 'then he will never care for the white *mem-log*. I hate them all
– I hate them all.'

'He will go back to his own people in time,' said the mother;
'but by the blessing of God that time is yet afar off.'

Holden sat silent on the couch thinking of the future, and his
thoughts were not pleasant. The drawbacks of a double life are
manifold. The Government, with singular care, had ordered him
out of the station for a fortnight on special duty in the place of a
man who was watching by the bedside of a sick wife. The verbal
notification of the transfer had been edged by a cheerful remark
that Holden ought to think himself lucky in being a bachelor and a
free man. He came to break the news to Ameera.

'It is not good,' she said slowly, 'but it is not all bad. There is my
mother here, and no harm will come to me – unless indeed I die of
pure joy. Go thou to thy work and think no troublesome
thoughts. When the days are done I believe . . . nay, I am sure. And
– and then I shall lay *him* in thy arms, and thou wilt love me for
ever. The train goes tonight, at midnight is it not? Go now, and do
not let thy heart be heavy by cause of me. But thou wilt not delay
in returning? Thou wilt not stay on the road to talk to the bold
white *mem-log*. Come back to me swiftly, my life.'

As he left the courtyard to reach his horse that was tethered to
the gate-post, Holden spoke to the white-haired old watchman
who guarded the house, and bade him under certain contingencies
despatch the filled-up telegraph-form that Holden gave him. It
was all that could be done, and with the sensations of a man who
has attended his own funeral Holden went away by the night mail
to his exile. Every hour of the day he dreaded the arrival of the
telegram, and every hour of the night he pictured to himself the
death of Ameera. In consequence his work for the State was not of
first-rate quality, nor was his temper towards his colleagues of the
most amiable. The fortnight ended without a sign from his home,
and, torn to pieces by his anxieties, Holden returned to be
swallowed up for two precious hours by a dinner at the club,
wherein he heard, as a man hears in a swoon, voices telling him
how execrably he had performed the other man's duties, and how
he had endeared himself to all his associates. Then he fled on
horseback through the night with his heart in his mouth. There

was no answer at first to his blows on the gate, and he had just wheeled his horse round to kick it in when Pir Khan appeared with a lantern and held his stirrup.

'Has aught occurred?' said Holden.

'The news does not come from my mouth. Protector of the Poor, but –' He held out his shaking hand as befitted the bearer of good news who is entitled to a reward.

Holden hurried through the courtyard. A light burned in the upper room. His horse neighed in the gateway, and he heard a shrill little wail that sent all the blood into the apple of his throat. It was a new voice, but it did not prove that Ameera was alive.

'Who is there?' he called up the narrow brick staircase.

There was a cry of delight from Ameera, and then the voice of the mother, tremulous with old age and pride – 'We be two women and – the man – thy – son.'

On the threshold of the room Holden stepped on a naked dagger, that was laid there to avert ill-luck, and it broke at the hilt under his impatient heel.

'God is great!' cooed Ameera in the half-light. 'Thou hast taken his misfortunes on thy head.'

'Ay, but how is it with thee, life of my life? Old woman, how is it with her?'

'She has forgotten her sufferings for joy that the child is born. There is no harm; but speak softly,' said the mother.

'It only needed thy presence to make me all well,' said Ameera. 'My king, thou hast been very long away. What gifts hast thou for me? Ah, ah! It is I that bring gifts this time. Look, my life, look. Was there ever such a babe? Nay, I am too weak even to clear my arm from him.'

'Rest then, and do not talk. I am here, *bachari* [little woman].'

'Well said, for there is a bond and a heel-rope [*peecharee*] between us now that nothing can break. Look – canst thou see in this light? He is without spot or blemish. Never was such a man-child. *Ya illah!* he shall be a pundit – no, a trooper of the Queen. And, my life, dost thou love me as well as ever, though I am faint and sick and worn? Answer truly.'

'Yea, I love as I have loved, with all my soul. Lie still, pearl, and rest.'

'Then do not go. Sit by my side here – so. Mother, the lord of this house needs a cushion. Bring it.' There was an almost imperceptible movement on the part of the new life that lay in the hollow of Ameera's arm. 'Aho!' she said, her voice breaking with love. 'The babe is a champion from his birth. He is kicking me in the side with mighty kicks. Was there ever such a babe? And he is ours to us – thine and mine. Put thy hand on his head, but carefully, for he is very young, and men are unskilled in such matters.'

Very cautiously Holden touched with the tips of his fingers the downy head.

'He is of the faith,' said Ameera; 'for lying here in the night-watches I whispered the call to prayer and the profession of faith into his ears. And it is most marvellous that he was born upon a Friday, as I was born. Be careful of him, my life; but he can almost grip with his hands.'

Holden found one helpless little hand that closed feebly on his finger. And the clutch ran through his body till it settled about his heart. Till then his sole thought had been for Ameera. He began to realise that there was someone else in the world, but he could not feel that it was a veritable son with a soul. He sat down to think, and Ameera dozed lightly.

'Get hence, Sahib,' said her mother under her breath. 'It is not good that she should find you here on waking. She must be still.'

'I go,' said Holden submissively. 'Here be rupees. See that my *baba* gets fat and finds all that he needs.'

The chink of the silver roused Ameera. 'I am his mother, and no hireling,' she said weakly. 'Shall I look to him more or less for the sake of money? Mother, give it back. I have born my lord a son.'

The deep sleep of weakness came upon her almost before the sentence was completed. Holden went down to the courtyard very softly with his heart at ease. Pir Khan, the old watchman, was chuckling with delight. 'This house is now complete,' he said, and without further comment thrust into Holden's hands the hilt of a sabre worn many years ago when he, Pir Khan, served the Queen in the police. The bleat of a tethered goat came from the well-kerb.

'There be two,' said Pir Khan, 'two goats of the best. I bought them, and they cost much money; and since there is no birth-party assembled their flesh will be all mine. Strike craftily, Sahib! 'Tis an ill-balanced sabre at the best. Wait till they raise their heads from cropping the marigolds.'

'And why?' said Holden, bewildered.

'For the birth-sacrifice. What else? Otherwise the child being unguarded from fate may die. The Protector of the Poor knows the fitting words to be said.'

Holden had learned them once with little thought that he would ever speak them in earnest. The touch of the cold sabre-hilt in his palm turned suddenly to the clinging grip of the child up-stairs – the child that was his own son – and a dread of loss filled him.

'Strike!' said Pir Khan. 'Never life came into the world but life was paid for it. See, the goats have raised their heads. Now! With a drawing cut!'

Hardly knowing what he did Holden cut twice as he muttered the Mahomedan prayer that runs: 'Almighty! In place of this my son I offer life for life, blood for blood, head for head, bone for bone, hair for hair, skin for skin.' The waiting horse snorted and bounded in his pickets at the smell of the raw blood that spurted over Holden's riding-boots.

'Well smitten!' said Pir Khan, wiping the sabre. 'A swordsman was lost in thee. Go with a light heart, Heaven-born. I am thy servant, and the servant of thy son. May the Presence live a thousand years and . . . the flesh of the goats is all mine?' Pir Khan drew back richer by a month's pay. Holden swung himself into the saddle and rode off through the low-hanging wood-smoke of the evening. He was full of riotous exultation, alternating with a vast vague tenderness directed towards no particular object, that made him choke as he bent over the neck of his uneasy horse. 'I never felt like this in my life,' he thought. 'I'll go to the club and pull myself together.'

A game of pool was beginning, and the room was full of men. Holden entered, eager to get to the light and the company of his fellows, singing at the top of his voice –

'In Baltimore a-walking, a lady I did meet!'

'Did you?' said the club-secretary from his corner. 'Did she happen to tell you that your boots were wringing wet? Great goodness, man, it's blood!'

'Bosh!' said Holden, picking his cue from the rack. 'May I cut in? It's dew. I've been riding through high crops. My faith! my boots are in a mess though!

> 'And if it be a girl she shall wear a wedding-ring,
> And if it be a boy he shall fight for his king,
> With his dirk, and his cap, and his little jacket blue,
> He shall walk the quarter-deck –'

'Yellow on blue – green next player,' said the marker monotonously.

' "He shall walk the quarter-deck," – Am I green, marker? "He shall walk the quarter-deck," – eh! that's a bad shot, – "As his daddy used to do!" '

'I don't see that you have anything to crow about,' said a zealous junior civilian acidly. 'The Government is not exactly pleased with your work when you relieved Sanders.'

'Does that mean a wigging from headquarters?' said Holden with an abstracted smile. 'I think I can stand it.'

The talk beat up round the ever-fresh subject of each man's work, and steadied Holden till it was time to go to his dark empty bungalow, where his butler received him as one who knew all his affairs. Holden remained awake for the greater part of the night, and his dreams were pleasant ones.

II

'How old is he now?'

'*Ya illah!* What a man's question! He is all but six weeks old; and on this night I go up to the housetop with thee, my life, to count the stars. For that is auspicious. And he was born on a Friday under the sign of the Sun, and it has been told to me that he will outlive us both and get wealth. Can we wish for aught better, beloved?'

'There is nothing better. Let us go up to the roof, and thou shalt count the stars – but a few only, for the sky is heavy with cloud.'

'The winter rains are late, and maybe they come out of season.

Come, before all the stars are hid. I have put on my richest jewels.'

'*Ai!* Ours. He comes also. He has never yet seen the skies.'

Ameera climbed the narrow staircase that led to the flat roof. The child, placid and unwinking, lay in the hollow of her right arm, gorgeous in silver-fringed muslin with a small skull-cap on his head. Ameera wore all that she valued most. The diamond nose-stud that takes the place of the Western patch in drawing attention to the curve of the nostril, the gold ornament in the centre of the forehead studded with tallow-drop emeralds and flawed rubies, the heavy circlet of beaten gold that was fastened round her neck by the softness of the pure metal, and the chinking curb-patterned silver anklets hanging low over the rosy ankle-bone. She was dressed in jade-green muslin as befitted a daughter of the Faith, and from shoulder to elbow and elbow to wrist ran bracelets of silver tied with floss silk, frail glass bangles slipped over the wrist in proof of the slenderness of the hand, and certain heavy gold bracelets that had no part in her country's ornaments but, since they were Holden's gift and fastened with a cunning European snap, delighted her immensely.

They sat down by the low white parapet of the roof, overlooking the city and its lights.

'They are happy down there,' said Ameera. 'But I do not think that they are as happy as we. Nor do I think the white *mem-log* are as happy. And thou?'

'I know they are not.'

'How dost thou know?'

'They give their children over to the nurses.'

'I have never seen that,' said Ameera with a sigh, 'nor do I wish to see. *Ahi!*' she dropped her head on Holden's shoulder – 'I have counted forty stars, and I am tired. Look at the child, love of my life, he is counting too.'

The baby was staring with round eyes at the dark of the heavens. Ameera placed him in Holden's arms, and he lay there without a cry.

'What shall we call him among ourselves?' she said. 'Look! Art thou ever tired of looking? He carries thy very eyes. But the mouth –'

'Is thine, most dear. Who should know better than I?'

''Tis such a feeble mouth. Oh, so small! And yet it holds my heart between its lips. Given him to me now. He has been too long away.'

'Nay, let him lie; he has not yet begun to cry.'

'When he cries thou wilt give him back – eh? What a man of mankind thou art! If he cried he were only the dearer to me. But, my life, what little name shall we give him?'

The small body lay close to Holden's heart. It was utterly helpless and very soft. He scarcely dared to breathe for fear of crushing it. The caged green parrot that is regarded as a sort of guardian-spirit in most native households moved on its perch and fluttered a drowsy wing.

'There is the answer,' said Holden. 'Mian Mittu has spoken. He shall be the parrot. When he is ready he will talk mightily and run about. Mian Mittu is the parrot in thy – in the Mussulman tongue, is it not?'

'Why put me so far off?' said Ameera fretfully. 'Let it be like unto some English name – but not wholly. For he is mine.'

'Then call him Tota, for that is likest English.'

'Ay, Tota, and that is still the parrot. Forgive me, my lord, for a minute ago, but in truth he is too little to wear all the weight of Mian Mittu for name. He shall be Tota – our Tota to us. Hearest thou, O small one? Littlest, thou art Tota.' She touched the child's cheek, and he waking wailed, and it was necessary to return him to his mother, who soothed him with the wonderful rhyme of *Aré koko, Jaré koko!* which says:

> Oh crow! Go crow! Baby's sleeping sound,
> And the wild plums grow in the jungle,
>   only a penny a pound.
> Only a penny a pound, *baba*, only a penny a pound.

Reassured many times as to the price of those plums, Tota cuddled himself down to sleep. The two sleek, white well-bullocks in the courtyard were steadily chewing the cud of their evening meal; old Pir Khan squatted at the head of Holden's horse, his police sabre across his knees, pulling drowsily at a big water-pipe that croaked like a bull-frog in a pond. Ameera's mother sat spinning in the lower verandah, and the wooden gate was shut and barred. The music of a marriage-procession came to the roof above the gentle hum of the city, and a string of flying-foxes crossed the face of the low moon.

'I have prayed,' said Ameera after a long pause, 'I have prayed for two things. First, that I may die in thy stead if thy death is demanded, and in the second that I may die in the place of the child. I have prayed to the Prophet and to Beebee Miriam [the Virgin Mary]. Thinkest thou either will hear?'

'From thy lips who would not hear the lightest word?'

'I asked for straight talk, and thou hast given me sweet talk. Will my prayers be heard?'

'How can I say? God is very good.'

'Of that I am not sure. Listen now. When I die, or the child dies, what is thy fate? Living, thou wilt return to the bold white *mem-log*, for kind calls to kind.'

'Not always.'

'With a woman, no; with a man it is otherwise. Thou wilt in this life, later on, go back to thine own folk. That I could almost endure, for I should be dead. But in thy very death thou wilt be taken away to a strange place and a paradise that I do not know.'

'Will it be paradise?'

'Surely, for who would harm thee? But we two – I and the child – shall be elsewhere, and we cannot come to thee, nor canst thou come to us. In the old days, before the child was born, I did not think of these things; but now I think of them always. It is very hard talk.'

'It will fall as it will fall. Tomorrow we do not know, but today and love we know well. Surely we are happy now.'

'So happy that it were well to make our happiness assured. And thy Beebee Miriam should listen to me; for she is also a woman. But then she would envy me! It is not seemly for men to worship a woman.'

Holden laughed aloud at Ameera's little spasm of jealousy.

'Is it not seemly? Why didst thou not turn me from worship of thee, then?'

'Thou a worshipper! And of me? My king, for all thy sweet words, well I know that I am thy servant and thy slave, and the dust under thy feet. And I would not have it otherwise. See!'

Before Holden could prevent her she stooped forward and touched his feet; recovering herself with a little laugh she hugged Tota closer to her bosom. Then, almost savagely –

'Is it true that the bold white *mem-log* live for three times the length of my life? Is it true that they make their marriages not before they are old women?'

'They marry as do others – when they are women.'

'That I know, but they wed when they are twenty-five. Is that true?'

'That is true.'

'*Ya illah!* At twenty-five! Who would of his own will take a wife even of eighteen? She is a woman – aging every hour. Twenty-five! I shall be an old woman at that age, and – Those *mem-log* remain young for ever. How I hate them!'

'What have they to do with us?'

'I cannot tell. I know only that there may now be alive on this earth a woman ten years older than I who may come to thee and take thy love ten years after I am an old woman, greyheaded, and the nurse of Tota's son. That is unjust and evil. They should die too.'

'Now, for all thy years thou art a child, and shalt be picked up and carried down the staircase.'

'Tota! Have a care for Tota, my lord! Thou at least art as foolish as any babe!' Ameera tucked Tota out of harm's way in the hollow of her neck, and was carried downstairs laughing in Holden's arms, while Tota opened his eyes and smiled after the manner of the lesser angels:

He was a silent infant, and, almost before Holden could realise that he was in the world, developed into a small gold-coloured little god and unquestioned despot of the house overlooking the city. Those were months of absolute happiness to Holden and Ameera – happiness withdrawn from the world, shut in behind the wooden gate that Pir Khan guarded. By day Holden did his work with an immense pity for such as were not so fortunate as himself, and a sympathy for small children that amazed and amused many mothers at the little station-gatherings. At nightfall he returned to Ameera, – Ameera, full of the wondrous doings of Tota; how he had been seen to clap his hands together and move his fingers with intention and purpose – which was manifestly a miracle – how later, he had of his own initiative crawled out of his low bedstead on to the floor and swayed on both feet for the space of three breaths.

'And they were long breaths, for my heart stood still with delight,' said Ameera.

Then Tota took the beasts into his councils – the well-bullocks, the little gray squirrels, the mongoose that lived in a hole near the well, and especially Mian Mittu, the parrot, whose tail he grievously pulled, and Mian Mittu screamed till Ameera and Holden arrived.

'Oh villain! Child of strength! This to thy brother on the house-top! *Tobah tobah!* Fie! Fie! But I know a charm to make him wise as Suleiman and Aflatoun [Solomon and Plato]. Now look,' said Ameera. She drew from an embroidered bag a handful of almonds. 'See! we count seven. In the name of God!'

She placed Mian Mittu, very angry and rumpled, on the top of his cage, and seating herself between the babe and the bird she cracked and peeled an almond less white than her teeth. 'This is a true charm, my life, and do not laugh. See! I give the parrot one half and Tota the other.' Mian Mittu with careful beak took his share from between Ameera's lips, and she kissed the other half into the mouth of the child, who ate it slowly with wondering eyes. 'This I will do each day of seven, and without doubt he who is ours will be a bold speaker and wise. Eh, Tota, what wilt thou be when thou art a man and I am grey-headed?' Tota tucked his fat legs into adorable creases. He could crawl, but he was not going to waste the spring of his youth in idle speech. He wanted Mian Mittu's tail to tweak.

When he was advanced to the dignity of a silver belt – which, with a magic square engraved on silver and hung round his neck, made up the greater part of his clothing – he staggered on a perilous journey down the garden to Pir Khan and proffered him all his jewels in exchange for one little ride on Holden's horse, having seen his mother's mother chaffering with pedlars in the verandah. Pir Khan wept and set the untried feet on his own grey head in sign of fealty, and brought the bold adventurer to his mother's arms, vowing that Tota would be a leader of men ere his beard was grown.

One hot evening, while he sat on the roof between his father and mother watching the never-ending warfare of the kites that the city boys flew, he demanded a kite of his own with Pir Khan to fly it, because he had a fear of dealing with anything larger than himself, and when Holden called him a 'spark,' he rose to his feet and answered slowly in defence of his new-found individuality, '*Hum 'park nahin bai. Hum admi bai* [I am no spark, but a man].'

The protest made Holden choke and devote himself very seriously to a consideration of Tota's future. He need hardly have taken the trouble. The delight of that life was too perfect to endure. Therefore it was taken away as many things are taken away in India – suddenly and without warning. The little lord of the house, as Pir Khan called him, grew sorrowful and complained of pains who had never known the meaning of pain. Ameera, wild with terror, watched him through the night, and in the dawning of the second day the life was shaken out of him by fever – the seasonal autumn fever. It seemed altogether impossible that he could die, and neither Ameera nor Holden at first believed the evidence of the little body on the bedstead. Then Ameera beat her head against the wall and would have flung herself down the well in the garden had Holden not restrained her by main force.

One mercy only was granted to Holden. He rode to his office in broad daylight and found waiting him an unusually heavy mail that demanded concentrated attention and hard work. He was not, however, alive to this kindness of the gods.

III

The first shock of a bullet is not more than a brisk pinch. The wrecked body does not send in its protest to the soul till ten or fifteen seconds later. Holden realised his pain slowly, exactly as he had realised his happiness, and with the same imperious necessity for hiding all trace of it. In the beginning he only felt that there had been a loss, and that Ameera needed comforting, where she sat with her head on her knees shivering as Mian Mittu from the house-top called *Tota! Tota! Tota!* Later all his world and the daily life of it rose up to hurt him. It was an outrage that any one of the children at the band-stand in the evening should be alive and clamorous, when his own child lay dead. It was more than mere pain when one of them touched him, and stories told by overfond fathers of their children's latest performances cut him to the quick. He could not declare his pain. He had neither help, comfort, nor sympathy; and Ameera at the end of each weary day would lead him through the hell of self-questioning reproach which is reserved for those who have lost a child, and believe that with a little – just a little – more care it might have been saved.

'Perhaps,' Ameera would say, 'I did not take sufficient heed. Did I, or did I not? The sun on the roof that day when he played so long alone and I was – *ahi!* braiding my hair – it may be that the sun then bred the fever. If I had warned him from the sun he might have lived. But, oh my life, say that I am guiltless! Thou knowest that I loved him as I love thee. Say that there is no blame on me, or I shall die – I shall die!'

'There is no blame, – before God, none. It was written and how could we do aught to save? What has been, has been. Let it go, beloved.'

'He was all my heart to me. How can I let the thought go when my arm tells me every night that he is not here? *Ahi! Ahi!* O Tota, come back to me – come back again, and let us be all together as it was before!'

'Peace, peace! For thine own sake, and for mine also, if thou lovest me – rest.'

'By this I know thou dost not care; and how shouldst thou? The white men have hearts of stone and souls of iron. Oh, that I had married a man of mine own people – though he beat me – and had never eaten the bread of an alien!'

'Am I an alien – mother of my son?'

'What else – Sahib? . . . Oh, forgive me – forgive! The death has driven me mad. Thou art the life of my heart, and the light of my eyes, and the breath of my life, and – and I have put thee from me, though it was but for a moment. If thou goest away to whom shall I look for help? Do not be angry. Indeed, it was the pain that spoke and not thy slave.'

'I know, I know. We be two who were three. The greater need therefore that we should be one.'

They were sitting on the roof as of custom. The night was a

warm one in early spring, and sheet-lightning was dancing on the horizon to a broken tune played by far-off thunder. Ameera settled in Holden's arms.

'The dry earth is lowing like a cow for the rain, and I – I am afraid. It was not like this when we counted the stars. But thou lovest me as much as before, though a bond is taken away? Answer!'

'I love more because a new bond has come out of the sorrow that we have eaten together, and that thou knowest.'

'Yea, I knew,' said Ameera in a very small whisper. 'But it is good to hear thee say so, my life, who art so strong to help. I will be a child no more, but a woman and an aid to thee. Listen! Give me my *sitar* and I will sing bravely.'

She took the light silver-studded *sitar* and began a song of the great hero Rajah Rasalu. The hand failed on the strings, the tune halted, checked, and at a low note turned off to the poor little nursery-rhyme about the wicked crow –

> And the wild plums grow in the jungle,
>   only a penny a pound.
> Only a penny a pound, *baba* – only . . .

Then came the tears, and the piteous rebellion against fate till she slept, moaning a little in her sleep, with the right arm thrown clear of the body as though it protected something that was not there. It was after this night that life became a little easier for Holden. The ever-present pain of loss drove him into his work, and the work repaid him by filling up his mind for nine or ten hours a day. Ameera sat alone in the house and brooded, but grew happier when she understood that Holden was more at ease, according to the custom of women. They touched happiness again, but this time with caution.

'It was because we loved Tota that he died. The jealousy of God was upon us,' said Ameera. 'I have hung up a large black jar before our window to turn the evil eye from us, and we must make no protestations of delight, but go softly underneath the stars, lest God find us out. Is that not good talk, worthless one?'

She had shifted the accent on the word that means 'beloved', in proof of the sincerity of her purpose. But the kiss that followed the new christening was a thing that any deity might have envied. They went about hence-forward saying, 'It is naught, it is naught', and hoping that all the Powers heard.

The Powers were busy on other things. They had allowed thirty million people four years of plenty wherein men fed well and the crops were certain, and the birth-rate rose year by year; the districts reported a purely agricultural population varying from nine hundred to two thousand to the square mile of the overburdened earth; and the Member for Lower Tooting, wandering about India in pot-hat and frock-coat, talked largely of the benefits of British rule and suggested as the one thing needful the establishment of a duly qualified electoral system and a general bestowal of the franchise. His long-suffering hosts smiled and made him welcome, and when he paused to admire, with pretty picked words, the blossom of the blood-red *dhak*-tree that had flowered untimely for a sign of what was coming, they smiled more than ever.

It was the Deputy Commissioner of Kot-Kumharsen, staying at the club for a day, who lightly told a tale that made Holden's blood run cold as he overheard the end.

'He won't bother any one any more. Never saw a man so astonished in my life. By Jove, I thought he meant to ask a question in the House about it. Fellow-passenger in his ship – dined next him – bowled over by cholera and died in eighteen hours. You needn't laugh, you fellows. The Member for Lower Tooting is awfully angry about it; but he's more scared. I think he's going to take his enlightened self out of India.'

'I'd give a good deal if he were knocked over. It might keep a few vestrymen of his kidney to their own parish. But what's this about cholera? It's full early for anything of that kind,' said the warden of an unprofitable salt-lick.

'Don't know,' said the Deputy Commissioner reflectively. 'We've got locusts with us. There's sporadic cholera all along the north – at least we're calling it sporadic for decency's sake. The spring crops are short in five districts, and nobody seems to know where the rains are. It's nearly March now. I don't want to scare anybody, but it seems to me that Nature's going to audit her accounts with a big red pencil this summer.'

'Just when I wanted to take leave, too!' said a voice across the room.

'There won't be much leave this year, but there ought to be a great deal of promotion. I've come in to persuade the Government to put my pet canal on the list of famine-relief works. It's an ill wind that blows no good. I shall get that canal finished at last.'

'Is it the old programme then,' said Holden; 'famine, fever, and cholera?'

'Oh, no. Only local scarcity and an unusual prevalence of seasonal sickness. You'll find it all in the reports if you live till next year. You're a lucky chap. *You* haven't got a wife to send out of harm's way. The hill-stations ought to be full of women this year.'

'I think you're inclined to exaggerate the talk in the *bazars*,' said a young civilian in the Secretariat. 'Now I have observed —'

'I daresay you have,' said the Deputy Commissioner, 'but you've a great deal more to observe, my son. In the meantime, I wish to observe to you —' and he drew him aside to discuss the construction of the canal that was so dear to his heart. Holden went to his bungalow and began to understand that he was not alone in the world, and also that he was afraid for the sake of another — which is the most soul-satisfying fear known to man.

Two months later, as the Deputy had foretold, Nature began to audit her accounts with a red pencil. On the heels of the spring-reapings came a cry for bread, and the Government, which had decreed that no man should die of want, sent wheat. Then came the cholera from all four quarters of the compass. It struck a pilgrim-gathering of half a million at a sacred shrine. Many died at the feet of their god; the others broke and ran over the face of the land, carrying the pestilence with them. It smote a walled city and killed two hundred a day. The people crowded the trains, hanging on to the footboards and squatting on the roofs of the carriages, and the cholera followed them, for at each station they dragged out the dead and the dying. They died by the roadside, and the horses of the Englishmen shied at the corpses in the grass. The rains did not come, and the earth turned to iron lest man should escape death by hiding in her. The English sent their wives away to the hills and went about their work, coming forward as they were bidden to fill the gaps in the fighting-line. Holden, sick

with fear of losing his chiefest treasure on earth, had done his best
to persuade Ameera to go away with her mother to the Hima-
layas.

'Why should I do?' said she one evening on the roof.

'There is sickness, and people are dying, and all the white
mem-log have gone.'

'All of them?'

'All – unless perhaps there remain some old scald-head who
vexes her husband's heart by running risk of death.'

'Nay; who stays is my sister, and thou must not abuse her, for I
will be a scald-head too. I am glad all the bold *mem-log* are gone.'

'Do I speak to a woman or a babe? Go to the hills and I will see
to it that thou goest like a queen's daughter. Think, child. In a
red-lacquered bullock-cart, veiled and curtained, with brass
peacocks upon the pole and red cloth hangings. I will send two
orderlies for guard, and –'

"Peace! Thou art the babe in speaking thus. What use are those
toys to me? *He* would have patted the bullocks and played with
the housings. For his sake, perhaps, – thou hast made me very
English – I might have gone. Now, I will not. Let the *mem-log*
run.'

'Their husbands are sending them, beloved.'

'Very good talk. Since when has thou been my husband to tell
me what to do? I have but borne thee a son. Thou art only all the
desire of my soul to me. How shall I depart when I know that if
evil befall thee by the breadth of so much as my littlest fingernail –
is that not small? – I should be aware of it though I were in
paradise. And here, this summer thou mayest die – *ai, janee,* die! –
and in dying they might call to tend thee a white woman, and she
would rob me in the last of thy love!'

'But love is not born in a moment or on a death-bed!'

'What dost thou know of love, stoneheart? She would take thy
thanks at least, and, by God and the Prophet and Beebee Miriam
the mother of thy Prophet, that I will never endure. My lord and
my love, let there be no more foolish talk of going away. Where
thou art, I am. It is enough.' She put an arm round his neck and a
hand on his mouth.

There are not many happinesses so complete as those that are snatched under the shadow of the sword. They sat together and laughed, calling each other openly by every pet name that could move the wrath of the gods. The city below them was locked up in its own torments. Sulphur fires blazed in the streets; the conches in the Hindu temples screamed and bellowed, for the gods were inattentive in those days. There was a service in the great Mahomedan shrine, and the call to prayer from the minarets was almost unceasing. They heard the wailing in the houses of the dead, and once the shriek of a mother who had lost a child and was calling for its return. In the grey dawn they saw the dead borne out through the city gates, each litter with its own little knot of mourners. Wherefore they kissed each other and shivered.

It was a red and heavy audit, for the land was very sick and needed a little breathing-space ere the torrent of cheap life should flood it anew. The children of immature fathers and undeveloped mothers made no resistance. They were cowed and sat still, waiting till the sword should be sheathed in November if it were so willed. There were gaps among the English, but the gaps were filled. The work of superintending famine-relief, cholera-sheds, medicine-distribution, and what little sanitation was possible, went forward because it was so ordered.

Holden had been told to keep himself in readiness to move to replace the next man who should fall. There were twelve hours in each day when he could not see Ameera, and she might die in three. He was considering what his pain would be if he could not see her for three months, or if she died out of his sight. He was absolutely certain that her death would be demanded – so certain that when he looked up from the telegram and saw Pir Khan breathless in the doorway, he laughed aloud. 'And?' said he, –

'When there is a cry in the night and the spirit flutters into the throat, who has a charm that will restore? Come swiftly, Heaven-born! It is the black cholera.'

Holden galloped to his home. The sky was heavy with clouds, for the long-deferred rains were near and the heat was stifling. Ameera's mother met him in the courtyard, whimpering, 'She is dying. She is nursing herself into death. She is all but dead. What shall I do, Sahib?'

Ameera was lying in the room in which Tota had been born. She made no sign when Holden entered, because the human soul is a very lonely thing, and, when it is getting ready to go away, hides itself in a misty borderland where the living may not follow. The black cholera does its work quietly and without explanation. Ameera was being thrust out of life as though the Angel of Death had himself put his hand upon her. The quick breathing seemed to show that she was either afraid or in pain, but neither eyes nor mouth gave any answer to Holden's kisses. There was nothing to be said or done. Holden could only wait and suffer. The first drops of the rain began to fall on the roof, and he could hear shouts of joy in the parched city.

The soul came back a little and the lips moved. Holden bent down to listen. 'Keep nothing of mine,' said Ameera. 'Take no hair from my head. *She* would make thee burn it later on. That flame I should feel. Lower! Stoop lower! Remember only that I was thine and bòre thee a son. Though thou wed a white woman tomorrow, the pleasure of receiving in thy arms thy first son is taken from thee for ever. Remember me when thy son is born – the one that shall carry thy name before all men. His misfortunes be on my head. I bear witness – I bear witness' – the lips were forming the words on his ear – 'that there is no God but – thee, beloved!'

Then she died. Holden sat still, and all thought was taken from him, – till he heard Ameera's mother lift the curtain.

'Is she dead, Sahib?'

'She is dead.'

'Then I will mourn, and afterwards take an inventory of the furniture in this house. For that will be mine. The Sahib does not mean to resume it? It is so little, so very little, Sahib, and I am an old woman. I would like to lie softly.'

'For the mercy of God be silent a while. Go out and mourn where I cannot hear.'

'Sahib, she will be buried in four hours.'

'I know the custom. I shall go ere she is taken away. That matter is in thy hands. Look to it, that the bed on which – on which she lies –'

'Ah! That beautiful red-lacquered bed. I have long desired –'

'That the bed is left here untouched for my disposal. All else in the house is thine. Hire a cart, take everything, go hence, and before sunrise let there be nothing in this house but that which I have ordered thee to respect.'

'I am an old woman. I would stay at least for the days of mourning, and the rains have just broken. Whither shall I go?'

'What is that to me? My order is that there is a going. The house gear is worth a thousand rupees, and my orderly shall bring thee a hundred rupees tonight.'

'That is very little. Think of the cart-hire.'

'It shall be nothing unless thou goest, and with speed. O woman, get hence and leave me with my dead!'

The mother shuffled down the staircase, and in her anxiety to take stock of the house-fittings forgot to mourn. Holden stayed by Ameera's side and the rain roared on the roof. He could not think connectedly by reason of the noise, though he made many attempts to do so. Then four sheeted ghosts glided dripping into the room and stared at him through their veils. They were the washers of the dead. Holden left the room and went out to his horse. He had come in a dead, stifling calm through ankle-deep dust. He found the courtyard a rain-lashed pond alive with frogs; a torrent of yellow water ran under the gate, and a roaring wind drove the bolts of the rain like buckshot against the mud walls. Pir Khan was shivering in his little hut by the gate, and the horse was stamping uneasily in the water.

'I have been told the Sahib's order,' said Pir Khan. 'It is well. This house is now desolate. I go also, for my monkey-face would be a reminder of that which has been. Concerning the bed, I will bring that to thy house yonder in the morning; but remember, Sahib, it will be to thee a knife turning in a green wound. I go upon a pilgrimage, and I will take no money. I have grown fat in the protection of the Presence whose sorrow is my sorrow. For the last time I hold his stirrup.'

He touched Holden's foot with both hands and the horse sprang out into the road, where the creaking bamboos were whipping the sky, and all the frogs were chuckling. Holden could not see for the rain in his face. He put his hands before his eyes and muttered—

'Oh, you brute! You utter brute!'

The news of his trouble was already in his bungalow. He read the knowledge in his butler's eyes when Ahmed Khan brought in food, and for the first and last time in his life laid a hand upon his master's shoulder, saying, 'Eat, Sahib, eat. Meat is good against sorrow. I also have known. Moreover, the shadows come and go, Sahib; the shadows come and go. These be curried eggs.'

Holden could neither eat nor sleep. The heavens sent down eight inches of rain in that night and washed the earth clean. The waters tore down walls, broke roads, and scoured open the shallow graves on the Mahomedan burying-ground. All next day it rained, and Holden sat still in his house considering his sorrow. On the morning of the third day he received a telegram which said only, 'Ricketts, Myndonie. Dying. Holden relieve. Immediate.' Then he thought that before he departed he would look at the house wherein he had been master and lord. There was a break in the weather, and the rank earth steamed with vapour.

He found that the rains had torn down the mud pillars of the gateway, and the heavy wooden gate that had guarded his life hung lazily from one hinge. There was grass three inches high in the courtyard; Pir Khan's lodge was empty, and the sodden thatch sagged between the beams. A gray squirrel was in possession of the verandah, as if the house had been untenanted for thirty years instead of three days. Ameera's mother had removed everything except some mildewed matting. The *tick-tick* of the little scorpions as they hurried across the floor was the only sound in the house. Ameera's room and the other one where Tota had lived were heavy with mildew; and the narrow staircase leading to the roof was streaked and stained with rain-borne mud. Holden saw all these things, and came out again to meet in the road Durga Dass, his landlord, – portly, affable, clothed in white muslin, and driving a Cee-spring buggy. He was overlooking his property to see how the roofs stood the stress of the first rains.

'I have heard,' said he, 'you will not take this place any more, Sahib?'

'What are you going to do with it?'

'Perhaps I shall let it again.'

'Then I will keep it on while I am away.'

Durga Dass was silent for some time. 'You shall not take it on,

Sahib,' he said. 'When I was a young man I also –, but today I am a member of the Municipality. Ho! Ho! No. When the birds have gone what need to keep the nest? I will have it pulled down – the timber will sell for something always. It shall be pulled down, and the Municipality shall make a road across, as they desire, from the burning-ghaut to the city wall, so that no man may say where this house stood.'

Thomas Hardy

THE SON'S VETO

I

To the eyes of a man viewing it from behind, the nut-brown hair was a wonder and a mystery. Under the black beaver hat, surmounted by its tuft of black feathers, the long locks, braided and twisted and coiled like the rushes of a basket, composed a rare, if somewhat barbaric, example of ingenious art. One could understand such weavings and coilings being wrought to last intact for a year, or even a calendar month; but that they should be all demolished regularly at bedtime, after a single day of permanence, seemed a reckless waste of successful fabrication.

And she had done it all herself, poor thing. She had no maid, and it was almost the only accomplishment she could boast of. Hence the unstinted pains.

She was a young invalid lady – not so very much of an invalid – sitting in a wheeled chair, which had been pulled up in the front part of a green enclosure, close to a bandstand, where a concert was going on, during a warm June afternoon. It had place in one of the minor parks or private gardens that are to be found in the suburbs of London, and was the effort of a local association to raise money for some charity. There are worlds within worlds in the great city, and though nobody outside the immediate district had ever heard of the charity, or the band, or the garden, the enclosure was filled with an interested audience sufficiently informed on all these.

As the strains proceeded many of the listeners observed the chaired lady, whose back hair, by reason of her prominent position, so challenged inspection. Her face was not easily discernible, but the aforesaid cunning tress-weavings, the white ear and poll, and the curve of a cheek which was neither flaccid nor sallow, were signals that led to the expectation of good beauty in front. Such expectations are not infrequently disappointed as soon as the disclosure comes; and in the present case, when the lady, by a turn of the head, at length revealed herself, she was not so handsome as the people behind her had supposed, and even hoped – they did not know why.

For one thing (alas! the commonness of this complaint), she was less young than they had fancied her to be. Yet attractive her face unquestionably was, and not at all sickly. The revelation of its details came each time she turned to talk to a boy of twelve or thirteen who stood beside her, and the shape of whose hat and jacket implied that he belonged to a well-known public school. The immediate by-standers could hear that he called her 'Mother'.

When the end of the programme was reached, and the audience withdrew, many chose to find their way out by passing at her elbow. Almost all turned their heads to take a full and near look at the interesting woman, who remained stationary in the chair till the way should be clear enough for her to be wheeled out without obstruction. As if she expected their glances, and did not mind gratifying their curiosity, she met the eyes of several of her observers by lifting her own, showing these to be soft, brown, and affectionate orbs, a little plaintive in their regard.

She was conducted out of the garden, and passed along the pavement till she disappeared from view, the school-boy walking beside her. To inquiries made by some persons who watched her away, the answer came that she was the second wife of the incumbent of a neighbouring parish, and that she was lame. She was generally believed to be a woman with a story – an innocent one, but a story of some sort or other.

In conversing with her on their way home the boy who walked at her elbow said that he hoped his father had not missed them.

'He have been so comfortable these last few hours that I am sure he cannot have missed us,' she replied.

'*Has*, dear mother – not *have!*' exclaimed the public-school boy, with an impatient fastidiousness that was almost harsh. 'Surely you know that by this time!'

His mother hastily adopted the correction, and did not resent his making it, or retaliate, as she might well have done, by bidding him to wipe that crumby mouth of his, whose condition had been caused by surreptitious attempts to eat a piece of cake without taking it out of the pocket wherein it lay concealed. After this the pretty woman and the boy went onward in silence.

That question of grammar bore upon her history, and she fell into reverie, of a somewhat sad kind to all appearance. It might have been assumed that she was wondering if she had done wisely in shaping her life as she had shaped it, to bring out such a result as this.

In a remote nook in North Wessex, forty miles from London, near the thriving county-town of Aldbrickham, there stood a pretty village with its church and parsonage, which she knew well enough, but her son had never seen. It was her native village, Gaymead, and the first event bearing upon her present situation had occurred at that place when she was only a girl of nineteen.

How well she remembered it, that first act in her little tragi-comedy, the death of her reverend husband's first wife. It happened on a spring evening, and she who now and for many years had filled that first wife's place was then parlour-maid in the parson's house.

When everything had been done that could be done, and the death was announced, she had gone out in the dusk to visit her parents, who were living in the same village, to tell them the sad news. As she opened the white swing-gate and looked towards the trees which rose westward, shutting out the pale light of the evening sky, she discerned, without much surprise, the figure of a man standing in the hedge, though she roguishly exclaimed, as a matter of form, 'Oh, Sam, how you frightened me!'

He was a young gardener of her acquaintance. She told him the particulars of the late event, and they stood silent, these two young people, in that elevated, calmly philosophic mind which is engendered when a tragedy has happened close at hand, and has not happened to the philosophers themselves. But it had its bearings upon their relations.

'And will you stay on now at the Vicarage, just the same?' asked he.

She had hardly thought of that. 'Oh yes – I suppose,' she said. 'Everything will be just as usual, I imagine.'

He walked beside her towards her mother's. Presently his arm stole round her waist. She gently removed it; but he placed it there again, and she yielded the point. 'You see, dear Sophy, you don't know that you'll stay on; you may want a home; and I shall be ready to offer one some day, though I may not be ready just yet.'

'Why, Sam, how can you be so fast? I've never even said I liked 'ee; and it is all your own doing, coming after me.'

'Still, it is nonsense to say I am not to have a try at you, like the rest.' He stooped to kiss her a farewell, for they had reached her mother's door.

'No, Sam; you sha'n't!' she cried, putting her hand over his mouth. 'You ought to be more serious on such a night as this.' And she bade him adieu without allowing him to kiss her or to come indoors.

The vicar just left a widower was at this time a man about forty years of age, of good family, and childless. He had led a secluded existence in this college living, partly because there were no resident land-owners; and his loss now intensified his habit of withdrawal from outward observation. He was still less seen than heretofore, kept himself still less in time with the rhythm and racket of the movements called progress in the world without. For many months after his wife's decease the economy of his house-hold remained as before; the cook, the house-maid, the parlour-maid, and the man out-of-doors performed their duties or left them undone, just as nature prompted them – the vicar knew not which. It was then represented to him that his servants seemed to have nothing to do in his small family of one. He was struck with the truth of this representation, and decided to cut down his establishment. But he was forestalled by Sophy, the parlour-maid, who said one evening that she wished to leave him.

'And why?' said the parson.

'Sam Hobson has asked me to marry him, sir.'

'Well – do you want to marry?'

'Not much. But it would be a home for me. And we have heard that one of us will have to leave.'

A day or two after she said: 'I don't want to leave just yet sir, if you don't wish it. Sam and I have quarrelled.'

He looked up at her. He had hardly ever observed her before, though he had been frequently conscious of her soft presence in the room. What a kitten-like, flexuous, tender creature she was! She was the only one of the servants with whom he came into immediate and continuous relation. What should he do if Sophy were gone?

Sophy did not go, but one of the others did, and things proceeded quietly again.

When Mr Twycott, the vicar, was ill, Sophy brought up his meals to him, and she had no sooner left the room one day than he hard a noise on the stairs. She had slipped down with the tray, and so twisted her foot that she could not stand. The village surgeon was called in; the vicar got better, but Sophy was incapacitated for a long time; and she was informed that she must never again walk much or engage in any occupation which required her to stand long on her feet. As soon as she was comparatively well she spoke to him alone. Since she was forbidden to walk and bustle about, and, indeed, could not do so, it became her duty to leave. She could very well work at something sitting down, and she had an aunt a seamstress.

The parson had been very greatly moved by what she had suffered on his account, and he exclaimed, 'No Sophy; lame or not lame, I cannot let you go. You must never leave me again.'

He came close to her, and, though she could never exactly tell how it happened, she became conscious of his lips upon her cheek. He then asked her to marry him. Sophy did not exactly love him, but she had a respect for him which almost amounted to veneration. Even if she had wished to get away from him she hardly dared refuse a personage so reverend and august in her eyes, and she assented forthwith to be his wife.

Thus it happened that one fine morning, when the doors of the church were naturally open for ventilation, and the singing birds fluttered in and alighted on the tie-beams of the roof, there was a marriage-service at the communion rails which hardly a soul knew of. The parson and neighbouring curate had entered at one door, and Sophy at another, followed by two necessary persons, whereupon in a short time there emerged a newly-made husband and wife.

Mr Twycott knew perfectly well that he had committed social suicide by this step, despite Sophy's spotless character, and he had taken his measures accordingly. An exchange of livings had been arranged with an acquaintance who was incumbent of a church in the south of London, and as soon as possible the couple removed thither, abandoning their pretty country home with trees and shrubs and glebe for a narrow, dusty house in a long, straight street, and their fine peal of bells for the wretchedest one-tongued clangour that ever tortured mortal ears. It was all on her account. They were, however, away from every one who had known her former position, and also under less observation from without than they would have had to put up with in any country parish.

Sophy the woman was as charming a partner as a man could possess, though Sophy the lady had her deficiencies. She showed a natural aptitude for little domestic refinements, so far as related to things and manners; but in what is called culture she was less intuitive. She had now been married more than fourteen years, and her husband had taken much trouble with her education; but she still held confused ideas on the use of 'was' and 'were', which did not beget a respect for her among the few acquaintances she made. Her great grief in this relation was that her only child, on whose education no expense had been or would be spared, was now old enough to perceive these deficiencies in his mother, and not only to see them but to feel irritated at their existence.

Thus she lived on in the city, and wasted hours in braiding her beautiful hair, till her once apple cheeks waned to pink of the very faintest. Her foot had never regained its natural strength after the accident, and she was mostly obliged to avoid walking altogether. Her husband had grown to like London for its freedom and its domestic privacy; but he was twenty years his Sophy's senior, and had latterly been seized with a serious illness. On this day, however, he had seemed to be well enough to justify her accompanying her son Randolph to the concert.

II

The next time we get a glimpse of her is when she appears in the mournful attire of a widow.

Mr Twycott had never rallied, and now lay in a well-packed cemetery to the south of the great city, where, if all the dead it contained had stood erect and alive, not one would have known him or recognized his name. The boy had dutifully followed him to the grave, and was now again at school.

Throughout these changes Sophy had been treated like the child she was in nature though not in years. She was left with no control over anything that had been her husband's beyond her modest personal income. In his anxiety lest her inexperience should be overreached he had safeguarded with trustees all he possibly could. The completion of the boy's course at the public school, to be followed in due time by Oxford and ordination, had been all previsioned and arranged, and she really had nothing to occupy her in the world but to eat and drink, and make a business of indolence, and go on weaving and coiling the nut-brown hair, merely keeping a home open for the son whenever he came to her during vacations.

Foreseeing his probable decease long years before her, her husband in his lifetime had purchased for her use a semi-detached villa in the same long, straight road whereon the church and parsonage faced, which was to be hers as long as she chose to live in it. Here she now resided, looking out upon the fragment of lawn in front, and through the railings at the ever-flowing traffic; or, bending forward over the window-sill on the first floor, stretching her eyes far up and down the vista of sooty trees, hazy air, and drab house façades, along which echoed the noises common to a suburban main thoroughfare.

Somehow, her boy, with his aristocratic school-knowledge, his grammars, and his aversions, was losing those wide infantine sympathies, extending as far as to the sun and moon themselves, with which he, like other children, had been born, and which his mother, a child of nature herself, had loved in him; he was reducing their compass to a population of a few thousand wealthy and titled people, the mere veneer of a thousand million or so of others who did not interest him at all. He drifted further and further away from her. Sophy's *milieu* being a suburb of minor tradesmen and under-clerks, and her almost only companions the two servants of her own house, it was not surprising that after her husband's death she soon lost the little artificial tastes she had acquired from him, and became – in her son's eyes – a mother whose mistakes and origin it was his painful lot as a gentleman to blush for. As yet he was far from being man enough – if he ever would be – to rate these sins of hers at their true infinitesimal value beside the yearning fondness that welled up and remained penned in her heart till it should be more fully accepted by him, or by some other person or thing. If he had lived at home with her he would have had all of it; but he seemed to require so very little in present circumstances, and it remained stored.

Her life became insupportably dreary; she could not take walks, and had no interest in going for drives, or, indeed, in travelling anywhere. Nearly two years passed without an event, and still she looked on that suburban road, thinking of the village in which she had been born, and whither she would have gone back – oh, how gladly! even to work in the fields.

Taking no exercise, she often could not sleep, and would rise in the night or early morning and look out upon the then vacant thoroughfare, where the lamps stood like sentinels waiting for some procession to go by. An approximation to such a procession was indeed made every early morning about one o'clock, when the country vehicles passed up with loads of vegetables for Covent Garden market. She often saw them creeping along at this silent and dusky hour – wagon after wagon, bearing green bastions of cabbages nodding to their fall, yet never falling; walls of baskets enclosing masses of beans and pease; pyramids of snow-white turnips, swaying howdahs of mixed produce – creeping along behind aged night-horses, who seemed ever patiently wondering between their hollow coughs why they had always to work at that still hour when all other sentient creatures were privileged to rest. Wrapped in a cloak, it was soothing to watch and sympathize with them when depression and nervousness hindered sleep, and to see how the fresh green-stuff brightened to life as it came opposite the lamp, and how the sweating animals steamed and shone with their miles of travel.

They had an interest, almost a charm, for Sophy, these semi-rural people and vehicles moving in an urban atmosphere, leading a life quite distinct from that of the daytime toilers on the same road. One morning a man who accompanied a wagon-load of potatoes gazed rather hard at the house fronts as he passed, and with a curious emotion she thought his form was familiar to her. She looked out for him again. His being an old-fashioned conveyance with a yellow front, it was easily recongizable, and on the third night after she saw it a second time. The man alongside was, as she had fancied, Sam Hobson, formerly gardener at Gaymead, who would at one time have married her.

She had occasionally thought of him, and wondered if life in a cottage with him would not have been a happier lot than the life she had accepted. She had not thought of him passionately, but her now dismal situation lent an interest to his resurrection – a tender interest which it is impossible to exaggerate. She went back to bed, and began thinking. When did these market-gardeners, who travelled up to town so regularly at one or two in the morning, come back? She dimly recollected seeing their empty wagons, hardly noticeable among the ordinary day-traffic, passing down at some hour before noon.

It was only April, but that morning, after breakfast, she had the window opened, and sat looking out, the feeble sun shining full upon her. She affected to sew, but her eyes never left the street. Between ten and eleven the desired wagon, now unladen, reappeared on its return journey. But Sam was not looking round him then, and drove on in a reverie.

'Sam!' cried she.

Turning with a start, his face lighted up. He called to him a little boy to hold the horse, alighted, and came and stood under her window.

'I can't come down easily, Sam or I would!' she said. 'Did you know I lived here?

'Well, Mrs Twycott, I knew you lived along here somewhere. I have often looked out for 'ee.'

He briefly explained his own presence on the scene. He had long since given up his gardening in the village near Aldbrickham, and was now manager at a market-gardener's on the south side of London, it being part of his duty to go up to Covent Garden with wagon-loads of produce two or three times a week. In answer to her curious inquiry, he admitted that he had come to this particular district because he had seen in the Aldbrickham paper a year or two before the announcement of the death in South London of the aforetime vicar of Gaymead, which had revived an interest in her dwelling-place that he could not extinguish, leading him to hover about the locality till his present post had been secured.

They spoke of their native village in dear old North Wessex, the spots in which they had played together as children. She tried to feel that she was a dignified personage now, that she must not be too confidential with Sam. But she could not keep it up, and the tears hanging in her eyes were indicated in her voice.

'You are not happy, Mrs Twycott, I'm afraid,' he said.

'Oh, of course not! I lost my husband only the year before last.'

'Ah! I meant in another way. You'd like to be home again?'

'This is my home – for life. The house belongs to me. But I understand –' She let it out then. 'Yes, Sam. I long for home – *our* home! I *should* like to be there, and never leave it, and die there.' But she remembered herself. 'That's only a momentary feeling. I have a son, you know, a dear boy. He's at school now.'

'Somewhere handy, I suppose? I see there's lots on 'em along this road.'

'Oh no! Not in one of these wretched holes! At a public school – one of the most distinguished in England.'

'Chok it all! of course! I forget, ma'am, that you've been a lady for so many years.'

'No, I am not a lady,' she said, sadly. 'I never shall be. But he's a gentleman, and that – makes it – oh, how difficult for me!'

III

The acquaintance thus oddly reopened proceeded apace. She often looked out to get a few words with him, by night or by day. Her sorrow was that she could not accompany her one old friend on foot a little way, and talk more freely than she could do while he paused before the house. One night, at the beginning of June, when she was again on the watch after an absence of some days from the window, he entered the gate and said, softly, 'Now, wouldn't some air do you good? I've only half a load this morning. Why not ride up to Covent Garden with me? There's a nice seat on the cabbages, where I've spread a sack. You can be home again in a cab before anybody is up.'

She refused at first, and then, trembling with excitement, hastily finished her dressing, and wrapped herself up in cloak and veil, afterwards sidling downstairs by the aid of the handrail, in a way she could adopt on an emergency. When she had opened the door she found Sam on the step, and he lifted her bodily on his strong arm across the little forecourt into his vehicle. Not a soul was visible or audible in the infinite length of the straight, flat highway, with its ever-waiting lamps converging to points in each direction. The air was fresh as country air at this hour, and the stars shone, except to the north-eastward, where there was a whitish light – the dawn. Sam carefully placed her in the seat and drove on.

They talked as they had talked in old days, Sam pulling himself up now and then, when he thought himself too familiar. More than once she said with misgiving that she wondered if she ought to have indulged in the freak. 'But I am so lonely in my house,' she added, 'and this makes me so happy!'

'You must come again, dear Mrs Twycott. There is no time o' day for taking the air like this.'

It grew lighter and lighter. The sparrows became busy in the streets, and the city waxed denser around them. When they approached the river it was day, and on the bridge they beheld the full blaze of morning sunlight in the direction of St Paul's, the river glistening towards it, and not a craft stirring.

Near Covent Garden he put her into a cab, and they parted, looking into each other's faces like the very old friends they were. She reached home without adventure, limped to the door, and let herself in with her latch-key unseen.

The air and Sam's presence had revived her; her cheeks were quite pink – almost beautiful. She had something to live for in addition to her son. A woman of pure instincts, she knew there had been nothing really wrong in the journey, but supposed it conventionally to be very wrong indeed.

Soon, however, she gave way to the temptation of going with him again, and on this occasion their conversation was distinctly tender, and Sam said he never should forget her, notwithstanding that she had served him rather badly at one time. After much hesitation he told her of a plan it was in his power to carry out, and one he should like to take in hand, since he did not care for London work; it was to set up as a master greengrocer down at Aldbrickham, the county-town of their native place. He knew of an opening – a shop kept by aged people who wished to retire.

'And why don't you do it, then, Sam?' she asked, with a slight heart-sinking.

'Because I'm not sure if – you'd join me. I know you wouldn't – couldn't! Such a lady as ye've been so long, you couldn't be a wife to a man like me.'

'I hardly suppose I could!' she assented, also frightened at the idea.

'If you could,' he said eagerly, 'you'd on'y have to sit in the back parlour and look through the glass partition when I was away sometimes – just to keep an eye on things. The lameness wouldn't hinder that. I'd keep you as genteel as ever I could, dear Sophy – if I might think of it,' he pleaded.

'Sam, I'll be frank,' she said, putting her hand on his. 'If it were only myself I would do it, and gladly, though everything I possess would be lost to me by marying again.'

'I don't mind that. It's more independent.'

'That's good of you, dear, dear Sam. But there's something else. I have a son. I almost fancy when I am miserable sometimes that he is not really mine, but one I hold in trust for my late husband. He seems to belong so little to me personally, so entirely to his dead father. He is so much educated and I so little that I do not feel dignified enough to be his mother. Well, he would have to be told.'

'Yes. Unquestionably.' Sam saw her thought and her fear. 'Still, you can do as you like, Sophy – Mrs Twycott,' he added. 'It is not you who are the child, but he.'

'Ah, you don't know! Sam, if I could, I would marry you, some day. But you must wait awhile, and let me think.'

It was enough for him, and he was blithe at their parting. Not so she. To tell Randolph seemed impossible. She could wait, till he had gone up to Oxford, when what she did would affect his life but little. But would he ever tolerate the idea? And if not, could she defy him?

She had not told him a word when the yearly cricket-match

came on at Lord's between the public schools, though Sam had already gone back to Aldbrickham. Mrs Twycott felt stronger than usual. She went to the match with Randolph, and was able to leave her chair and walk about occasionally. The bright idea occurred to her that she could casually broach the subject while moving round among the spectators, when the boy's spirits were high with interest in the game, and he would weigh domestic matters as feathers in the scale beside the day's victory. They promenaded under the lurid July sun, this pair, so wide apart, yet so near, and Sophy saw the large proportion of boys like her own, in their broad white collars and dwarf hats, and all around the rows of great coaches under which was jumbled the débris of luxurious luncheons – bones, pie-crusts, champagne-bottles, glasses, plates, napkins, and the family silver; while on the coaches sat the proud fathers and mothers; but never a poor mother like her. If Randolph had not appertained to these, had not centred all his interests in them, had not cared exclusively for the class they belonged to, how happy would things have been! A great huzza at some small performance with the bat burst from the multitide of relatives, and Randolph jumped wildly into the air to see what had happened. Sophy fetched up the sentence that had been already shaped; but she could not get it out. The occasion was, perhaps, an inopportune one. The contrast between her story and the display of fashion to which Randolph had grown to regard himself as akin would be fatal. She awaited a better time.

It was on an evening when they were alone in their plain suburban residence, where life was not blue but brown, that she ultimately broke silence, qualifying her announcement of a probable second marriage by assuring him that it would not take place for a long time to come, when he would be living quite independently of her.

The boy thought the idea a very reasonable one, and asked if she had chosen anybody. She hesitated; and he seemed to have a misgiving. He hoped his step-father would be a gentleman, he said.

'Not what you call a gentleman,' she answered, timidly. 'He'll be much as I was before I knew your father;' and by degrees she acquainted him with the whole. The youth's face remained fixed for a moment; then he flushed, leaned on the table, and burst into passionate tears.

His mother went up to him, kissed all of his face that she could get at, and patted his back as if he were still the baby he once had been, crying herself the while. When he had somewhat recovered from his paroxysm he went hastily to his own room and fastened the door.

Parleyings were attempted through the key-hole, outside which she waited and listened. It was long before he would reply, and when he did it was to say sternly at her from within: 'I am ashamed of you! It will ruin me! A miserable boor! a churl! a clown! It will degrade me in the eyes of all the gentlemen of England!'

'Say no more — perhaps I am wrong! I will struggle against it!' she cried, miserably.

Before Randolph left her that summer a letter arrived from Sam to inform her that he had been unexpectedly fortunate in obtaining the shop. He was in possession; it was the largest in the town, combining fruit with vegetables, and he thought it would form a home worthy even of her some day. Might he not run up to town to see her?

She met him by stealth, and said he must still wait for her final answer. The autumn dragged on, and when Randolph was home at Christmas for the holidays she broached the matter again. But the young gentleman was inexorable.

It was dropped for months; renewed again; abandoned under his repugnance; again attempted, and thus the gentle creature reasoned and pleaded till four or five long years had passed. Then the faithful Sam revived his suit with some peremptoriness. Sophy's son, now an undergraduate, was down from Oxford one Easter, when she again opened the subject. As soon as he was ordained, she argued, he would have a home of his own, wherein she, with her bad grammar and her ignorance, would be an encumbrance to him. Better obliterate her as much as possible.

He showed a more manly anger now, but would not agree. She on her side was more persistent, and he had doubts whether she could be trusted in his absence. But by indignation and contempt for her taste he completely maintained his ascendency; and finally taking her before a little cross and shrine that he had erected in his bedroom for his private devotions, there bade her kneel, and swear that she would not wed Samuel Hobson without his consent. 'I owe this to my father!' he said.

The poor woman swore, thinking he would soften as soon as he was ordained and in full swing of clerical work. But he did not. His education had by this time sufficiently ousted his humanity to keep him quite firm; though his mother might have led an idyllic life with her faithful fruiterer and green-grocer, and nobody have been anything the worse in the world.

Her lameness became more confirmed as time went on, and she seldom or never left the house in the long southern thoroughfare, where she seemed to be pining her heart away. 'Why mayn't I say to Sam that I'll marry him? Why mayn't I?' she would murmur plaintively to herself when nobody was near.

Some four years after this date a middle-aged man was standing at the door of the largest fruiterer's shop in Aldbrickham. He was the proprietor, but today, instead of his usual business attire, he wore a neat suit of black; and his window was partly shuttered. From the railway-station a funeral procession was seen approaching: it passed his door and went out of the town towards the village of Gaymead. The man, whose eyes were wet, held his hat in his hand as the vehicles moved by; while from the mourning coach a young smooth-shaven priest in a high waistcoat looked black as a cloud at the shopkeeper standing there.

THE REAL THING

I

When the porter's wife, who used to answer the house-bell, announced 'A gentleman and a lady, sir,' I had, as I often had in those days – the wish being father to the thought – an immediate vision of sitters. Sitters my visitors in this case proved to be; but not in the sense I should have preferred. There was nothing at first however to indicate that they mightn't have come for a portrait. The gentleman, a man of fifty, very high and very straight, with a moustache slightly grizzled and a dark grey walking-coat admirably fitted, both of which I noted professionally – I don't mean as a barber or yet as a tailor – would have struck me as a celebrity if celebrities often were striking. It was a truth of which I had for some time been conscious that a figure with a good deal of frontage was, as one might say, almost never a public institution. A glance at the lady helped to remind me of this paradoxical law: she also looked too distinguished to be a 'personality'. Moreover one would scarcely come across two variations together.

Neither of the pair immediately spoke – they only prolonged the preliminary gaze suggesting that each wished to give the other a chance. They were visibly shy; they stood there letting me take them in – which, as I afterwards perceived, was the most practical thing they could have done. In this way their embarrassment served their cause. I had seen people painfully reluctant to mention that they desired anything so gross as to be represented on canvas; but the scruples of my new friends appeared almost insurmountable. Yet the gentleman might have said 'I should like a portrait of my wife,' and the lady might have said 'I should like a portrait of my husband.' Perhaps they weren't husband and wife – this naturally would make the matter more delicate. Perhaps they wished to be done together – in which case they ought to have brought a third person to break the news.

'We come from Mr Rivet,' the lady finally said with a dim smile that had the effect of a moist sponge passed over a 'sunk' piece of painting, as well as of a vague allusion to vanished beauty. She was as tall and straight, in her degree, as her companion, and with ten years less to carry. She looked as sad as a woman could look whose face was not charged with expression; that is her tinted oval mask showed waste as an exposed surface shows friction. The hand of time had played over her freely, but to an effect of elimination. She was slim and stiff, and so well-dressed, in dark blue cloth, with lappets and pockets and buttons, that it was clear she employed the same tailor as her husband. The couple had an indefinable air of prosperous thrift – they evidently got a good deal of luxury for their money. If I was to be one of their luxuries it would behoove me to consider my terms.

'Ah Claude Rivet recommended me?' I echoed; and I added that it was very kind of him, though I could reflect that, as he only painted landscape, this wasn't a sacrifice.

The lady looked very hard at the gentleman, and the gentleman looked round the room. Then staring at the floor a moment and stroking his moustache, he rested his pleasant eyes on me with the remark: 'He said you were the right one.'

'I try to be, when people want to sit.'

'Yes, we should like to,' said the lady anxiously.

'Do you mean together?'

My visitors exchanged a glance. 'If you could do anything with *me* I suppose it would be double,' the gentleman stammered.

'Oh yes, there's naturally a higher charge for two figures than for one.'

'We should like to make it pay,' the husband confessed.

'That's very good of you,' I returned, appreciating so unwonted a sympathy – for I supposed he meant pay the artist.

A sense of strangeness seemed to dawn on the lady. 'We mean for the illustrations – Mr Rivet said you might put one in.'

'Put in – an illustration?' I was equally confused.

'Sketch her off, you know,' said the gentleman, colouring.

It was only then that I understood the service Claude Rivet had rendered me; he had told them how I worked in black-and-white, for magazines, for storybooks, for sketches of contemporary life, and consequently had copious employment for models. These things were true, but it was not less true – I may confess it now; whether because the aspiration was to lead to everything or to nothing I leave the reader to guess – that I couldn't get the honours, to say nothing of the emoluments, of a great painter of portraits out of my head. My 'illustrations' were my pot-boilers; I looked to a different branch of art – far and away the most interesting it had always seemed to me – to perpetuate my fame. There was no shame in looking to it also to make my fortune; but that fortune was by so much further from being made from the moment my visitors wished to be 'done' for nothing. I was disappointed; for in the pictorial sense I had immediately *seen* them. I had seized their type – I had already settled what I would do with it. Something that wouldn't absolutely have pleased them, I afterwards reflected.

'Ah you're – you're – a?' I began as soon as I had mastered my surprise. I couldn't bring out the dingy word 'models': it seemed so little to fit the case.

We haven't had much practice,' said the lady.

'We've got to *do* something, and we've thought that an artist in your line might perhaps make something of us,' her husband threw off. He further mentioned that they didn't know many artists and that they had gone first, on the off-chance – he painted views of course, but sometimes put in figures; perhaps I remembered – to Mr Rivet, whom they had met a few years before at a place in Norfolk where he was sketching.

'We used to sketch a little ourselves,' the lady hinted.

'It's very awkward, but we absolutely *must* do something,' her husband went on.

'Of course we're not so *very* young,' she admitted with a wan smile.

With the remark that I might as well know something more about them the husband had handed me a card extracted from a neat new pocket-book – their appurtenances were all of the freshest – and inscribed with the words 'Major Monarch'. Impressive as these words were they didn't carry my knowledge much further; but my visitor presently added: 'I've left the army and we've had the misfortune to lose our money. In fact our means are dreadfully small.'

'It's awfully trying – a regular strain,' said Mrs Monarch.

They evidently wished to be discreet – to take care not to swagger because they were gentlefolk. I felt them willing to recognise this as something of a drawback, at the same time that I guessed at an underlying sense – their consolation in adversity – that they *had* their points. They certainly had; but these advantages struck me as preponderantly social; such for instance as would help to make a drawing-room look well. However, a drawing-room was always, or ought to be, a picture.

In consequence of his wife's allusion to their age Major Monarch observed: 'Naturally it's more for the figure that we thought of going in. We can still hold ourselves up.' On the instant I saw that the figure was indeed their strong point. His 'naturally' didn't sound vain, but it lighted up the question. '*She* has the best one,' he continued, nodding at his wife with a pleasant after-dinner absence of circumlocution. I could only reply, as if we were in fact sitting over our wine, that this didn't prevent his own from being very good; which led him in turn to make answer: 'We thought that if you ever have to do people like us we might be something like it. *She* particularly – for a lady in a book, you know.'

I was so amused by them that, to get more of it, I did my best to take their point of view; and thought it was an embarrassment to find myself appraising physically, as if they were animals on hire or useful blacks, a pair whom I should have expected to meet only in one of the relations in which criticism is tacit, I looked at Mrs Monarch judicially enough to be able to exclaim after a moment with conviction: 'Oh yes, a lady in a book!' She was singularly like a bad illustration.

'We'll stand up, if you like,' said the Major; and he raised himself before me with a really grand air.

I could take his measure at a glance – he was six feet two and a perfect gentleman. It would have paid any club in process of formation and in want of a stamp to engage him at a salary to stand in the principal window. What struck me at once was that in coming to me they had rather missed their vocation; they could surely have been turned to better account for advertising purposes. I couldn't of course see the thing in detail, but I could see them make somebody's fortune – I don't mean their own. There was something in them for a waistcoat-maker, an hotel-keeper or a soap-vendor. I could imagine 'We always use it' pinned on their bosoms with the greatest effect; I had a vision of the brilliancy with which they would launch a table d'hôte.

Mrs Monarch sat still, not from pride but from shyness, and presently her husband said to her: 'Get up, my dear, and show how smart you are.' She obeyed, but she had no need to get up to show it. She walked to the end of the studio and then came back blushing, her fluttered eyes on the partner of her appeal. I was reminded of an incident I had accidentally had a glimpse of in Paris – being with a friend there, a dramatist about to produce a play, when an actress came to him to ask to be entrusted with a part. She went through her paces before him, walked up and down as Mrs Monarch was doing. Mrs Monarch did it quite as well, but I abstained from applauding. It was very odd to see such people apply for such poor pay. She looked as if she had ten thousand a year. Her husband had used the word that described her: she was in the London current jargon essentially and typically 'smart'. Her figure was, in the same order of ideas, conspicuously and irreproachably 'good'. For a woman of her age her waist was surprisingly small; her elbow moreover had the orthodox crook. She held her head at the conventional angle, but why did she come to *me*? She ought to have tried on jackets at a big shop. I feared my visitors were not only destitute but 'artistic' – which would be a great complication. When she sat down again I thanked her, observing that what a draughtsman most valued in his model was the faculty of keeping quiet.

'Oh *she* can keep quiet,' said Major Monarch. Then he added jocosely: 'I've always kept her quiet.'

'I'm not a nasty fidget, am I?' It was going to wring tears from me, I felt, the way she hid her head, ostrich-like, in the other broad bosom.

The owner of this expanse addressed his answer to me. 'Perhaps it isn't out of place to mention – because we ought to be quite business-like, oughtn't we? – that when I married her she was known as the Beautiful Statue.'

'Oh dear!' said Mrs Monarch ruefully.

'Of course I should want a certain amount of expression,' I rejoined.

'Of *course*!' – and I had never heard such unanimity.

'And then I suppose you know that you'll get awfully tired.'

'Oh we *never* get tired!' they eagerly cried.

'Have you had any kind of practice?'

They hesitated – they looked at each other. 'We've been photographed – *immensely*,' said Mrs Monarch.

'She means the fellows have asked us themselves,' added the Major.

'I see – because you're so good-looking.'

'I don't know what they thought, but they were always after us.'

'We always got our photographs for nothing,' smiled Mrs Monarch.

'We might have brought some, my dear,' her husband remarked.

'I'm not sure we have any left. We've given quantities away,' she explained to me.

'With our autographs and that sort of thing,' said the Major.

'Are they to be got in the shops?' I enquired as a harmless pleasantry.

'Oh yes, *hers* – they used to be.'

'Not now,' said Mrs Monarch with her eyes on the floor.

II

I could fancy the 'sort of thing' they put on the presentation copies of their photographs, and I was sure they wrote a beautiful hand. It was odd how quickly I was sure of everything that concerned them. If they were now so poor as to have to earn shillings and pence they could never have had much of a margin. Their good looks had been their capital, and they had good-humouredly made the most of the career that this resource marked out for them. It was in their faces, the blankness, the deep intellectual repose of the twenty years of country-house visiting that had given them pleasant intonations. I could see the sunny drawing-rooms, sprinkled with periodicals she didn't read, in which Mrs Monarch had continuously sat; I could see the wet shrubberies in which she had walked, equipped to admiration for either exercise. I could see the rich covers the Major had helped to shoot and the wonderful garments in which, late at night, he repaired to the smoking-room to talk about them. I could imagine their leggings and waterproofs, their knowing tweeds and rugs, their rolls of sticks and cases of tackle and neat umbrellas; and I could evoke the exact appearance of their servants and the compact variety of their luggage on the platforms of country stations.

They gave small tips, but they were liked; they didn't do anything themselves, but they were welcome. They looked so well everywhere; they gratified the general relish for stature, complexion and 'form'. They knew it without fatuity or vulgarity, and they respected themselves in consequence. They weren't superficial; they were thorough and kept themselves up – it had been their line. People with such a taste for activity had to have some line. I could feel how even in a dull house they could have been counted on for the joy of life. At present something had happened – it didn't matter what, their little income had grown less, it had grown least – and they had to do something for pocket-money. Their friends could like them, I made out, without liking to support them. There was something about them that represented credit – their clothes, their manners, their type; but if credit is a large empty pocket in which an occasional chink reverberates, the chink at least must be audible. What they wanted of me was to help to make it so. Fortunately they had no children – I soon divined that. They would also perhaps wish our relations to be kept secret: this was why it was 'for the figure' – the reproduction of the face would betray them.

I liked them – I felt, quite as their friends must have done – they were so simple; and I had no objection to them if they would suit. But somehow with all their perfections I didn't easily believe in them. After all they were amateurs, and the ruling passion of my life was the detestation of the amateur. Combined with this was another perversity – an innate preference for the represented subject over the real one: the defect of the real one was so apt to be a lack of representation. I like things that appeared; then one was sure. Whether they *were* or not was a subordinate and almost always a profitless question. There were other considerations, the first of which was that I already had two or three recruits in use, notably a young person with big feet, in alpaca, from Kilburn, who for a couple of years had come to me regularly for my illustrations and with whom I was still – perhaps ignobly – satisfied. I frankly explained to my visitors how the case stood, but they had taken more precautions than I supposed. They had reasoned out their opportunity, for Claude Rivet had told them of the projected *édition de luxe* of one of the writers of our day – the rarest of the novelists – who, long neglected by the multitudinous vulgar and dearly prized by the attentive (need I mention Philip Vincent?) had had the happy fortune of seeing, late in life, the dawn and then the full light of a higher criticism; an estimate in which on the part of the public there was something really of expiation. The edition preparing, planned by a publisher of taste, was practically an act of high reparation; the wood-cuts with which it was to be enriched were the homage of English art to one of the most independent representatives of English letters. Major and Mrs Monarch confessed to me they had hoped I might be able to work *them* into my branch of the enterprise. They knew I was to do the first of the books, 'Rutland Ramsay', but I had to make clear to them that my participation in the rest of the affair – this first book was to be a test – must depend on the satisfaction I should give. If this should be limited my employers would drop me with scarce common forms. It was therefore a crisis for me, and naturally I was making special preparations, looking about for new people, should they be necessary, and securing the best types. I admitted however that I should like to settle down to two or three good models who would do for everything.

'Should we have often to – a – put on special clothes?' Mrs Monarch timidly demanded.

'Dear yes – that's half the business.'

'And should we be expected to supply our own costumes?'

'Oh no; I've got a lot of things. A painter's models put on – or put off – anything he likes.'

'And you mean – a – the same?'

'The same?'

Mrs Monarch looked at her husband again.

'Oh she was just wondering,' he explained, 'if the costumes are in *general* use.' I had to confess that they were, and I mentioned further that some of them – I had a lot of genuine greasy last-century things – had served their time, a hundred years ago, on living world-stained men and women; on figures not perhaps so far removed, in that vanished world, from *their* type, the Monarchs', *quoi!* of a breeched and bewigged age. 'We'll put on anything that *fits*,' said the Major.

'Oh I arrange that – they fit in the pictures.'

'I'm afraid I should do better for the modern books. I'd come as you like,' said Mrs Monarch.

'She has got a lot of clothes at home: they might do for contemporary life,' her husband continued.

'Oh I can fancy scenes in which you'd be quite natural.' And indeed I could see the slipshod rearrangements of stale properties – the stories I tried to produce pictures for without the exasperation of reading them – whose sandy tracts the good lady might help to people. But I had to return to the fact that for this sort of work – the daily mechanical grind – I was already equipped: the people I was working with were fully adequate.

'We only thought we might be more like *some* characters,' said Mrs Monarch mildly, getting up.

Her husband also rose; he stood looking at me with a dim wistfulness that was touching in so fine a man. 'Wouldn't it be rather a pull sometimes to have – a – to have ?' He hung fire; he wanted me to help him by phrasing what he meant. But I couldn't – I didn't know. So he brought it out awkwardly: 'The *real* thing; a gentleman, you know, or a lady.' I was quite ready to give a general assent – I admitted that there was a great deal in that. This encouraged Major Monarch to say, following up his appeal with an unacted gulp: 'It's awfully hard – we've tried everything.' The gulp was communicative; it proved too much for his wife. Before I knew it Mrs Monarch had dropped again upon a divan and burst into tears. Her husband sat down beside her, holding one of her hands; whereupon she quickly dried her eyes with the other, while I felt embarrassed as she looked up at me. 'There isn't a confounded job I haven't applied for – waited for – prayed for. You can

fancy we'd be pretty bad first. Secretaryships and that sort of
thing? You might as well ask for a peerage. I'd be *anything* – I'm
strong; a messenger or a coalheaver. I'd put on a gold-laced cap
and open carriage-doors in front of the haberdasher's; I'd hang
about a station to carry portmanteaux; I'd be a postman. But they
won't *look* at you; there are thousands as good as yourself already
on the ground. *Gentlemen,* poor beggars, who've drunk their
wine, who've kept their hunters!'

I was as reassuring as I knew how to be, and my visitors were
presently on their feet again while, for the experiment, we agreed
on an hour. We were discussing it when the door opened and Miss
Churm came in with a wet umbrella. Miss Churm had to take the
omnibus to Maida Vale and then walk half a mile. She looked a
trifle blowsy and slightly splashed. I scarcely ever saw her come in
without thinking afresh how odd it was that, being so little in
herself, she should yet be so much in others. She was a meagre
little Miss Churm, but was such an ample heroine of romance. She
was only a freckled cockney, but she could represent everything,
from a fine lady to a shepherdess; she had the faculty as she might
have had a fine voice or long hair. She couldn't spell and she loved
beer, but she had two or three 'points', and practice, and a knack,
and mother-wit, and a whimsical sensibility, and a love of the
theatre, and seven sisters, and not an ounce of respect, especially
for the *h*. The first thing my visitors saw was that her umbrella
was wet, and in their spotless perfection they visibly winced at it.
The rain had come on since their arrival.

'I'm all in a soak; there *was* a mess of people in the 'bus. I wish
you lived near a stytion,' said Miss Churm. I requested her to get
ready as quickly as possible, and she passed into the room in
which she always changed her dress. But before going out she
asked me what she was to get into this time.

'It's the Russian princess, don't you know?' I answered; 'the
one with the "golden eyes," in black velvet, for the long thing in
the *Cheapside*.'

'Golden eyes? I *say!*' cried Miss Churm, while my companions
watched her with intensity as she withdrew. She always arranged
herself, when she was late, before I could turn round; and I kept
my visitors a little on purpose, so that they might get an idea, from

seeing her, what would be expected of themselves. I mentioned that she was quite my notion of an excellent model – she was really very clever.

'Do you think she looks like a Russian princess?' Major Monarch asked with lurking alarm.

'When I make her, yes.'

'Oh, if you have to *make* her –!' he reasoned, not without point.

'That's the most you can ask. There are so many who are not makeable.'

'Well now, *here's* a lady' – and with a persuasive smile he passed his arm into his wife's – 'who's already made!'

'Oh, I'm not a Russian princess,' Mrs Monarch protested a little coldly. I could see she had known some and didn't like them. There at once was a complication of a kind I never had to fear with Miss Churm.

This young lady came back in black velvet – the gown was rather rusty and very low on her lean shoulders – and with a Japanese fan in her red hands. I reminded her that in the scene I was doing she had to look over some one's head. 'I forget whose it is; but it doesn't matter. Just look over a head.'

'I'd rather look over a stove,' said Miss Churm; and she took her station near the fire. She fell into position, settled herself into a tall attitude, gave a certain backward inclination to her head and a certain forward droop to her fan, and looked, at least to my prejudiced sense, distinguished and charming, foreign and dangerous. We left her looking so while I went downstairs with Major and Mrs Monarch.

'I believe I could come about as near it as that,' said Mrs Monarch.

'Oh you think she's shabby, but you must allow for the alchemy of art.'

However, they went off with an evident increase of comfort founded on their demonstrable advantage in being the real thing. I could fancy them shuddering over Miss Churm. She was very droll about them when I went back, for I told her what they wanted.

'Well, if *she* can sit I'll tyke to book-keeping,' said my model.

'She's very ladylike,' I replied as an innocent form of aggravation.

'So much the worse for *you*. That means she can't turn round.'

'She'll do for the fashionable novels.'

'Oh yes, she'll *do* for them!' my model humorously declared. 'Ain't they bad enough without her?' I had often sociably denounced them to Miss Churm.

III

It was for the elucidation of a mystery in one of these works that I first tried Mrs Monarch. Her husband came with her, to be useful if necessary – it was sufficiently clear that as a general thing he would prefer to come with her. At first I wondered if this were for 'propriety's' sake – if he were going to be jealous and meddling. The idea was too tiresome, and if it had been confirmed it would speedily have brought our acquaintance to a close. But I soon saw there was nothing in it and that if he accompanied Mrs Monarch it was – in addition to the chance of being wanted – simply because he had nothing else to do. When they were separate his occupation was gone and they never *had* been separate. I judged rightly that in their awkward situation their close union was their main comfort and that this union had no weak spot. It was a real marriage, an encouragement to the hesitating, a nut for pessimists to crack. Their address was humble – I remember afterwards thinking it had been the only thing about them that was really professional – and I could fancy the lamentable lodgings in which the Major would have been left alone. He could sit there more or less grimly with his wife – he couldn't sit there anyhow without her.

He had too much tact to try and make himself agreeable when he couldn't be useful; so when I was too absorbed in my work to talk he simply sat and waited. But I liked to hear him talk – it made my work, when not interrupting it, less mechanical, less special. To listen to him was to combine the excitement of going out with the economy of staying at home. There was only one hindrance – that I seemed not to know any of the people this brilliant couple had known. I think he wondered extremely, during the term of our intercourse, whom the deuce I *did* know. He hadn't a stray sixpence of an idea to fumble for, so we didn't spin it very fine; we confined ourselves to questions of leather and even of liquor – saddlers and breeches-makers and how to get excellent claret cheap – and matters like 'good trains' and the habits of small game. His lore on these last subjects was astonishing – he managed to interweave the station-master with the ornithologist. When he couldn't talk about greater things he could talk cheerfully about smaller, and since I couldn't accompany him into reminiscences of the fashionable world he could lower the conversation without a visible effort to my level.

So earnest a desire to please was touching in a man who could so easily have knocked one down. He looked after the fire and had an opinion on the draught of the stove without my asking him, and I could see that he thought many of my arrangements not half knowing. I remember telling him that if I were only rich I'd offer him a salary to come and teach me how to live. Sometimes he gave a random sigh of which the essence might have been: 'Give me even such a bare old barrack as *this*, and I'd do something with it!' When I wanted to use him he came alone; which was an illustration of the superior courage of women. His wife could bear her solitary second floor, and she was in general more discreet; showing by various small reserves that she was alive to the propriety of keeping our relations markedly professional – not letting them slide into sociability. She wished it to remain clear that she and the Major were employed, not cultivated, and if she approved of me as a superior, who could be kept in his place, she never thought me quite good enough for an equal.

She sat with great intensity, giving the whole of her mind to it, and was capable of remaining for an hour almost as motionless as before a photographer's lens. I could see she had been photographed often, but somehow the very habit that made her good for that purpose unfitted her for mine. At first I was extremely pleased with her ladylike air, and it was a satisfaction, on coming to follow her lines, to see how good they were and how far they could lead the pencil. But after a little skirmishing I began to find her too insurmountably stiff; do what I would with it my drawing looked like a photograph or a copy of a photograph. Her figure had no variety of expression – she herself had no sense of variety. You may say that this was my business and was only a question of placing her. Yet I placed her in every conceivable position and she managed to obliterate their differences. She was always a lady certainly, and into the bargain was always the same lady. She was the real thing, but always the same thing. There were moments when I rather writhed under the serenity of her confidence that she *was* the real thing. All her dealings with me and all her husband's were an implication that this was lucky for *me*. Meanwhile I found myself trying to invent types that approached her own, instead of making her own transform itself – in the clever way that was not impossible for instance to poor Miss Churm. Arrange as I would and take the precautions I would, she always came out, in my pictures, too tall – landing me in the dilemma of having represented a fascinating woman as seven feet high, which (out of respect perhaps to my own very much scantier inches) was far from my idea of such a personage.

The case was worse with the Major – nothing I could do would keep *him* down, so that he became useful only for the representation of brawny giants. I adored variety and range, I cherished human accidents, the illustrative note; I wanted to characterise closely, and the thing in the world I most hated was the danger of being ridden by a type. I had quarrelled with some of my friends about it; I had parted company with them for maintaining that one *had* to be, and that if the type was beautiful – witness Raphael and Leonardo – the servitude was only a gain. I was neither Leonardo nor Raphael – I might only be a presumptuous young modern searcher; but I held that everything was to be sacrificed sooner than character. When they claimed that the obsessional form could easily *be* character I retorted, perhaps superficially, 'Whose?' It couldn't be everybody's – it might end in being nobody's.

After I had drawn Mrs Monarch a dozen times I felt surer even than before that the value of such a model as Miss Churm resided precisely in the fact that she had no positive stamp, combined of course with the other fact that what she did have was a curious and inexplicable talent for imitation. Her usual appearance was like a curtain which she could draw up at request for a capital performance. This performance was simply suggestive; but it was a word to the wise – it was vivid and pretty. Sometimes even I thought it, though she was plain herself, too insipidly pretty; I made it a reproach to her that the figures drawn from her were monotonously (*bêtement*, as we used to say) graceful. Nothing made her more angry; it was so much her pride to feel she could sit for characters that had nothing in common with each other. She would accuse me at such moments of taking away her 'reputytion'.

It suffered a certain shrinkage, this queer quantity, from the repeated visits of my new friends. Miss Churm was greatly in demand, never in want of employment, so I had no scruple in putting her off occasionally, to try them more at my ease. It was certainly amusing at first to do the real thing – it was amusing to do Major Monarch's trousers. They *were* the real thing, even if he did come out colossal. It was amusing to do his wife's back hair – it was so mathematically neat – and the particular 'smart' tension of her tight stays. She lent herself especially to positions in which the face was somewhat averted or blurred; she abounded in ladylike back views and *profils perdus*. When she stood erect she took naturally one of the attitudes in which court-painters represent queens and princesses; so that I found myself wondering whether, to draw out this accomplishment, I couldn't get the editor of the *Cheapside* to publish a really royal romance, 'A Tale of Buckingham Palace'. Sometimes however the real thing and the make-believe came into contact; by which I mean that Miss Churm, keeping an appointment or coming to make one on days when I had much work in hand, encountered her invidious rivals. The encounter was not on their part, for they noticed her no more than if she had been the housemaid; not from intentional loftiness, but simply because as yet, professionally, they didn't know how to fraternise, as I could imagine they would have liked – or at least that the Major would. They couldn't talk about the omnibus – they always walked; and they didn't know what else to try – she wasn't interested in good trains or cheap claret. Besides, they must have felt – in the air – that she was amused at them, secretly derisive of their ever knowing how. She wasn't a person to conceal the limits of her faith if she had had a chance to show them. On the other hand Mrs Monarch didn't think her tidy; for why else did she take pains to say to me – it was going out of the way, for Mrs Monarch – that she didn't like dirty women?

One day when my young lady happened to be present with my other sitters – she even dropped in, when it was convenient, for a chat – I asked her to be so good as to lend a hand in getting tea, a service with which she was familiar and which was one of a class that, living as I did in a small way, with slender domestic resources, I often appealed to my models to render. They liked to lay hands on my property, to break the sitting, and sometimes the china – it made them feel Bohemian. The next time I saw Miss Churm after this incident she surprised me greatly by making a scene about it – she accused me of having wished to humiliate her. She hadn't resented the outrage at the time, but had seemed obliging and amused, enjoying the comedy of asking Mrs Monarch, who sat vague and silent, whether she would have cream and sugar, and putting an exaggerated simper into the question. She had tried intonations – as if she too wished to pass for the real thing – till I was afraid my other visitors would take offence.

Oh they were determined not to do this, and their touching patience was the measure of their great need. They would sit by the hour, uncomplaining, till I was ready to use them; they would come back on the chance of being wanted and would walk away cheerfully if it failed. I used to go to the door with them to see in what magnificent order they retreated. I tried to find other employment for them – I introduced them to several artists. But they didn't 'take', for reasons I could appreciate, and I became rather anxiously aware that after such disappointments they fell back upon me with a heavier weight. They did me the honour to think me most *their* form. They weren't romantic enough for the painters, and in those days there were few serious workers in black-and-white. Besides, they had an eye to the great job I had mentioned to them – they had secretly set their hearts on supplying the right essence for my pictorial vindication of our fine novelist. They knew that for this undertaking I should want no costume-effects, none of the frippery of past ages – that it was a case in which everything would be contemporary and satirical and presumably genteel. If I could work them into it their future would be assured, for the labour would of course be long and the occupation steady.

One day Mrs Monarch came without her husband – she explained his absence by his having had to go to the City. While she sat there in her usual relaxed majesty there came at the door a knock which I immediately recognised as the subdued appeal of a model out of work. It was followed by the entrance of a young man whom I at once saw to be a foreigner and who proved in fact an Italian acquainted with no English word but my name, which he uttered in a way that made it seem to include all others. I hadn't then visited his country, nor was I proficient in his tongue; but as he was not so meanly constituted – what Italian is? – as to depend only on that member for expression he conveyed to me, in familiar but graceful mimicry, that he was in search of exactly the employment in which the lady before me was engaged. I was not struck with him at first, and while I continued to draw I dropped few signs of interest or encouragement. He stood his ground however – not importunately, but with a dumb dog-like fidelity in his eyes that amounted to innocent impudence, the manner of a devoted servant – he might have been in the house for years – unjustly suspected. Suddenly it struck me that this very attitude and expression made a picture; whereupon I told him to sit down and wait till I should be free. There was another picture in the way he obeyed me, and I observed as I worked that there were others still in the way he looked wonderingly, with his head thrown back, about the high studio. He might have been crossing himself in Saint Peter's. Before I finished I said to myself 'The fellow's a bankrupt orange-monger, but a treasure.'

When Mrs Monarch withdrew he passed across the room like a flash to open the door for her, standing there with the rapt pure gaze of the young Dante spellbound by the young Beatrice. As I never insisted, in such situations, on the blankness of the British domestic, I reflected that he had the making of a servant – and I needed one, but couldn't pay him to be only that – as well as of a model; in short I resolved to adopt my bright adventurer if he would agree to officiate in the double capacity. He jumped at my offer, and in the event my rashness – for I had really known nothing about him – wasn't brought home to me. He proved a sympathetic though a desultory ministrant, and had in a wonderful degree the *sentiment de la pose*. It was uncultivated, instinctive, a part of the happy instinct that had guided him to my door and helped him to spell out my name on the card nailed to it. He had had no other introduction to me than a guess, from the shape of my high north window, seen outside, that my place was a studio and that as a studio it would contain an artist. He had wandered to England in search of fortune, like other itinerants, and had embarked, with a partner and a small green hand-cart, on the sale of penny ices. The ices had melted away and the partner had dissolved in their train. My young man wore tight yellow trousers with reddish stripes and his name was Oronte. He was sallow but fair, and when I put him into some old clothes of my own he looked like an Englishman. He was as good as Miss Churm, who could look, when requested, like an Italian.

IV

I thought Mrs Monarch's face slightly convulsed when, on her coming back with her husband, she found Oronte installed. It was strange to have to recognize in a scrap of a lazzarone a competitor to her magnificent Major. It was she who scented danger first, for the Major was anecdotically unconscious. But Oronte gave us tea, with a hundred eager confusions – he had never been concerned in so queer a process – and I think she thought better of me for having at last an 'establishment'. They saw a couple of drawings that I had made of the establishment, and Mrs Monarch hinted that it never would have struck her he had sat for them. 'Now the drawings you make from *us*, they look exactly like us,' she reminded me, smiling in triumph; and I recognised that this was indeed just their defect. When I drew the Monarchs I couldn't anyhow get away from them – get into the character I wanted to represent; and I hadn't the least desire my model should be discoverable in my picture. Miss Churm never was, and Mrs Monarch thought I hid her, very properly, because she was vulgar; whereas if she was lost it was only as the dead who go to heaven are lost – in the gain of an angel the more.

By this time I had got a certain start with 'Rutland Ramsay', the first novel in the great projected series; that is I had produced a dozen drawings, several with the help of the Major and his wife, and I had sent them in for approval. My understanding with the publishers, as I have already hinted, had been that I was to be left to do my work, in this particular case, as I liked, with the whole book committed to me; but my connexion with the rest of the series was only contingent. There were moments when, frankly, it *was* a comfort to have the real thing under one's hand; for there were characters in 'Rutland Ramsay' that were very much like it. There were people presumably as erect as the Major and women of as good a fashion as Mrs Monarch. There was a great deal of country-house life – treated, it is true, in a fine fanciful ironical generalised way – and there was a considerable implication of knickerbockers and kilts. There were certain things I had to settle at the outset; such things for instance as the exact appearance of the hero and the particular bloom and figure of the heroine. The author of course gave me a lead, but there was a margin for interpretation. I took the Monarchs into my confidence, I told them frankly what I was about, I mentioned my embarrassments and alternatives. 'Oh take *him!*' Mrs Monarch murmured sweetly, looking at her husband; and 'What could you want better than my wife?' the Major enquired with the comfortable candour that now prevailed between us.

I wasn't obliged to answer these remarks – I was only obliged to place my sitters. I wasn't easy in mind, and I postponed a little timidly perhaps the solving of my question. The book was a large canvas, the other figures were numerous, and I worked off at first some of the episodes in which the hero and the heroine were not concerned. When once I had set *them* up I should have to stick to them – I couldn't make my young man seven feet high in one place and five feet nine in another. I inclined on the whole to the latter measurement, though the Major more than once reminded me that *he* looked about as young as any one. It was indeed quite possible to arrange him, for the figure, so that it would have been difficult to detect his age. After the spontaneous Oronte had been with me a month, and after I had given him to understand several times over that his native exuberance would presently constitute an insurmountable barrier to our further intercourse, I waked to a sense of his heroic capacity. He was only five feet seven, but the remaining inches were latent. I tried him almost secretly at first, for I was really rather afraid of the judgment my other models would pass on such a choice. If they regarded Miss Churm as little better than a snare what would they think of the representation by a person so little the real thing as an Italian street-vendor of a protagonist formed by a public school?

If I went a little in fear of them it wasn't because they bullied me, because they had got an oppressive foothold, but because in their really pathetic decorum and mysteriously permanent newness they counted on me so intensely. I was therefore very glad when Jack Hawley came home: he was always of such good counsel. He painted badly himself, but there was no one like him for putting his finger on the place. He had been absent from England for a year; he had been somewhere – I don't remember where – to get a fresh eye. I was in a good deal of dread of any such organ, but we were old friends; he had been away for months and a sense of emptiness was creeping into my life. I hadn't dodged a missile for a year.

He came back with a fresh eye, but with the same old black velvet blouse, and the first evening he spent in my studio we smoked cigarettes till the small hours. He had done no work himself, he had only got the eye; so the field was clear for the production of my little things. He wanted to see what I had produced for the *Cheapside*, but he was disappointed in the exhibition. That at least seemed the meaning of two or three comprehensive groans which, as he lounged on my big divan, his leg folded under him, looking at my latest drawings, issued from his lips with the smoke of the cigarette.

'What's the matter with you?' I asked.

'What's the matter with *you*?'

'Nothing save that I'm mystified.'

'You are indeed. You're quite off the hinge. What's the meaning of this new fad?' And he tossed me, with visible irreverence, a drawing in which I happened to have depicted both my elegant models. I asked if he didn't think it good, and he replied that it struck him as execrable, given the sort of thing I had always represented myself to him as wishing to arrive at; but I let that pass – I was so anxious to see exactly what he meant. The two figures in the picture looked colossal, but I supposed this was *not* what he meant, inasmuch as, for aught he knew to the contrary, I might have been trying for some such effect. I maintained that I was working exactly in the same way as when he last had done me the honour to tell me I might do something some day. 'Well, there's a screw loose somewhere,' he answered; 'wait a bit and I'll discover it.' I depended upon him to do so: where else was the fresh eye? But he produced at last nothing more luminous than 'I don't know – I don't like your types.' This was lame for a critic who had never consented to discuss with me anything but the question of execution, the direction of strokes and the mystery of values.

'In the drawings you've been looking at I think my types are very handsome.'

'Oh they won't do!'

'I've been working with new models.'

'I see you have. *They* won't do.'

'Are you very sure of that?'

'Absolutely – they're stupid.'

'You mean *I* am – for I ought to get round that.'

'You *can't* – with such people. Who are they?'

I told him, so far as was necessary, and he concluded heartlessly: 'Ce sont des gens qu'il faut mettre à la porte.'

'You've never seen them; they're awfully good' – I flew to their defence.

'Not seen them? Why all this recent work of yours drops to pieces with them. It's all I want to see of them.'

'No one else has said anything against it – the *Cheapside* people are pleased.'

'Every one else is an ass, and the *Cheapside* people the biggest asses of all. Come, don't pretend at this time of day to have pretty illusions about the public, especially about publishers and editors. It's not for *such* animals you work – it's for those who know, *coloro che sanno*; so keep straight for *me* if you can't keep straight for yourself. There was a certain sort of thing you used to try for – and a very good thing it was. But this twaddle isn't *in* it.' When I talked with Hawley later about 'Rutland Ramsay' and its possible successors he declared that I must get back into my boat again or I should go to the bottom. His voice in short was the voice of warning.

I noted the warning, but I didn't turn my friends out of doors. They bored me a good deal; but the very fact that they bored me admonished me not to sacrifice them – if there was anything to be done with them – simply to irritation. As I look back at this phase they seem to me to have pervaded my life not a little. I have a vision of them as most of the time in my studio, seated against the wall on an old velvet bench to be out of the way, and resembling the while a pair of patient courtiers in a royal antechamber. I'm convinced that during the coldest weeks of the winter they held their ground because it saved them fire. Their newness was losing its gloss, and it was impossible not to feel them objects of charity. Whenever Miss Churm arrived they went away, and after I was fairly launched in 'Rutland Ramsay' Miss Churm arrived pretty often. They managed to express to me tacitly that they supposed I wanted her for the low life of the book, and I let them suppose it, since they had attempted to study the work – it was lying about the studio – without discovering that it dealt only with the highest circles. They had dipped into the most brilliant of our novelists without deciphering many passages. I still took an hour from them, now and again, in spite of Jack Hawley's warning: it would be time enough to dismiss them, if dismissal should be necessary, when the rigour of the season was over. Hawley had made their acquaintance – he had met them at my fireside – and thought them a ridiculous pair. Learning that he was a painter they tried to approach him, to show him too that they were the real thing; but he looked at them, across the big room, as if they were miles away: they were a compendium of everything he most objected to in the social system of his country. Such people as that, all convention and patent-leather, with ejaculations that stopped conversation, had no business in a studio. A studio was a place to learn to see, and how could you see through a pair of feather-beds?

The main inconvenience I suffered at their hands was that at first I was shy of letting it break upon them that my artful little servant had begun to sit to me for 'Rutland Ramsay'. They knew I had been odd enough – they were prepared by this time to allow oddity to artists – to pick a foreign vagabond out of the streets when I might have had a person with whiskers and credentials; but it was some time before they learned how high I rated his accomplishments. They found him in an attitude more than once, but they never doubted I was doing him as an organ-grinder. There were several things they never guessed, and one of them was that for a striking scene in the novel, in which a footman briefly figured, it occurred to me to make use of Major Monarch as the menial. I kept putting this off, I didn't like to ask him to don the livery – besides the difficulty of finding a livery to fit him. At last, one day late in the winter, when I was at work on the despised Oronte, who caught one's idea on the wing, and was in the glow of feeling myself go very straight, they came in, the Major and his wife, with their society laugh about nothing (there was less and less to laugh at); came in like country-callers – they always reminded me of that – who have walked across the park after church and are presently persuaded to stay to luncheon. Luncheon was over, but they could stay to tea – I knew they wanted it. The fit was on me, however, and I couldn't let my ardour cool and my work wait, with the fading daylight, while my model prepared it. So I asked Mrs Monarch if she would mind laying it out – a request which for an instant brought all the blood to her face. Her eyes were on her husband's for a second, and some mute telegraphy passed between them. Their folly was over the next instant; his cheerful shrewdness put an end to it. So far from pitying their wounded pride, I must add, I was moved to give it as complete a lesson as I could. They bustled about together and got out the cups and saucers and made the kettle boil. I know they felt as if they were waiting on my servant, and when the tea was prepared I said: 'He'll have a cup, please – he's tired.' Mrs Monarch brought him one where he stood, and he took it from her as if he had been a gentleman at a party squeezing a crush-hat with an elbow.

Then it came over me that she had made a great effort for me – made it with a kind of nobleness – and that I owed her a compensation. Each time I saw her after this I wondered what the compensation could be. I couldn't go on doing the wrong thing to oblige them. Oh it *was* the wrong thing, the stamp of the work for which they sat – Hawley was not the only person to say it now. I sent in a large number of the drawings I had made for 'Rutland Ramsay', and I received a warning that was more to the point than

Hawley's. The artistic adviser of the house for which I was working was of opinion that many of my illustrations were not what had been looked for. Most of these illustrations were the subjects in which the Monarchs had figured. Without going into the question of what *had* been looked for, I had to face the fact that at this rate I shouldn't get the other books to do. I hurled myself in despair on Miss Churm – I put her through all her paces. I not only adopted Oronte publicly as my hero, but one morning when the Major looked in to see if I didn't require him to finish a *Cheapside* figure for which he had begun to sit the week before, I told him I had changed my mind – I'd do the drawing from my man. At this my visitor turned pale and stood looking at me. 'Is *he* your idea of an English gentleman?' he asked.

I was disappointed, I was nervous, I wanted to get on with my work; so I replied with irritation; 'Oh my dear Major – I can't be ruined for *you!*'

It was a horrid speech, but he stood another moment – after which, without a word, he quitted the studio. I drew a long breath, for I said to myself that I shouldn't see him again. I hadn't told him definitely that I was in danger of having my work rejected, but I was vexed at his not having felt the catastrophe in the air, read with me the moral of our fruitless collaboration, the lesson that in the deceptive atmosphere of art even the highest respectability may fail of being plastic.

I didn't owe my friends money, but I did see them again. They reappeared together three days later, and, given all the other facts, there was something tragic in that one. It was a clear proof they could find nothing else in life to do. They had threshed the matter out in a dismal conference – they had digested the bad news that they were not in for the series. If they weren't useful to me even for the *Cheapside* their function seemed difficult to determine, and I could only judge at first that they had come, forgivingly, de-corously, to take a last leave. This made mè rejoice in secret that I had little leisure for a scene; for I had placed both my other models in position together and I was pegging away at a drawing from which I hoped to derive glory. It had been suggested by the passage in which Rutland Ramsay, drawing up a chair to Artemi-sia's piano-stool, says extraordinary things to her while she ostensibly fingers out a difficult piece of music. I had done Miss Churm at the piano before – it was an attitude in which she knew how to take on an absolutely poetic grace. I wished the two figures to 'compose' together with intensity, and my little Italian had entered perfectly into my conception. The pair were vividly before me, the piano had been pulled out; it was a charming show of blended youth and murmured love, which I had only to catch and keep. My visitors stood and looked at it, and I was friendly to them over my shoulder.

They made no response, but I was used to silent company and went on with my work, only a little disconcerted – even though exhilarated by the sense that *this* was at least the ideal thing – at not having got rid of them after all. Presently I heard Mrs Monarch's sweet voice beside or rather above me: 'I wish her hair were a little better done.' I looked up and she was staring with a strange fixedness at Miss Churm, whose back was turned to her. 'Do you mind my just touching it?' she went on – a question which made me spring up for an instant as with the instinctive fear that she might do the young lady a harm. But she quieted me with a glance I shall never forget – I confess I should like to have been able to paint *that* – and went for a moment to my model. She spoke to her softly, laying a hand on her shoulder and bending over her; and as the girl, understanding, gratefully assented, she disposed her rough curls, with a few quick passes, in such a way as to make Miss Churm's head twice as charming. It was one of the most heroic personal services I've ever seen rendered. Then Mrs Monarch turned away with a low sigh and, looking about her as if for something to do, stooped to the floor with a noble humility and picked up a dirty rag that had dropped out of my paint-box.

The Major meanwhile had also been looking for something to do, and, wandering to the other end of the studio, saw before him my breakfast-things neglected, unremoved. 'I say, can't I be useful *here*?' he called out to me with an irrepressible quaver. I assented with a laugh that I fear was awkward, and for the next ten minutes, while I worked, I heard the light clatter of china and the tinkle of spoons and glass. Mr Monarch assisted her husband – they washed up my crockery, they put it away. They wandered off into my little scullery, and I afterwards found that they had cleaned my knives and that my slender stock of plate had an unprecedented surface. When it came over me, the latent eloquence of what they were doing, I confess that my drawing was blurred for a moment – the picture swam. They had accepted their failure, but they couldn't accept their fate. They had bowed their heads in bewilderment to the perverse and cruel law in virtue of which the real thing could be so much less precious than the unreal; but they didn't want to starve. If my servants were my models, then my models might be my servants. They would reverse the parts – the others would sit for the ladies and gentlemen and *they* would do the work. They would still be in the studio – it was an intense dumb appeal to me not to turn them out. 'Take us on,' they wanted to say – 'we'll do *anything*.'

My pencil dropped from my hand; my sitting was spoiled and I got rid of my sitters, who were also evidently rather mystified and awestruck. Then, alone with the Major and his wife I had a most uncomfortable moment. He put their prayer into a single sentence: 'I say, you know – just let *us* do for you, can't you?' I couldn't – it was dreadful to see them emptying my slops; but I pretended I could, to oblige them, for about a week. Then I gave them a sum of money to go away, and I never saw them again. I obtained the remaining books, but my friend Hawley repeats that Major and Mrs Monarch did me a permanent harm, got me into false ways. If it be true I'm content to have paid the price – for the memory.

'George Egerton'
(Mary Chavelita Dunne)

VIRGIN SOIL

The bridegroom is waiting in the hall; with a trifle of impatience he is tracing the pattern of the linoleum with the point of his umbrella. He curbs it and laughs, showing his strong white teeth at a remark of his best man; then compares the time by his hunter with the clock on the stairs. He is florid, bright-eyed, loose-lipped, inclined to stoutness, but kept in good condition; his hair is crisp, curly, slightly grey; his ears peculiar, pointed at their tops like a faun's. He looks very big and well-dressed, and, when he smiles, affable enough.

Upstairs a young girl, with the suns of seventeen summers on her brown head, is lying with her face hidden on her mother's shoulder; she is sobbing with great childish sobs, regardless of reddened eyes and the tears that have splashed on the silk of her grey, going-away gown.

The mother seems scarcely less disturbed than the girl. She is a fragile-looking woman with delicate fair skin, smoothly parted thin chestnut hair, dove-like eyes, and a monotonous piping voice. She is flushing painfully, making a strenuous effort to say something to the girl, something that is opposed to the whole instincts of her life.

She tries to speak, parts her lips only to close them again, and clasp her arms tighter round the girl's shoulders; at length she manages to say with trembling, uncertain pauses:

'You are married now, darling, and you must obey' – she lays a stress upon the word – 'your husband in all things – there are – there are things you should know – but – marriage is a serious thing, a sacred thing' – with desperation – 'you must believe that what your husband tells you is right – let him guide you – tell you –'

There is such acute distress in her usually unemotional voice that the girl looks up and scans her face – her blushing, quivering, faded face. Her eyes are startled, fawn-like eyes as her mother's, her skin too is delicately fair, but her mouth is firmer, her jaw squarer, and her piquant, irregular nose is full of character. She is slightly built, scarcely fully developed in her fresh youth.

'What is it that I do not know, mother? What is it?' — with anxious impatience. 'There is something more — I have felt it all these last weeks in your and the others' looks — in his, in the very atmosphere — but why have you not told me before — I —' Her only answer is a gush of helpless tears from the mother, and a sharp rap at the door, and the bridegroom's voice, with an imperative note that it strikes the nervous girl is new to it, that makes her cling to her mother in a close, close embrace, drop her veil and go out to him.

She shakes hands with the best man, kisses the girl friend who has acted as bridesmaid — the wedding has been a very quiet one — and steps into the carriage. The Irish cook throws an old shoe after them from the side door, but it hits the trunk of an elder-tree, and falls back on to the path, making that worthy woman cross herself and mutter of ill-omens and bad luck to follow; for did not a magpie cross the path first thing this morning when she went to open the gate, and wasn't a red-haired woman the first creature she clapped eyes on as she looked down the road?

Half-an-hour later the carriage pulls up at the little station and the girl jumps out first; she is flushed, and her eyes stare helplessly as the eyes of a startled child, and she trembles with quick running shudders from head to foot. She clasps and unclasps her slender, grey-gloved hands so tightly that the stitching on the back of one bursts.

He has called to the station-master, and they go into the refreshment-room together; the latter appears at the door and, beckoning to a porter, gives him an order.

She takes a long look at the familiar little place. They have lived there three years, and yet she seems to see it now for the first time; the rain drips, drips monotonously off the zinc roof, the smell of the dust is fresh, and the white pinks in the borders are beaten into the gravel.

Then the train runs in; a first-class carriage, marked 'engaged', is attached, and he comes for her; his hot breath smells of champagne, and it strikes her that his eyes are fearfully big and bright, and he offers her his arm with such a curious amused proprietary air that the girl shivers as she lays her hand in it.

The bell rings, the guard locks the door, the train steams out, and as it passes the signal-box, a large well-kept hand, with a signet ring on the little finger, pulls down the blind on the window of an engaged carriage.

Five years later, one afternoon on an autumn day, when the rain is falling like splashing tears on the rails, and the smell of the dust after rain fills the mild air with freshness, and the white chrysan-themums struggle to raise their heads from the gravel path into which the sharp shower has beaten them, the same woman, for there is no trace of girlhood in her twenty-two years, slips out of a first-class carriage; she has a dressing-bag in her hand.

She walks with her head down and a droop in her shoulders; her quickness of step is due rather to nervous haste than elasticity of frame. When she reaches the turn of the road, she pauses and looks at the little villa with the white curtains and gay tiled window-boxes. She can see the window of her old room; disting-uish every shade in the changing leaves of the creeper climbing up the south wall; hear the canary's shrill note from where she stands.

Never once has she set foot in the peaceful little house with its air of genteel propriety since that eventful morning when she left it with him; she has always framed an excuse.

Now as she sees it a feeling of remorse fills her heart, and she thinks of the mother living out her quiet years, each day a replica of the one gone before, and her resolve weakens; she feels inclined to go back, but the waning sun flickers over the panes in the window of the room she occupied as a girl. She can recall how she used to run to the open window on summer mornings and lean out and draw in the dewy freshness and welcome the day, how she has stood on moonlight nights and danced with her bare white feet in the strip of moonlight, and let her fancies fly out into the silver night, a young girl's dreams of the beautiful, wonderful world that lay outside.

A hard dry sob rises in her throat at the memory of it, and the fleeting expression of softness on her face changes to a bitter disillusion.

She hurries on, with her eyes down, up the neat gravelled path, through the open door into the familiar sitting-room.

The piano is open with a hymn-book on the stand; the grate is filled with fresh green ferns, a bowl of late roses perfume the room from the centre of the table. The mother is sitting in her easy chair, her hands folded across a big white Persian cat on her lap; she is fast asleep. Some futile lace work, her thimble, and bright scissor are placed on a table near her.

Her face is placid, not a day older than that day five years ago. Her glossy hair is no greyer, her skin is clear, she smiles in her sleep. The smile rouses a sort of sudden fury in the breast of the woman standing in her dusty travelling cloak at the door, noting every detail in the room. She throws back her veil and goes over and looks at herself in the mirror over the polished chiffonnier – scans herself pitilessly. Her skin is sallow with the dull sallowness of a fair skin in ill-health, and the fringe of her brown hair is so lacking in lustre that it affords no contrast. The look of fawn-like shyness has vanished from her eyes, they burn sombrefully and resentfully in their sunken orbits, there is a dragged look about the mouth; and the keynote of her face is a cynical disillusion. She looks from herself to the reflection of the mother, and then turning sharply with a suppressed exclamation goes over, and shaking the sleeping woman not too gently, says:

'Mother, wake up, I want to speak to you!'

The mother starts with frightened eyes, stared at the other woman as if doubting the evidence of her sight, smiles, then cowed by the unresponsive look in the other face, grows grave again, sits still and stares helplessly at her, finally bursting into tears with a

'Flo, my dear, Flo, is it really you?'

The girl jerks her head impatiently and says drily:

'Yes, that is self-evident. I am going on a long journey. I have something to say to you before I start! Why on earth are you crying?'

There is a note of surprised wonder in her voice mixed with impatience.

The older woman has had time to scan her face and the dormant motherhood in her is roused by its weary anguish. She is ill, she thinks, in trouble. She rises to her feet; it is characteristic of the habits of her life, with its studied regard for the observance of small proprieties, and distrust of servants as a class, that she goes over and closes the room door carefully.

This hollow-eyed, sullen women is so unlike the fresh girl who left her five years ago that she feels afraid. With the quiet selfishness that has characterized her life she has accepted the excuses her daughter has made to avoid coming home, as she has accepted the presents her son-in-law has sent her from time to time. She has found her a husband well-off in the world's goods, and there her responsibility ended. She approaches her hesitatingly; she feels she ought to kiss her, there is something unusual in such a meeting after so long an absence; it shocks her, it is so unlike the one she has pictured; she has often looked forward to it, often; to seeing Flo's new frocks, to hearing of her town life.

'Won't you take off your things? You will like to go to your room?'

She can hear how her own voice shakes; it is really inconsiderate of Flo to treat her in this strange way.

'We will have some tea,' she adds.

Her colour is coming and going, the lace at her wrist is fluttering. The daughter observes it with a kind of dull satisfaction, she is taking out her hat-pins carefully. She notices a portrait in a velvet case upon the mantelpiece; she walks over and looks at it intently. It is her father, the father who was killed in India in a hill skirmish when she was a little lint-locked maid barely up to his knee. She studies it with new eyes, trying to read what man he was, what soul he had, what part of him is in her, tries to find herself by reading him. Something in his face touches her, strikes some underlying chord in her, and she grinds her teeth at a thought it rouses.

'She must be ill, she must be very ill,' says the mother, watching her, 'to think I daren't offer to kiss my own child!' She checks the tears that keep welling up, feeling that they may offend this woman who is so strangely unlike the girl who left her. The latter has turned from her scrutiny of the likeness and sweeps her with a

cold criticizing look as she turns towards the door, saying:
'I *should* like some tea. I will go upstairs and wash off the dust.'

Half an hour later the two women sit opposite one another in
the pretty room. The younger one is leaning back in her chair
watching the mother pour out the tea, following the graceful
movements of the white, blue-veined hands amongst the tea
things – she lets her wait on her; they have not spoken beyond a
commonplace remark about the heat, the dust, the journey.

'How is Philip, is he well?' The mother ventures to ask with a
feeling of trepidation, but it seems to her that she ought to ask
about him.

'He is quite well, men of his type usually are; I may say he is
particularly well just now, he has gone to Paris with a girl from the
Alhambra!'

The older woman flushes painfully, and pauses with her cup
half way to her lips and lets the tea run over unheeded on to her
dainty silk apron.

'You are spilling your tea,' the girl adds with malicious enjoy-
ment.

The woman gasps: 'Flo, but Flo, my dear, it is dreadful! What
would your poor father have said! *no wonder* you look ill, dear,
how shocking! Shall I – ask the vicar to – to remonstrate with
him? —'

'My dear mother, what an extraordinary idea! These little trips
have been my one solace. I assure you, I have always hailed them
as lovely oases in the desert of matrimony, resting-places on the
journey. My sole regret was their infrequency. That is very good
tea, I suppose it is the cream.'

The older woman puts her cup on the tray and stares at her with
frightened eyes and paled cheeks.

'I am afraid I don't understand you, Florence. I am old-
fashioned' – with a little air of frigid propriety – 'I have always
looked upon matrimony as a sacred thing. It is dreadful to hear
you speak this way; you should have tried to save Philip – from –
from such a shocking sin.'

The girl laughs, and the woman shivers as she hears her. She
cries —

'I would never have thought it of Philip. My poor dear, I am afraid you must be very unhappy.

'Very,' with a grim smile, 'but it is over now, I have done with it. I am not going back.'

If a bomb had exploded in the quiet, pretty room the effect could hardly have been more startling than her almost cheerful statement. A big bee buzzes in and bangs against the lace of the older woman's cap and she never heeds it, then she almost screams:

'Florence, Florence, my dear, you can't mean to desert your husband! Oh, think of the disgrace, the scandal, what people will say, the' – with an uncertain quaver – 'the sin. You took a solemn vow, you know, and you are going to break it —'

'My dear mother, the ceremony had no meaning for me, I simply did not know what I was signing my name to, or what I was vowing to do. I might as well have signed my name to a document drawn up in Choctaw. I have no remorse, no prick of conscience at the step I am taking; my life must be my own. They say sorrow chastens, I don't believe it; it hardens, embitters; joy is like the sun, it coaxes all that is loveliest and sweetest in human nature. No, I am not going back.'

The older woman cries, wringing her hands helplessly:

'I can't understand it. You must be very miserable to dream of taking such a serious step.'

'As I told you, I am. It is a defect of my temperament. How many women really take the man nearest to them as seriously as I did! I think few. They finesse and flatter and wheedle and coax, but truth there is none. I couldn't do that, you see, and so I went to the wall. I don't blame them; it must be so, as long as marriage is based on such unequal terms, as long as man demands from a wife as a right, what he must sue from a mistress as a favour; until marriage becomes for many women a legal prostitution, a nightly degradation, a hateful yoke under which they age, mere bearers of children conceived in a sense of duty, not love. They bear them, birth them, nurse them, and begin again without choice in the matter, growing old, unlovely, with all joy of living swallowed in a senseless burden of reckless maternity, until their love, granted they started with that, the mystery, the crowning glory of their lives, is turned into a duty they submit to with distaste instead of a favour granted to a husband who must become a new lover to obtain it.'

'But men are different, Florence; you can't refuse a husband, you might cause him to commit sin.'

'Bosh, mother, he is responsible for his own sins, we are not bound to dry-nurse his morality. Man is what we have made him, his very faults are of our making. No wife is bound to set aside the demands of her individual soul for the sake of imbecile obedience. I am going to have some more tea.'

The mother can only whimper:

'It is dreadful! I thought he made you such an excellent husband, his position too is so good, and he is so highly connected.'

'Yes, and it is as well to put the blame in the right quarter. Philip is as God made him, he is an animal with strong passions, and he avails himself of the latitude permitted him by the laws of society. Whatever of blame, whatever of sin, whatever of misery is in the whole matter rests *solely* and *entirely* with you, mother' – the woman sits bolt upright – 'and with no one else – that is why I came here – to tell you that – I have promised myself over and over again that I would tell you. It is with you, and you alone the fault lies.'

There is so much of cold dislike in her voice that the other woman recoils and whimpers piteously:

'You must be ill, Florence, to say such wicked things. What have I done? I am sure I devoted myself to you from the time you were little; I refused' – dabbing her eyes with her cambric handkerchief – 'ever so many good offers. There was young Fortescue in the artillery, such a good-looking man, and such an elegant horseman, he was quite infatuated about me; and Jones, to be sure he was in business, but he was most attentive. Every one said I was a devoted mother; I can't think what you mean, I —'

A smile of cynical amusement checks her.

'Perhaps not. Sit down, and I'll tell you.'

She shakes off the trembling hand, for the mother has risen and is standing next to her, and pushes her into a chair, and paces up and down the room. She is painfully thin, and drags her limbs as she walks.

'I say it is your fault, because you reared me a fool, an idiot, ignorant of everything I ought to have known, everything that concerned me and the life I was bound to lead as a wife; my physical needs, my coming passion, the very meaning of my sex, my wifehood and motherhood to follow. You gave me not one weapon in my hand to defend myself against the possible attacks of man at his worst. You sent me out to fight the biggest battle of a woman's life, the one in which she ought to know every turn of the game, with a white gauze' – she laughs derisively – 'of maiden purity as a shield.'

Her eyes blaze, and the woman in the chair watches her as one sees a frog watch a snake when it is put into its case.

'I was fourteen when I gave up the gooseberry-bush theory as the origin of humanity; and I cried myself ill with shame when I learnt what maternity meant, instead of waking with a sense of delicious wonder at the great mystery of it. You gave me to a man, nay more, you told me to obey him, to believe that whatever he said would be right, would be my duty; knowing that the meaning of marriage was a sealed book to me, that I had no real idea of what union with a man meant. You delivered me body and soul into his hands without preparing me in any way for the ordeal I was to go through. You sold me for a home, for clothes, for food; you played upon my ignorance, I won't say innocence, that is different. You told me, you and your sister, and your friend the vicar's wife, that it would be an anxiety off your mind if I were comfortably settled —'

'It is wicked of you to say such dreadful things!' the mother cries, 'and besides' – with a touch of asperity – 'you married him willingly, you seemed to like his attentions —'

'How like a woman! What a thorough woman you are, mother! The good old-fashioned kitten with a claw in her paw! Yes, I married him willingly; I was not eighteen, I had known no men; was pleased that you were pleased – and, as you say, I liked his attentions. He had tact enough not to frighten me, and I had not the faintest conception of what marriage with him meant. I had an idea' – with a laugh – 'that the words of the minister settled the matter. Do you think that if I had realised how fearfully close the intimacy with him would have been that my whole soul would not have stood up in revolt, the whole woman in me cried out against such a degradation of myself?' Her words tremble with passion, and the woman who bore her feels as if she is being lashed by a whip. 'Would I not have shuddered at the thought of *him* in such a relationship? – and waited, waited until I found the man who would satisfy me, body and soul – to whom I would have gone without any false shame, of whom I would think with gladness as the father of a little child to come, for whom the white fire of love or passion, call it what you will, in my heart would have burned clearly and saved me from the feeling of loathing horror that has made my married life a nightmare to me – ay, made me a murderess in heart over and over again. This is not exaggeration. It has killed the sweetness in me, the pure thoughts of woman-hood – has made me hate myself and *hate you*. Cry, mother, if you will; you don't know how much you have to cry for – I have cried myself barren of tears. Cry over the girl you killed' – with a gust of passion – 'why didn't you strangle me as a baby? It would have been kinder; my life has been a hell, mother – I felt it vaguely as I stood on the platform waiting, I remember the mad impulse I had to jump down under the engine as it came in, to escape from the dread that was chilling my soul. What have these years been? One long crucifixion, one long submittal to the desires of a man I bound myself to in ignorance of what it meant; every caress' – with a cry – 'has only been the first note of that. Look at me' – stretching out her arms – 'look at this wreck of my physical self; I wouldn't dare to show you the heart or the soul underneath. He has stood on his rights; but do you think, if I had known, that I would have given such insane obedience, from a mistaken sense of duty, as would lead to this? I have my rights too, and my duty to myself; if I had only recognized them in time.'

'Sob away, mother; I don't even feel for you – I have been burnt too badly to feel sorry for what will only be a tiny scar to you; I have all the long future to face with all the world against me. Nothing will induce me to go back. Better anything than that; food and clothes are poor equivalents for what I have had to suffer – I can get them at a cheaper rate. When he comes to look for me, give him that letter. He will tell you he has only been an uxorious husband, and that you reared me a fool. You can tell him too, if you like, that I loathe him, shiver at the touch of his lips, his breath, his hands; that my whole body revolts at his touch; that when he has turned and gone to sleep, I have watched him with such growing hatred that at times the temptation to kill him has been so strong that I have crept out of bed and walked the cold passage in my bare feet until I was too benumbed to feel anything; that I have counted the hours to his going away, and cried out with delight at the sight of the retreating carriage!'

'You are very hard, Flo; the Lord soften your heart! Perhaps' – with trepidation – 'if you had had a child —'

'Of his – that indeed would have been the last straw – no, mother.'

There is such a peculiar expression of satisfaction over something – of some inner understanding, as a man has when he dwells on the successful accomplishment of a secret purpose – that the mother sobs quietly, wringing her hands.

'I did not know, Flo, I acted for the best; you are very hard on me!'

Later, when the bats are flitting across the moon, and the girl is asleep – she has thrown herself half-dressed on the narrow white bed of her girlhood, with her arms folded across her breast and her hands clenched – the mother steals into the room. She has been turning over the contents of an old desk; her marriage certificate, faded letters on foreign paper, and a bit of Flo's hair cut off each birthday, and a sprig of orange blossom she wore in her hair. She looks faded and grey in the silver light, and she stands and gazes at the haggard face in its weary sleep. The placid current of her life is disturbed, her heart is roused, something of her child's soul-agony has touched the sleeping depths of her nature. She feels as if scales have dropped from her eyes, as if the instincts and conventions of her life are toppling over, as if all the needs of protesting women of whom she has read with a vague displeasure have come home to her. She covers the girl tenderly, kisses her hair, and slips a little roll of notes into the dressing-bag on the table and steals out, with the tears running down her cheeks.

When the girl looks into her room as she steals by, when the morning light is slanting in, she sees her kneeling, her head, with its straggling grey hair, bowed in tired sleep. It touches her. Life is too short, she thinks, to make any one's hours bitter; she goes down and writes a few kind words in pencil and leaves them near her hand, and goes quickly out into the road.

The morning is grey and misty, with faint yellow stains in the east, and the west wind blows with a melancholy sough in it – the first whisper of the fall, the fall that turns the world of nature into a patient suffering from phthisis – delicate season of decadence, when the lovelist scenes have a note of decay in their beauty; when a poisoned arrow pierces the marrow of insect and plant, and the leaves have a hectic flush and fall, fall and shrivel and curl in the night's cool; and the chrysanthemums, the 'goodbye summers' of the Irish peasants, have a sickly tinge in their white. It affects her, and she finds herself saying: 'Wither and die, wither and die, make compost for the loves of the spring, as the old drop out and make place for the new, who forget them, to be in their turn forgotten.' She hurries on, feeling that her autumn has come to her in her spring, and a little later she stands once more on the platform where she stood in the flush of her girlhood, and takes the train in the opposite direction.

Hubert Crackanthorpe

MODERN MELODRAMA

The pink shade of a single lamp supplied an air of subdued mystery; the fire burned red and still; in place of door and windows hung curtains, obscure, formless; the furniture, dainty, but sparse, stood detached and incoördinate like the furniture of a stage-scene; the atmosphere was heavy with heat, and a scent of stale tobacco; some cut flowers, half-withered, tissue-paper still wrapping their stalks, lay on a gilt, cane-bottomed chair.

'Will you give me a sheet of paper, please?'

He had crossed the room, to seat himself before the principal table. He wore a fur-lined overcoat, and he was tall, and broad, and bald; a sleek face, made grave by gold-rimmed spectacles.

The other man was in evening dress; his back leaning against the mantelpiece, his hands in his pockets: he was moodily scraping the hearthrug with his toe. Clean-shaved; stolid and coarsely regular features; black, shiny hair, flattened on to his head; undersized eyes, moist and glistening; the tint of his face uniform, the tint of discoloured ivory; he looked a man who ate well and lived hard.

'Certainly, sir, certainly,' and he started to hurry about the room.

'Daisy,' he exclaimed roughly, a moment later, 'where the deuce do you keep the notepaper?'

'I don't know if there is any, but the girl always has some.' She spoke in a slow tone – insolent and fatigued.

A couple of bed-pillows were supporting her head, and a scarlet plush cloak, trimmed with white down, was covering her feet, as she lay curled on the sofa. The fire-light glinted on the metallic gold of her hair, which clashed with the black of her eyebrows; and the full, blue eyes, wide-set, contradicted the hard line of her vivid-red lips. She drummed her fingers on the sofa-edge, nervously.

'Never mind,' said the bald man shortly, producing a notebook from his breast-pocket, and tearing a leaf from it.

He wrote, and the other two stayed silent; the man returned to the hearthrug, lifting his coat-tails under his arms; the girl went on drumming the sofa edge.

'There,' sliding back his chair, and looking from the one to the other, evidently uncertain which of the two he should address. 'Here is the prescription. Get it made up tonight, a tablespoonful at a time, in a wine-glassful of water at lunch-time, at dinner-time and before going to bed. Go on with the port wine twice a day, and' (to the girl deliberately and distinctly) 'you *must* keep quite quiet; avoid all sort of excitement – that is extremely important. Of course you must on no account go out at night. Go to bed early, take regular meals, and keep always warm.'

'I say,' broke in the girl, 'tell us, it isn't bad – dangerous, I mean?'

'Dangerous! – no, not if you do what I tell you.'

He glanced at his watch, and rose, buttoning his coat.

'Good-evening,' he said gravely.

At first she paid no heed; she was vacantly staring before her: then, suddenly conscious that he was waiting, she looked up at him.

'Good-night, doctor.'

She held out her hand, and he took it.

'I'll get all right, won't I?' she asked, still looking up at him.

'All right – of course you will – of course. But remember you must do what I tell you.'

The other man handed him his hat and umbrella, opened the door for him, and it closed behind them.

The girl remained quiet, sharply blinking her eyes, her whole expression eager, intense.

A murmur of voices, a muffled tread of footsteps descending the stairs – the gentle shutting of a door – stillness.

She raised herself on her elbow, listening; the cloak slipped noiselessly to the floor. Quickly her arm shot out to the bell-rope: she pulled it violently; waited, expectant; and pulled again.

A slatternly figure appeared – a woman of middle age – her arms, bared to the elbows, smeared with dirt; a grimy apron over her knees.

'What's up? – I was smashin' coal,' she explained.

'Come here,' hoarsely whispered the girl – 'here – no – nearer – quite close. Where's he gone?'

'Gone? 'oo?'

'That man that was here.'

'I s'ppose 'ee's in the downstairs room. I ain't 'eard the front door slam.'

'And Dick, where's he?'

'They're both in there together, I s'ppose.'

'I want you to go down – quietly – without making a noise – listen at the door – come up, and tell me what they're saying.'

'What? Down there?' jerking her thumb over her shoulder.

'Yes, of course – at once,' answered the girl, impatiently.

'And if they catches me – a nice fool I looks. No, I'm jest blowed if I do!' she concluded. 'Whatever's up?'

'You must,' the girl broke out excitedly. 'I tell you, you must.'

'Must – must – an' if I do, what am I goin' to get out of it?' She paused, reflecting; then added: 'Look 'ere – I tell yer what – I'll do it for half a quid, there!'

'Yes – yes – all right – only make haste.'

'An' 'ow d' I know as I'll git it?' she objected doggedly. 'It's a jolly risk, yer know.'

The girl sprang up, flushed and feverish.

'Quick – or he'll be gone. I don't know where it is – but you shall have it – I promise – quick – please go – quick.'

The other hesitated, her lips pressed together; turned, and went out.

And the girl, catching at her breath, clutched a chair.

A flame flickered up in the fire, buzzing spasmodically. A creak outside. She had come up. But the curtains did not move. Why didn't she come in? She was going past. The girl hastened across the room, the intensity of the impulse lending her strength.

'Come – come in,' she gasped. 'Quick – I'm slipping.'

She struck at the wall; but with the flat of her hand, for there was no grip. The woman bursting in, caught her, and led her back to the sofa.

'There, there, dearie,' tucking the cloak round her feet. 'Lift up the piller, my 'ands are that mucky. Will yer 'ave anythin'?'

She took her head. 'It's gone,' she muttered. 'Now – tell me.'

'Tell yer? – tell yer what? Why – why – there ain't jest nothin' to tell yer.'

'What were they, saying? Quick.'

'I didn't 'ear nothin'. They was talkin' about some ballet-woman.'

The girl began to cry, feebly, helplessly, like a child in pain.

'You might tell me, Liz. You might tell me. I've been a good sort to you.'

'That yer 'ave. I knows yer 'ave, dearie. There, there, don't yer take on like that. Yer'll only make yerself bad again.'

'Tell me – tell me,' she wailed. 'I've been a good sort to you, Liz.'

'Well, they wasn't talkin' of no ballet-woman – that's straight,' the woman blurted out savagely.

'What did he say? – tell me.' Her voice was weaker now.

'I can't tell yer – don't yer ask me – for God's sake, don't yer ask me.'

With a low crooning the girl cried again.

'Oh! for God's sake, don't yer take on like that – it's awful – I can't stand it. There, dearie, stop that cryin' an' I'll tell yer – I will indeed. It was jest this way – I slips my shoes off, an' I goes down as careful – jest as careful as a cat – an' when I gets to the door I crouches myself down, listenin' as 'ard as ever I could. The first thing as I 'ears was Mr Dick speakin' thick-like – like as if 'ee'd bin drinkin' – an t'other chap 'ee says somethin' about lungs, using some long word – I missed that – there was a van or somethin' rackettin' on the road. Then 'ee says 'gallopin', gallopin',' jest like as if 'ee was talkin' of a 'orse. An' Mr Dick, 'ee says, 'ain't there no chance – no'ow?' and 'ee give a sort of a grunt. I was awful sorry for 'im, that I was, 'ee must 'ave been crool bad, 'ee's mostly so quiet-like, ain't 'ee? An', in a minute, 'ee sort o' groans out somethin', an' t'other chap 'ee answer 'im quite cool-like that 'ee don't properly know: but, anyways, it 'ud be over afore the end of February. There, I've done it. Oh! dearie, its awful, awful, that's jest what it is. An' I 'ad no intention to tell yer – not a blessed word – that I didn't – may God strike me blind if I did! Some'ow it all come out, seein' yer chokin' that 'ard an' feelin' at the wall there. Yer 'ad no right to ask me to do it – 'ow was I to know 'ee was a doctor?'

She put the two corners of her apron to her eyes, gurgling loudly.

'Look 'ere, don't yer b'lieve a word of it – I don't – I tell yer they're a 'umbuggin' lot, them doctors, all together. I know it. Yer take my word for that – yer'll git all right again. Yer'll be as well as I am, afore yer've done – Oh, Lord! – it's jest awful – I feel that upset – I'd like to cut my tongue out, for 'avin' told yer – but I jest couldn't 'elp myself.' She was retreating towards the door, wiping her eyes, and snorting out loud sobs – 'An' don't yer offer me that half-quid – I couldn't take it of yer – that I couldn't.'

She shivered, sat up, and dragged the cloak tight round her shoulders. In her desire to get warm she forgot what had happened. She extended the palms of her hands towards the grate: the heat was delicious. A smoking lump of coal clattered on to the fender: she lifted the tongs, but the sickening remembrance arrested her. The things in the room were receding, dancing round: the fire was growing taller and taller. The woollen scarf chafed her skin: she wrenched if off. Then hope, keen and bitter, shot up, hurting her. 'How could he know? Of course he couldn't know. She'd been a lot better this last fortnight – the other doctor said so – she didn't believe it – she didn't care — Anyway, it would be over before the end of February!'

Suddenly the crooning wail started again: next, spasms of weeping, harsh and gasping.

By-and-bye she understood that she was crying noisily, and that she was alone in the room: like a light in a wind, the sobbing fit ceased.

'Let me live – let me live – I'll be straight – I'll go to church – I'll do anything! Take it away – it hurts – I can't bear it!'

Once more the sound of her own voice in the empty room calmed her. But the tension of emotion slackened, only to tighten again: immediately she was jeering at herself. What was she wasting her breath for? What had Jesus ever done for her? She'd had her fling, and it was no thanks to Him.

' "*Dy-sy – Dy-sy —*" '

From the street below, boisterous and loud, the refrain came up. And, as the footsteps tramped away, the words reached her once more, indistinct in the distance:

' "*I'm jest cry-zy, all for the love o'you.*" '

She felt frightened. It was like a thing in a play. It was as if some one was there, in the room – hiding – watching her.

Then a coughing fit started, racking her. In the middle, she struggled to cry for help; she thought she was going to suffocate.

Afterwards she sank back, limp, tired, and sleepy.

The end of February – she was going to die – it was important, exciting – what would it be like? Everybody else died. Midge had died in the summer – but that was worry and going the pace. And they said that Annie Evans was going off too. Damn it! she wasn't going to be chicken-hearted. She'd face it. She had had a jolly time. She'd be game till the end. Hell-fire – that was all stuff and nonsense – she knew that. It would be just nothing – like a sleep. Not even painful: she'd be just shut down in a coffin, and she wouldn't know that they were doing it. Ah! but they might do it before she was quite dead! It had happened sometimes. And she wouldn't be able to get out. The lid would be nailed, and there would be earth on the top. And if she called no one would hear.

Ugh! what a fit of the blues she was getting! It was beastly, being alone. Why the devil didn't Dick come back?

That noise! What was that?

Bah! only some one in the street. What a fool she was!

She winced again as the fierce feeling of revolt swept through her, the wild longing to fight. It was damned rough – four months! A year, six months even, was a long time. The pain grew acute, different from anything she had felt before,

'Good Lord! what am I maundering on about? Four months – I'll go out with a fizzle like a firework. Why the devil doesn't Dick come? – or Liz – or somebody? What do they leave me alone like this for?'

She dragged at the bell-rope.

He came in, white and blear-eyed.

'Whatever have you been doing all this time?' she began angrily.

'I've been chatting with the doctor.' He was pretending to read a newspaper: there was something funny about his voice.

'It's ripping. He says you'll soon be fit again, as long as you don't get colds, or that sort of thing. Yes, he says you'll soon be fit again' – a quick, crackling noise – he had gripped the newspaper in his fist.

She looked at him, surprised, in spite of herself. She would never have thought he'd have done it like that. He was a good sort, after all. But – she didn't know why – she broke out furiously:

'You infernal liar! – I know. I shall be done for by the end of February – ha! ha!'

Seizing a vase of flowers, she flung it into the grate. The crash and the shrivelling of the leaves in the flames brought her an instant's relief. Then she said quietly:

'There – I've made an idiot of myself; but' (weakly) 'I didn't know – I didn't know – I thought it was different.'

He hesitated, embarrassed by his own emotion. Presently he went up to her and put his hands round her cheeks.

'No,' she said, 'that's no good, I don't want that. Get me something to drink. I feel bad.'

He hurried to the cupboard and fumbled with the cork of a champagne bottle. It flew out with a bang. She started violently.

'You clumsy fool!' she exclaimed.

She drank off the wine at a gulp.

'Daisy,' he began.

She was staring stonily at the empty glass.

'Daisy,' he repeated.

She tapped her toe against the fender-rail.

At this sign, he went on –

'How did you know?'

'I sent Liz to listen,' she answered mechanically.

He looked about him, helpless.

'I think I'll smoke,' he said feebly.

She made no answer.

'Here, put the glass down,' she said.

He obeyed.

He lit a cigarette over the lamp, sat down opposite her, puffing dense clouds of smoke.

And, for a long while, neither spoke.

'Is that doctor a good man?'

'I don't know. People say so,' he answered.

H. G. Wells

THE CONE

The night was hot and overcast, the sky red-rimmed with the lingering sunset of mid-summer. They sat at the open window, trying to fancy the air was fresher there. The trees and shrubs of the garden stood stiff and dark; beyond in the roadway a gas-lamp burnt, bright orange against the hazy blue of the evening. Farther were the three lights of the railway signal against the lowering sky. The man and woman spoke to one another in low tones.

'He does not suspect?' said the man, a little nervously.

'Not he,' she said peevishly, as though that too irritated her. 'He thinks of nothing but the works and the prices of fuel. He has no imagination, no poetry.'

'None of these men of iron have,' he said sententiously. 'They have no hearts.'

'*He* has not,' she added. She turned her discontented face towards the window. The distant sound of a roaring and rushing drew nearer and grew in volume; the house quivered; one heard the metallic rattle of the tender. As the train passed, there was a glare of light above the cutting and a driving tumult of smoke; one, two, three, four, five, six, seven, eight black oblongs – eight trucks – passed across the dim grey of the embankment, and were suddenly extinguished one by one in the throat of the tunnel, which, with the last, seemed to swallow down train, smoke, and sound in one abrupt gulp.

'This country was all fresh and beautiful once,' he said; 'and now – it is Gehenna. Down that way – nothing but pot-banks and chimneys belching fire and dust into the face of heaven . . . But what does it matter? An end comes, and end to all this cruelty. . . . *Tomorrow*.' He spoke the last word in a whisper.

'*Tomorrow*,' she said, speaking in a whisper, too, and still staring out of the window.

'Dear!' he said, putting his hand on hers.

She turned with a start, and their eyes searched one another's. Hers softened to his gaze. 'My dear one!' she said, and then: 'It seems so strange – that you should have come into my life like this – to open' – She paused.

'To open?' he said.

'All this wonderful world' – she hesitated, and spoke still more softly – 'this world of *love* to me.'

Then suddenly the door clicked and closed. They turned their heads, and he started violently back. In the shadow of the room stood a great shadowy figure – silent. They saw the face dimly in the half-light, with unexpressive dark patches under the pent-house brows. Every muscle in Raut's body suddenly became tense. When could the door have opened? What had he heard. Had he heard all? What had he seen? A tumult of questions.

The newcomer's voice came at last, after a pause that seemed interminable. 'Well?' he said.

'I was afraid I had missed you, Horrocks,' said the man at the window, gripping the window-ledge with his hand. His voice was unsteady.

The clumsy figure of Horrocks came forward out of the shadow. He made no answer to Raut's remark. For a moment he stood above them.

The woman's heart was cold within her. 'I told Mr Raut it was just possible you might come back,' she said, in a voice that never quivered.

Horrocks, still silent, sat down abruptly in the chair by her little work-table. His big hands were clenched; one saw now the fire of his eyes under the shadow of his brows. He was trying to get his breath. His eyes went from the woman he had trusted to the friend he had trusted, and then back to the woman.

By this time and for the moment all three half understood one another. Yet none dared say a word to ease the pent-up things that choked them.

It was the husband's voice that broke the silence at last.

'You wanted to see me?' he said to Raut.

Raut started as he spoke. 'I came to see you,' he said, resolved to lie to the last.

'Yes,' said Horrocks.

'You promised,' said Raut, 'to show me some fine effects of moonlight and smoke.'

'I promised to show you some fine effects of moonlight and smoke,' repeated Horrocks, in a colourless voice.

'And I thought I might catch you tonight before you went down to the works,' proceeded Raut, 'and come with you.'

There was another pause. Did the man mean to take the thing coolly? Did he after all know? How long had he been in the room? Yet even at the moment when they heard the door, their attitudes . . . Horrocks glanced at the profile of the woman, shadowy pallid in the half-light. Then he glanced at Raut, and seemed to recover himself suddenly. 'Of course,' he said, 'I promised to show you the works under their proper dramatic conditions. It's odd how I could have forgotten.'

'If I am troubling you' – began Raut.

Horrocks started again. A new light had suddenly come into the sultry gloom of his eyes. 'Not in the least,' he said.

'Have you been telling Mr Raut of all these contrasts of flame and shadow you think so splendid?' said the woman, turning now to her husband for the first time, her confidence creeping back again, her voice just one half-note too high. 'That dreadful theory of yours that machinery is beautiful, and everything else in the world ugly. I thought he would not spare you Mr Raut. It's his great theory, his one discovery in art.'

'I am slow to make discoveries,' said Horrocks grimly, damping her suddenly. 'But what I discover . . .' He stopped.

'Well?' she said.

'Nothing;' and suddenly he rose to his feet.

'I promised to show you the works,' he said to Raut, and put his big, clumsy hand on his friend's shoulder. 'Are you ready to go?'

'Quite,' said Raut, and stood up also.

There was another pause. Each of them peered through the indistinctness of the dusk at the other two. Horrocks' hand still rested on Raut's shoulder. Raut half fancied still that the incident was trivial after all. But Mrs Horrocks knew her husband better, knew that grim quiet in his voice, and the confusion in her mind took a vague shape of physical evil. 'Very well,' said Horrocks, and, dropping his hand, turned towards the door.

'My hat?' Raut looked round in the half-light.

'That's my work-basket,' said Mrs Horrocks with a gust of hysterical laughter. Their hands came together on the back of the chair. 'Here it is!' he said. She had an impulse to warn him in an undertone, but she could not frame a word. 'Don't go!' and 'Beware of him!' struggled in her mind, and the swift moment passed.

'Got it?' said Horrocks, standing with the door half open.

Raut stepped towards him. 'Better say goodbye to Mrs Horrocks,' said the ironmaster, even more grimly quiet in his tone than before.

Raut started and turned. 'Good-evening, Mrs Horrocks,' he said, and their hands touched.

Horrocks held the door open with a ceremonial politeness unusual in him towards men. Raut went out, and then, after a wordless look at her, her husband followed. She stood motionless while Raut's light footfall and her husband's heavy tread, like bass and treble, passed down the passage together. The front door slammed heavily. She went to the window, moving slowly, and stood watching – leaning forward. The two men appeared for a moment at the gateway in the road, passed under the street lamp, and were hidden by the black masses of the shrubbery. The lamplight fell for a moment on their faces, showing only unmeaning pale patches, telling nothing of what she still feared, and doubted, and craved vainly to know. Then she sank down into a crouching attitude in the big armchair, her eyes wide open and staring out at the red lights from the furnaces that flickered in the sky. An hour after she was still there, her attitude scarcely changed.

The oppressive stillness of the evening weighed heavily upon Raut. They went side by side down the road in silence, and in silence turned into the cinder-made by-way that presently opened out the prospect of the valley.

A blue haze, half dust, half mist, touched the long valley with mystery. Beyond were Hanley and Etruria, grey and black masses, outlined thinly by the rare golden dots of the street-lamps, and here and there a gaslit window, or the yellow glare of some late-working factory or crowded public-house. Out of the masses, clear and slender against the evening sky, rose a multitude of tall chimneys, many of them reeking, a few smokeless during the season of 'play'. Here and there a pallid patch and ghostly stunted beehive shapes showed the position of a pot-bank, or a wheel, black and sharp against the hot lower sky, marked some colliery where they raise the iridescent coal of the place. Nearer at hand was the broad stretch of railway, and half invisible trains shunted – a steady puffing and rumbling, with every now and then a ringing concussion and a series of impacts, and a passage of intermittent puffs of white steam across the further view. And to the left, between the railway and the dark mass of the low hill beyond, dominating the whole view, colossal, inky-black, and crowned with smoke and fitful flames, stood the great cylinders of the Jeddah Company Blast Furnaces, the central edifices of the big ironworks of which Horrocks was the manager. They stood heavy and threatening, full of an incessant turmoil of flames and seething molten iron, and about the feet of them rattled the rolling-mills, and the steam-hammer beat heavily and splashed the white iron sparks hither and thither. Even as they looked, a truckful of fuel was shot into one of the giants, and red flames gleamed out, and a confusion of smoke and black dust came boiling upwards towards the sky.

'Certainly you get some fine effects of colour with your furnaces,' said Raut, breaking a silence that had become apprehensive.

Horrocks grunted. He stood with his hands in his pockets, frowning down at the dim steaming railway and the busy ironworks beyond, frowning as if he were thinking out some knotty problem.

Raut glanced at him and away again. 'At present your moonlight effect is hardly ripe,' he continued, looking upward: 'the moon is still smothered by the vestiges of daylight.'

Horrocks stared at him with the expression of a man who has suddenly awakened. 'Vestiges of daylight? . . . Of course, of course.' He too looked up at the moon, pale still in the midsummer sky. 'Come along,' he said suddenly, and, gripping Raut's arm in his hand, made a move towards the path that dropped from them to the railway.

Raut hung back. Their eyes met and saw a thousand things in a

moment that their lips came near to say. Horrocks' hand tight-
ened and then relaxed. He let go, and before Raut was aware of it,
they were arm in arm, and walking, one unwillingly enough,
down the path.

'You see the fine effect of the railway signals towards Burslem,'
said Horrocks, suddenly breaking into loquacity. striding fast and
tightening the grip of his elbow the while. 'Little green lights and
red and white lights, all against the haze. You have an eye for
effect, Raut. It's a fine effect. And look at those furnaces of mine,
how they rise upon us as we come down the hill. That to the right
is my pet — seventy feet of him. I packed him myself, and he's
boiled away cheerfully with iron in his guts for five long years. I've
a particular fancy for *him*. That line of red there — a lovely bit of
warm orange you'd call it, Raut — that's the puddlers' furnaces,
and there, in the hot light, three black figures — did you see the
white splash of the steam-hammer then? — that's the rolling-mills.
Come along! Clang, clatter, how it goes rattling across the floor!
Sheet tin, Raut, — amazing stuff. Glass mirrors are not in it when
that stuff comes from the mill. And, squelch! — there goes the
hammer again. Come along!'

He had to stop talking to catch at his breath. His arm twisted
into Raut's with benumbing tightness. He had come striding
down the black path towards the railway as though he was
possessed. Raut had not spoken a word, had simply hung back
against Horrocks' pull with all his strength.

'I say,' he said now, laughing nervously, but with an undertone
of snarl in his voice, 'why on earth are you nipping my arm off,
Horrocks, and dragging me along like this?'

At length Horrocks released him. His manner changed again.
'Nipping your arm off?' he said. 'Sorry. But it's you taught me
the trick of walking in that friendly way.'

'You haven't learnt the refinements of it yet then,' said Raut,
laughing artificially again. 'By Jove! I'm black and blue.' Horrocks offered no apology. They stood now near the bottom of the
hill, close to the fence that bordered the railway. The ironworks
had grown larger and spread out with their approach. They
looked up to the blast furnaces now instead of down; the further
view of Etruria and Hanley had dropped out of sight with their

descent. Before them, by the stile, rose a notice-board, bearing, still dimly visible, the words, 'BEWARE OF THE TRAINS', half hidden by splashes of coaly mud.

'Fine effects,' said Horrocks, waving his arm. 'Here comes a train. The puffs of smoke, the orange glare, the round eye of light in front of it, the melodious rattle. Fine effects! But these furnaces of mine used to be finer, before we shoved cones in their throats, and saved the gas.'

'How?' said Raut. 'Cones?'

'Cones, my man, cones. I'll show you one nearer. The flames used to flare out of the open throats, great — what is it? — pillars of cloud by day, red and black smoke, and pillars of fire by night. Now we run it off in pipes, and burn it to heat the blast, and the top is shut by a cone. You'll be interested in that cone.'

'But every now and then,' said Raut, 'you get a burst of fire and smoke up there.'

'The cone's not fixed, it's hung by a chain from a lever, and balanced by an equipoise. You shall see it nearer. Else, of course, there'd be now way of getting fuel into the thing. Every now and then the cone dips, and out comes the flare.'

'I see,' said Raut. He looked over his shoulder. 'The moon gets brighter,' he said.

'Come along,' said Horrocks abruptly, gripping his shoulder again, and moving him suddenly towards the railway crossing. And then came one of those swift incidents, vivid, but so rapid that they leave one doubtful and reeling. Halfway across, Horrocks' hand suddenly clenched upon him like a vice, and swung him backward and through a half-turn, so that he looked up the line. And there a chain of lamp-lit carriage-windows telescoped swiftly as it came towards them, and the red and yellow lights of an engine grew larger and larger, rushing down upon them. As he grasped what this meant, he turned his face to Horrocks, and pushed with all his strength against the arm that held him back between the rails. The struggle did not last a moment. Just as certain as it was that Horrocks held him there, so certain was it that he had been violently lugged out of danger.

'Out of the way,' said Horrocks, with a gasp, as the train came rattling by, and they stood panting by the gate into the ironworks.

'I did not see it coming,' said Raut, still, even in spite of his own apprehensions, trying to keep up an appearance of ordinary intercourse.

Horrocks answered with a grunt. 'The cone,' he said, and then, as one who recovers himself, 'I thought you did not hear.'

'I didn't,' said Raut.

'I wouldn't have had you run over then for the world,' said Horrocks.

'For a moment I lost my nerve,' said Raut.

Horrocks stood for a half a minute, then turned abruptly towards the ironworks again. 'See how fine these great mounds of mine, these slinker-heaps, look in the night! That truck yonder, up above there! Up it goes, and out-tilts the slag. See the palpitating red stuff go sliding down the slope. As we get nearer, the heap rises up and cuts the blast furnaces. See the quiver up above the big one. Not that way! This way, between the heaps. That goes to the puddling furnaces, but I want to show you the canal first.' He came and took Raut by the elbow, and so they went along side by side. Raut answered Horrocks vaguely. What, he asked himself, had really happened on the line? Was he deluding himself with his own fancies, or had Horrocks actually held him back in the way of the train? Had he just been within an ace of being murdered?

Suppose this slouching, scowling monster *did* know anything? For a minute or two then Raut was really afraid for his life, but the mood passed as he reasoned with himself. After all, Horrocks might have heard nothing. At any rate, he pulled him out of the way in time. His odd manner might be due to the mere vague jealousy he had shown once before. He was talking now of the ash-heaps and the canal. Eight?' said Horrocks.

'What?' said Raut. 'Rather! The haze in the moonlight. Fine!'

'Our canal,' said Horrocks, stopping suddenly. 'Our canal by moonlight and firelight is an immense effect. You've never seen it? Fancy that! You've spent too many of your evenings philandering up in Newcastle there. I tell you, for real florid effects – But you shall see. Boiling water . . .'

As they came out of the labyrinth of clinker-heaps and mounds of coal and ore, the noises of the rolling-mill sprang upon them suddenly, loud, near, and distinct. Three shadowy workmen went by and touched their caps to Horrocks. Their faces were vague in the darkness. Raut felt a futile impulse to address them, and before he could frame his words, they passed into the shadows. Horrocks pointed to the canal close before them now: a weird-looking place it seemed, in the blood-red reflections of the furnaces. The hot water that cooled the tuyères came into it, some fifty yards up – a tumultuous, almost boiling affluent, and the steam rose up from the water in silent white wisps and streaks, wrapping damply about them, an incessant succession of ghosts coming up from the black and red eddies, a white uprising that made the head swim. The shining black tower of the larger blast-furnace rose overhead out of the mist, and its tumultuous riot filled their ears. Raut kept away from the edge of the water, and watched Horrocks.

'Here it is red,' said Horrocks, 'blood-red vapour as red and hot as sin; but yonder there, where the moonlight falls on it, and it drives across the clinker-heaps, it is as white as death.'

Raut turned his head for a moment, and then came back hastily to his watch on Horrocks. 'Come along to the rolling-mills,' said Horrocks. The threatening hold was not so evident that time, and Raut felt a little reassured. But all the same, what on earth did Horrocks mean about 'white as death' and 'red as sin'? Coincidence, perhaps?

They went and stood behind the puddlers for a little while, and then through the rolling-mills, where amidst an incessant din the deliberate steam-hammer beat the juice out of the succulent iron, and black, half-naked Titans rushed the plastic bars, like hot sealing-wax, between the wheels. 'Come on,' said Horrocks in Raut's ear, and they went and peeped through the little glass hole behind the tuyères, and saw the tumbled fire writhing in the pit of the blast-furnace. It left one eye blinded for a while. Then, with green and blue patches dancing across the dark, they went to the lift by which the trucks of ore and fuel and lime were raised to the top of the big cylinder.

And out upon the narrow rail that overhung the furnace, Raut's doubts came upon him again. Was it wise to be here? If Horrocks did know – everything! Do what he would, he could not resist a violent trembling. Right under foot was a sheer depth of seventy feet. It was a dangerous place. They pushed by a truck of fuel to get to the railing that crowned the place. The reek of the furnace, a sulphorous vapour streaked with pungent bitterness, seemed to make the distant hillside of Hanley quiver. The moon was riding out now from among a drift of clouds, half-way up the sky above the undulating wooded outlines of Newcastle. The steaming canal ran away from below them under an indistinct bridge, and vanished into the dim haze of the flat fields towards Burslem.

'That's the cone I've been telling you of,' shouted Horrocks; 'and, below that, sixty feet of fire and molten metal, with the air of the blast frothing through it like gas in soda-water.'

Raut gripped the hand-rail tightly, and stared down at the cone. The heat was intense. The boiling of the iron and the tumult of the blast made a thunderous accompaniment to Horrocks' voice. But the thing had to be gone through now. Perhaps, after all . . .

'In the middle,' bawled Horrocks, 'temperature near a thousand degrees. If *you* were dropped into it . . . flash into flame like a pinch of gunpowder in a candle. Put your hand out and feel the heat of his breath. Why, even up here I've seen the rain-water boiling off the trucks. And that cone there. It's a damned sight too hot for roasting cakes. The top side of it's three hundred degrees.'

'Three hundred degrees!' said Raut.

'Three hundred centigrade, mind!' said Horrocks. 'It will boil the blood out of you in no time.'

'Eigh?' said Raut, and turned.

'Boil the blood out of you in . . . No, you don't!'

'Let me go!' screamed Raut. 'Let go my arm!'

With one hand he clutched at the hand-rail, then with both. For a moment the two men stood swaying. Then suddenly, with a violent jerk, Horrocks had twisted him from his hold. He clutched at Horrocks and missed, his foot went back into empty air; in mid-air he twisted himself, and then cheek and shoulder and knee struck the hot cone together.

He clutched the chain by which the cone hung, and the thing sank an infinitesimal amount as he struck it. A circle of of glowing red appeared about him, and a tongue of flame, released from the chaos within, flickered up towards him. An intense pain assailed him at the knees, and he could smell the singeing of his hands. He raised himself to his feet, and tried to climb up the chain, and then something struck his head. Black and shining with the moonlight, the throat of the furnace rose about him.

Horrocks, he saw, stood above him by one of the trucks of fuel on the rail. The gesticulating figure was bright and white in the moonlight, and shouting, 'Fizzle, you fool! Fizzle, you hunter of women! You hot-blooded hound! Boil! boil! boil!'

Suddenly he caught up a handful of coal out of the truck, and flung it deliberately, lump after lump, at Raut.

'Horrocks!' cried Raut. 'Horrocks!'

He clung crying to the chain, pulling himself up from the burning of the cone. Each missile Horrocks flung hit him. His clothes charred and glowed, and as he struggled the cone dropped, and a rush of hot suffocating gas whooped out and burned round him in a swift breath of flame.

His human likeness departed from him. When the momentary red had passed, Horrocks saw a charred, blackened figure, it head streaked with blood, still clutching and fumbling with the chain, and writhing in agony – a cindery animal, an inhuman, monstrous creature that began a sobbing intermittent shriek.

Abruptly, at the sight, the ironmaster's anger passed. A deadly sickness came upon him. The heavy odour of burning flesh came drifting up to his nostrils. His sanity returned to him.

'God have mercy upon me!' he cried. 'O God! what have I done?'

He knew the thing below him, save that it still moved and felt, was already a dead man – that the blood of the poor wretch must be boiling in his veins. An intense realisation of that agony came to his mind, and overcame every other feeling. For a moment he stood irresolute, and then, turning to the truck, he hastily tilted its contents upon the struggling thing that had once been a man. The mass fell with a thud, and went radiating over the cone. With the thud the shriek ended, and a boiling confusion of smoke, dust, and flame came rushing up towards him. As it passed, he saw the cone clear again.

Then he staggered back, and stood trembling, clinging to the rail with both hands. His lips moved, but no words came to them.

Down below was the sound of voices and running steps. The clangour of rolling in the shed ceased abruptly.

Arthur Conan Doyle

THE BRAZILIAN CAT

It is hard luck on a young fellow to have expensive tastes, great expectations, aristocratic connections, but no actual money in his pocket, and no profession by which he may earn any. The fact was that my father, a good, sanguine, easy-going man, had such confidence in the wealth and benevolence of his bachelor elder brother, Lord Southerton, that he took it for granted that I, his only son, would never be called upon to earn a living for myself. He imagined that if there were not a vacancy for me on the great Southerton Estates, at least there would be found some post in that diplomatic service which still remains the special preserve of our privileged classes. He died too early to realize how false his calculations had been. Neither my uncle nor the State took the slightest notice of me, or showed any interest in my career. An occasional brace of pheasants, or basket of hares, was all that ever reached me to remind me that I was heir to Otwell House and one of the richest estates in the country. In the meantime, I found myself a bachelor and man about town, living in a suite of apartments in Grosvenor Mansions, with no occupation save that of pigeon-shooting and polo-playing at Hurlingham. Month by month I realized that it was more and more difficult to get the brokers to renew my bills, or to cash any further post-obits upon an unentailed property. Ruin lay right across my path, and every day I saw it clearer, nearer, and more absolutely unavoidable.

What made me feel my own poverty the more was that, apart from the great wealth of Lord Southerton, all my other relations were fairly well-to-do. The nearest of these was Everard King, my father's nephew and my own first cousin, who had spent an adventurous life in Brazil, and had now returned to this country to settle down on his fortune. We never knew how he made his money, but he appeared to have plenty of it, for he bought the estate of Greylands, near Clipton-on-the-Marsh, in Suffolk. For the first year of residence in England he took no more notice of me than my miserly uncle; but at last one summer morning, to my very great relief and joy, I received a letter asking me to come down that very day and spend a short visit at Greylands Court. I was expecting a rather long visit to Bankruptcy Court at the time, and this interruption seemed almost providential. If I could only get on terms with this unknown relative of mine, I might pull through yet. For the family credit he could not let me go entirely to the wall. I ordered my valet to pack my valise, and I set off the same evening for Clipton-on-the-Marsh.

After changing at Ipswich, a little local train deposited me at a small, deserted station lying amidst a rolling grassy country, with a sluggish and winding river curving in and out amidst the valleys, between high, silted banks, which showed that we were within reach of the tide. No carriage was awaiting me (I found afterwards that my telegram had been delayed), so I hired a dog-cart at the local inn. The driver, an excellent fellow, was full of my relative's praises, and I learned from him that Mr Everard King was already a name to conjure with in that part of the country. He had entertained the schoolchildren, he had thrown his grounds open to visitors, he had subscribed to charities – in short, his benevolence had been so universal that my driver could only account for it on the supposition that he had Parliamentary ambitions.

My attention was drawn away from my driver's panegyric by the appearance of a very beautiful bird which settled on a telegraph-post beside the road. At first I thought that it was a jay, but it was larger, with a brighter plumage. The driver accounted for its presence at once by saying that it belonged to the very man whom we were about to visit. It seems that the acclimatization of foreign creatures was one of his hobbies, and that he had brought with him from Brazil a number of birds and beasts which he was endeavouring to rear in England. When once we had passed the gates of Greylands Park we had ample evidence of this taste of his. Some small spotted deer, a curious wild pig known, I believe, as a peccary, a gorgeously feathered oriole, some sort of armadillo, and a singular lumbering intoed beast like a very fat badger, were among the creatures which I observed as we drove along the winding avenue.

Mr Everard King, my unknown cousin, was standing in person upon the steps of his house, for he had seen us in the distance, and guessed that it was I. His appearance was very homely and benevolent, short and stout, forty-five years old, perhaps, with a round, good-humoured face, burned brown with the tropical sun, and shot with a thousand wrinkles. He wore white linen clothes, in true planter style, with a cigar between his lips, and a large Panama hat upon the back of his head. It was such a figure as one associates with a verandahed bungalow, and it looked curiously out of place in front of this broad, stone English mansion, with its solid wings and its Palladio pillars before the doorway.

'My dear!' he cried, glancing over his shoulder; 'my dear, here is our guest! Welcome, welcome to Greylands! I am delighted to make your acquaintance, Cousin Marshall, and I take it as a great compliment that you should honour this sleepy little country place with your presence.'

Nothing could be more hearty than his manner, and he set me at my ease in an instant. But it needed all his cordiality to atone for the frigidity and even rudeness of his wife, a tall, haggard woman, who came forward at his summons. She was, I believe, of Brazilian extraction, though she spoke excellent English, and I excused her manners on the score of her ignorance of our customs. She did not attempt to conceal, however, either then or afterwards, that I was no very welcome visitor at Greylands Court. Her actual words were, as a rule, courteous, but she was the possessor of a pair of particularly expressive dark eyes, and I read in them very clearly from the first that she heartily wished me back in London once more.

However, my debts were too pressing and my designs upon my wealthy relative were too vital for me to allow them to be upset by the ill-temper of his wife, so I disregarded her coldness and reciprocated the extreme cordiality of his welcome. No pains had been spared by him to make me comfortable. My room was a charming one. He implored me to tell him anything which could add to my happiness. It was on the tip of my tongue to inform him that a blank cheque would materially help towards that end, but I felt that it might be premature in the present state of our acquaintance. The dinner was excellent, and as we sat together afterwards over his Havanas and coffee, which latter he told me was specially prepared upon his own plantation, it seemed to me that all my driver's eulogies were justified, and that I had never met a more large-hearted and hospitable man.

But, in spite of his cheery good nature, he was a man with a strong will and a fiery temper of his own. Of this I had an example upon the following morning. The curious aversion which Mrs Everard King had conceived towards me was so strong, that her manner at breakfast was almost offensive. But her meaning became unmistakable when her husband had quitted the room.

'The best train in the day is at twelve fifteen,' said she.

'But I was not thinking of going today,' I answered, frankly – perhaps even defiantly, for I was determined not to be driven out by this woman.

'Oh, if it rests with you –' said she, and stopped with a most insolent expression in her eyes.

'I am sure,' I answered, 'that Mr Everard King would tell me if I were outstaying my welcome.'

'What's this? What's this?' said a voice, and there he was in the room. He had overheard my last words, and a glance at our faces had told him the rest. In an instant his chubby, cherry face set into an expression of absolute ferocity.

'Might I trouble you to walk outside, Marshall,' said he? (I may mention that my own name is Marshall King.)

He closed the door behind me, and then, for an instant, I heard him talking in a low voice of concentrated passon to his wife. This gross breach of hospitality had evidently hit upon his tenderest point. I am no eavesdropper, so I walked out on to the lawn. Presently I heard a hurried step behind me, and there was the lady, her face pale with excitement, and her eyes red with tears.

'My husband has asked me to apologize to you, Mr Marshall King,' said she, standing with downcast eyes before me.

'Please do not say another word, Mrs King.'

Her dark eyes suddenly blazed out at me.

'You fool!' she hissed, with frantic vehemence, and turning on her heel swept back to the house.

The insult was so outrageous, so insufferable, that I could only stand staring after her in bewilderment. I was still there when my host joined me. He was his cheery, chubby self once more.

'I hope that my wife has apologized for her foolish remarks,' said he.

'Oh, yes – yes, certainly!'

He put his hand through my arm and walked with me up and down the lawn.

'You must not take it seriously,' said he. 'It would grieve me inexpressibly if you curtailed your visit by one hour. The fact is – there is no reason why there should by any concealment between relatives – that my poor dear wife is incredibly jealous. She hates that anyone – male or female – should for an instant come between us. Her ideal is a desert island and an eternal *tête-à-tête*. That gives you the clue to her actions, which are, I confess, upon this particular point, not very far removed from mania. Tell me that you will think no more of it.'

'No, no; certainly not.'

'Then light this cigar and come round with me and see my little menagerie.'

The whole afternoon was occupied by this inspection, which included all the birds, beasts, and even reptiles which he had imported. Some were free, some in cages, a few actually in the house. He spoke with enthusiasm of his successes and his failures, his births and his deaths, and he would cry out in his delight, like a schoolboy, when, as we walked, some gaudy bird would flutter up from the grass, or some curious beast slink into the cover. Finally he led me down a corridor which extended from one wing of the house. At the end of this there was a heavy door with a sliding shutter in it, and beside it there projected from the wall an iron handle attached to a wheel and a drum. A line of stout bars extended across the passage.

'I am about to show you the jewel of my collection,' said he. 'There is only one other specimen in Europe, now that the Rotterdam cub is dead. It is a Brazilian cat.'

'But how does that differ from any other cat?'

'You will soon see that,' said he, laughing. 'Will you kindly draw that shutter and look through?'

I did so, and found that I was gazing into a large, empty room, with stone flags, and small, barred windows upon the farther wall. In the centre of this room, lying in the middle of a golden patch of sunlight, there was stretched a huge creature, as large as a tiger, but as black and sleek as ebony. It was simply a very enormous and very well-kept black cat, and it cuddled up and basked in that yellow pool of light exactly as a cat would do. It was so graceful, so sinewy, and so gently and smoothly diabolical, that I could not take my eyes from the opening.

'Isn't he splendid?' said my host, enthusiastically.

'Glorious! I never saw such a noble creature.'

'Some people call it a black puma, but really it is not a puma at all. That fellow is nearly eleven feet from tail to tip. Four years ago he was a little ball of black fluff, with two yellow eyes staring out of it. He was sold me as a new-born cub up in the wild country at the head-waters of the Rio Negro. They speared his mother to death after she had killed a dozen of them.'

'They are ferocious, then?'

'The most absolutely treacherous and bloodthirsty creatures upon earth. You talk about a Brazilian cat to an up-country Indian, and see him get the jumps. They prefer humans to game. This fellow has never tasted living blood yet, but when he does he will be a terror. At present he won't stand anyone but me in his den. Even Baldwin, the groom, dare not go near him. As to me, I am his mother and father in one.'

As he spoke he suddenly, to my astonishment, opened the door and slipped in, closing it instantly behind him. At the sound of his voice the huge, lithe creature rose, yawned and rubbed its round, black head affectionately against his side, while he patted and fondled it.

'Now Tommy, into your cage!' said he.

The monstrous cat walked over to one side of the room and coiled itself up under a grating. Everard King came out, and taking the iron handle which I have mentioned, he began to turn it. As he did so the line of bars in the corridor began to pass though a slot in the wall and closed up the front of this grating, so as to make an effective cage. When it was in position he opened the door once more and invited me into the room, which was heavy with the pungent, musty smell peculiar to the great carnivora.

'That's how we work it,' said he. 'We give him the run of the room for exercise, and then at night we put him in his cage. You can let him out by turning the handle from the passage, or you can, as you have seen coop him up in the same way. No, no, you should not do that!'

I had put my hand between the bars to pat the glossy, heaving flank. He pulled it back with a serious face.

'I assure you that he is not safe. Don't imagine that because I can take liberties with him anyone else can. He is very exclusive in his friends – aren't you Tommy? Ah, he hears his lunch coming to him! Don't you, boy?'

A step sounded in the stone-flagged passage, and the creature had sprung to his feet, and was pacing up and down the narrow cage, his yellow eyes gleaming, and his scarlet tongue rippling and quivering over the white line of his jagged teeth. A groom entered with a coarse joint upon a tray, and thust it through the bars to him. He pounced lightly upon it, carried it off to the corner, and there, holding it between his paws, tore and wrenched at it, raising his bloody muzzle every now and then to look at us. It was a malignant and yet fascinating sight.

'You can't wonder that I am fond of him, can you?' said my host, as we left the room, 'especially when you consider that I have had the rearing of him. It was no joke bringing him over from the centre of South America; but here he is safe and sound – and, as I have said, far the most perfect specimen in Europe. The people at the Zoo are dying to have him, but I really can't part with him. Now, I think that I have inflicted my hobby upon you long enough, so we cannot do better than follow Tommy's example, and go to our lunch.'

My South American relative was so engrossed by his grounds and their curious occupants, that I hardly gave him credit at first for having any interests outside them. That he had some, and pressing ones, was soon borne in upon me by the number of telegrams which he received. They arrived at all hours, and were always opened by him with the utmost eagerness and anxiety upon his face. Sometimes I imagined that it must be the Turf, and sometimes the Stock Exchange, but certainly he had some very urgent business going forwards which was not transacted upon the Downs of Suffolk. During the six days of my visit he had never fewer than three or four telegrams a day, and sometimes as many as seven or eight.

I had occupied these six days so well, that by the end of them I had succeeded in getting upon the most cordial terms with my cousin. Every night we had sat up late in the billiard-room, he telling me the most extraordinary stories of his adventures in America – stories so desperate and reckless, that I could hardly associate them with the brown little chubby man before me. In return, I ventured upon some of my own reminiscences of London life, which interested him so much, that he vowed he would come up to Grosvenor Mansions and stay with me. He was anxious to see the faster side of city life, and certainly, though I say it, he could not have chosen a more competent guide. It was not until the last day of my visit that I ventured to approach that which was on my mind. I told him frankly about my pecuniary difficulties and my impending ruin, and I asked his advice – though I hoped for something more solid. He listened attentively, puffing hard at his cigar.

'But surely,' said he, 'you are the heir of our relative, Lord Southerton?'

'I have every reason to believe so, but he would never make me any allowance.'

'No, no, I have heard of his miserly ways. My poor Marshall, your position has been a very hard one. By the way, have you heard any news of Lord Southerton's health lately?'

'He has always been in a critical condition ever since my childhood.'

'Exactly – a creaking hinge, if ever there was one. Your inheritance may be a long way off. Dear me, how awkwardly situated you are!'

'I had some hopes, sir, that you, knowing all the facts, might be inclined to advance —'

'Don't say another word, my dear boy,' he cried, with the utmost cordiality; 'we shall talk it over tonight, and I give you my word that whatever is in my power shall be done.'

I was not sorry that my visit was drawing to a close, for it is unpleasant to feel that there is one person in the house who eagerly desires your departure. Mrs King's sallow face and forbidding eyes had become more and more hateful to me. She was no longer actively rude – her fear of her husband prevented her – but she pushed her insane jealousy to the extent of ignoring me, never addressing me, and in every way making my stay at Greylands as uncomfortable as she could. So offensive was her manner during that last day, that I should certainly have left had it not been for that interview with my host in the evening which would, I hoped, retrieve my broken fortunes.

It was very late when it occurred, for my relative, who had been receiving even more telegrams than usual during the day, went off to his study after dinner, and only emerged when the household had retired to bed. I heard him go round locking the doors, as his custom was of a night, and finally he joined me in the billiard-room. His stout figure was wrapped in a dressing-gown, and he wore a pair of red Turkish slippers without any heels. Settling down into an armchair, he brewed himself a glass of grog, in which I could not help noticing that the whisky considerably predominated over the water.

'My word!' said he, 'what a night!'

It was, indeed. The wind was howling and screaming round the house, and the latticed windows rattled and shook as if they were coming in. The glow of the yellow lamps and the flavour of our cigars seemed the brighter and more fragrant for the contrast.

'Now, my boy,' said my host, 'we have the house and the night to ourselves. Let me have an idea of how your affairs stand, and I will see what can be done to set them in order. I wish to hear every detail.'

Thus encouraged, I entered into a long exposition, in which all my tradesmen and creditors from my landlord to my valet, figured in turn. I had notes in my pocket-book, and I marshalled my facts, and gave, I flatter myself, a very business-like statement of my own unbusinesslike ways and lamentable position. I was depressed, however, to notice that my companion's eyes were vacant and his attention elsewhere. When he did occasionally throw out a remark it was so entirely perfunctory and pointless, that I was sure he had not in the least followed my remarks. Every now and then he roused himself and put on some show of interest, asking me to repeat or to explain more fully, but it was always to sink once more into the same brown study. At last he rose and threw the end of his cigar into the grate.

'I'll tell you what, my boy,' said he. 'I never had a head for figures, so you will excuse me. You must jot it all down upon paper, and let me have a note of the amount. I'll understand it when I see it in black and white.'

The proposal was encouraging. I promised to do so.

'And now it's time we were in bed. By Jove, there's one o'clock striking in the hall.'

The tingling of the chiming clock broke thorugh the deep roar of the gale. The wind was sweeping past with the rush of a great river.

'I must see my cat before I go to bed,' said my host. 'A high wind excites him. Will you come?'

'Certainly,' said I.

'Then tread softly and don't speak, for everyone is asleep.'

We passed quietly down the lamp-lit Persian-rugged hall, and through the door at the farther end. All was dark in the stone corridor, but a stable lantern hung on a hook, and my host took it down and lit it. There was no grating visible in the passage, so I knew that the beast was in its cage.

'Come in!' said my relative, and opened the door.

A deep growling as we entered showed that the storm had really excited the creature. In the flickering light of the lantern, we saw it, a huge black mass coiled in the corner of its den and throwing a squat, uncouth shadow upon the whitewashed wall. Its tail switched angrily among the straw.

'Poor Tommy is not in the best of tempers,' said Everard King, holding up the lantern and looking in at him. 'What a black devil he looks, doesn't he? I must give him a little supper to put him in a better humour. Would you mind holding the lantern for a moment?'

I took it from his hand and he stepped to the door.

'His larder is just outside here,' said he. 'You will excuse me for an instant, won't you?' He passed out, and the door shut with a sharp metallic click behind him.

That hard, crisp sound made my heart stand still. A sudden wave of terror passed over me. A vague perception of some monstrous treachery turned me cold. I sprang to the door, but there was no handle upon the inner side.

'Here!' I cried. 'Let me out!'

'All right!' Don't make a row!' said my host from the passage. 'You've got the light all right.'

'Yes, but I don't care about being locked in alone like this.'

'Don't you?' I heard his hearty, chuckling laugh. 'You won't be alone long.'

'Let me out, sir!' I repeated angrily. 'I tell you I don't allow practical jokes of this sort.'

'Practical is the word,' said he, with another hateful chuckle. And then suddenly I heard, amidst the roar of the storm, the creak and whine of the winch-handle turning, and the rattle of the grating as it passed through the slot. Great God, he was letting loose the Brazilian cat!

In the light of the lantern I saw the bars sliding slowly before me. Already there was an opening a foot wide at the farther end. With a scream I seized the last bar with my hands and pulled with the strength of a madman. I *was* a madman with rage and horror. For a minute or more I held the thing motionless. I knew that he was straining with all his force upon the handle, and that the leverage was sure to overcome me. I gave inch by inch, my feet sliding along the stones, and all the time I begged and prayed this inhuman monster to save me from this horrible death. I conjured him by his kinship. I reminded him that I was his guest; I begged to know what harm I had ever done him. His only answers were the tugs and jerks upon the handle, each of which, in spite of all my struggles, pulled another bar through the opening. Clinging and clutching, I was dragged across the whole front of the cage, until at last, with aching wrists and lacerated fingers, I gave up the hopeless struggle. The grating clanged back as I released it, and an instant later I heard the shuffle of the Turkish slippers in the passage, and the slam of the distant door, Then everything was silent.

The creature had never moved during this time. He lay still in the corner, and his tail had ceased switching. This apparition of a man adhering to his bars and dragged screaming across him had apparently filled him with amazement. I saw his great eyes staring steadily at me. I had dropped the lantern when I seized the bars, but it still burned upon the floor, and I made a movement to grasp it, with some idea that its light might protect me. But the instant I moved, the beast gave a deep and menacing growl. I stopped and stood still, quivering with fear in every limb. The cat (if one may call so fearful a creature by so homely a name) was not more than ten feet from me. The eyes glimmered like two disks of phosphorus in the darkness. They appalled and yet fascinated me. I could not take my own eyes from them. Nature plays strange tricks with us at such moments of intensity, and those glimmering lights waxed and waned with a steady rise and fall. Sometimes they seemed to be tiny points of extreme brilliancy – little electric sparks in the black obscurity – then they would widen and widen until all that corner of the room was filled with their shifting and sinister light. And then suddenly they went out altogether.

The beast had closed its eyes. I do not know whether there may be any truth in the old idea of the dominance of the human gaze, or whether the huge cat was simply drowsy, but the fact remains that, far from showing any symptom of attacking me, it simply rested its sleek, black head upon its huge forepaws and seemed to sleep. I stood, fearing to move lest I should rouse it into malignant life once more. But at least I was able to think clearly now that the baleful eyes were off me. Here I was shut up for the night with the ferocious beast. My own instincts, to say nothing of the words of the plausible villain who laid this trap for me, warned me that the animal was as savage as its master. How could I stave it off until morning? The door was hopeless, and so were the narrow, barred windows. There was no shelter anywhere in the bare, stone-flagged room. To cry for assistance was absurd. I knew that this den was an outhouse, and that the corridor which connected it with the house was at least a hundred feet long. Besides, with that gale thundering outside, my cries were not likely to be heard. I had only my own courage and my own wits to trust to.

And then, with a fresh wave of horror, my eyes fell upon the lantern. The candle had burned low, and was already beginning to gutter. In ten minutes it would be out. I had only ten minutes then in which to do something, for I felt that if I were once left in the dark with that fearful beast I should be incapable of action. The very thought of it paralysed me. I cast my despairing eyes round this chamber of death, and they rested upon one spot which seemed to promise I will not say safety, but less immediate and imminent danger than the open floor.

I have said that the cage had a top as well as a front, and this top was left standing when the front was wound through the slot in the wall. It consisted of bars at a few inches' interval, with stout wire netting between, and it rested upon a strong stanchion at each end. It stood now as a great barred canopy over the crouching figure in the corner. The space between this iron shelf and the roof may have been from two to three feet. If I could only get up there, squeezed in between bars and ceiling, I should have only one vulnerable side. I should be safe from below, from behind, and from each side. Only on the open face of it could I be attacked. There it is true, I had no protection whatever; but, at least, I should be out of the brute's path when he began to pace about his den. He would have to come out of his way to reach me. It was now or never, for if once the light were out it would be impossible. With a gulp in my throat I sprang up, seized the iron edge of the top, and swung myself panting on to it. I writhed in face downwards, and found myself looking straight into the terrible eyes and yawning jaws of the cat. Its fetid breath came up into my face like the steam from some foul pot.

It appeared, however, to be rather curious than angry. With a sleek ripple of its long, black back it rose, stretched itself, and then rearing itself on its hind legs, with one forepaw against the wall, it raised the other, and drew its claws across the wire meshes beneath me. One sharp, white hook tore through my trousers – for I may mention that I was still in evening dress – and dug a furrow in my knee. It was not meant as an attack, but rather as an experiment, for upon my giving a sharp cry of pain he dropped down again, and springing lightly into the room, he began walking swiftly round it, looking up every now and again in my direction. For my part I shuffled backwards until I lay with my back against the wall, screwing myself into the smallest space possible. The farther I got the more difficult it was for him to attack me.

He seemed more excited now that he had begun to move about,

and he ran swiftly and noiselessly round and round the den, passing continually underneath the iron couch upon which I lay. It was wonderful to see so great a bulk passing like a shadow, with hardly the softest thudding of velvety pads. The candle was burning low – so low that I could hardly see the creature. And then, with a last flare and splutter it went out altogether. I was alone with the cat in the dark!

It helps one to face a danger when one knows that one has done all that possibly can be done. There is nothing for it then but to quietly await the result. In this case, there was no chance of safety anywhere except the precise spot where I was. I stretched myself out, therefore, and lay silently, almost breathlessly, hoping that the beast might forget my presence if I did nothing to remind him. I reckoned that it must already be two o'clock. At four it would be full dawn. I had not more than two hours to wait for daylight.

Outside, the storm was still raging, and the rain lashed continually against the little windows. Inside, the poisonous and fetid air was overpowering. I could neither hear nor see the cat. I tried to think about other things – but only one had power enough to draw my mind from my terrible position. That was the contemplation of my cousin's villainy, his unparalleled hypocrisy, his malignant hatred of me. Beneath that cheerful face there lurked the spirit of a medieval assassin. And as I thought of it I saw more clearly how cunningly the thing had been arranged. He had apparently gone to bed with the others. No doubt he had his witnesses to prove it. Then, unknown to them, he had slipped down, had lured me into this den and abandoned me. His story would be so simple. He had left me to finish my cigar in the billiard-room. I had gone down on my own account to have a last look at the cat. I had entered the room without observing that the cage was opened, and I had been cuaght. How could such a crime be brought home to him? Suspicion, perhaps – but proof, never!

How slowly those dreadful two hours went by! Once I heard a low, rasping sound, which I took to be the creature licking its own fur. Several times those greenish eyes gleamed at me through the darkness, but never in a fixed stare, and my hopes grew stronger that my presence had been forgotten or ignored. At last the least faint glimmer of light came through the windows – I first dimly saw them as two grey squares upon the black wall, then grey turned to white, and I could see my terrible companion once more. And he, alas, could see me!

It was evident to me at once that he was in a much more dangerous and aggressive mood than when I had seen him last. The cold of the morning had irritated him, and he was hungry as well. With a continual growl he paced swiftly up and down the side of the room which was farthest from my refuge, his whiskers bristling angrily, and his tail switching and lashing. As he turned at the corners his savage eyes always looked upwards at me with a dreadful menace. I knew then that he meant to kill me. Yet I found myself even at that moment admiring the sinuous grace of the devilish thing, its long, undulating, rippling movements, the gloss of its beautiful flanks, the vivid, palpitating scarlet of the glistening tongue which hung from the jet-black muzzle. And all the time that deep, threatening growl was rising and rising in an unbroken crescendo. I knew that the crisis was at hand.

It was a miserable hour to meet such a death – so cold, so comfortless, shivering in my light dress clothes upon this gridiron of torment upon which I was stretched. I tried to brace myself to it, to raise my soul above it, and at the same time, with the lucidity which comes to a perfectly desperate man, I cast round for some possible means of escape. One thing was clear to me. If that front of the cage was only back in its position once more, I could find a sure refuge behind it. Could I possibly pull it back? I hardly dared to move for fear of bringing the creature upon me. Slowly, very slowly, I put my hand forward, until it grasped the edge of the front, the final bar which protruded through the wall. To my surprise it came quite easily to my jerk. Of course the difficulty of drawing it out arose from the fact that I was clinging to it. I pulled again, and three inches of it came through. It ran apparently on wheels. I pulled again . . . and then the cat sprang!

It was so quick, so sudden, that I never saw it happen. I simply heard the savage snarl, and in an instant afterwards the blazing yellow eyes, the flattened black head with its red tongue and flashing teeth, were within reach of me. The impact of the creature shook the bars upon which I lay, until I thought (as far as I could think of anything at such a moment) that they were coming down.

The cat swayed there for an instant, the head and front paws quite close to me, the hind paws clawing to find a grip upon the edge of the grating. I heard the claws rasping as they clung to the wire-netting, and the breath of the beast made me sick. But its bound had been miscalculated. It could not retain its position. Slowly, grinning with rage, and scratching madly at the bars, it swung backwards and dropped heavily upon the floor. With a growl it instantly faced round to me and crouched for another spring.

I knew that the next few moments would decide my fate. The creature had learned by experience. It would not miscalculate again. I must act promptly, fearlessly, if I were to have a chance for life. In an instant I had formed my plan. Pulling off my dress-coat, I threw it down over the head of the beast. At the same moment I dropped over the edge, seized the end of the front grating, and pulled it frantically out of the wall.

It came more easily than I could have expected. I rushed across the room, bearing it with me; but, as I rushed, the accident of my position put me upon the outer side. Had it been the other way, I might have come off scathless. As it was, there was a moment's pause as I stopped it and tried to pass in through the opening which I had left. That moment was enough to give time to the creature to toss off the coat with which I had blinded him and to spring upon me. I hurled myself through the gap and pulled the rails to behind me, but he seized my leg before I could entirely withdraw it. One stroke of that huge paw tore off my calf as a shaving of wood curls off before a plane. The next moment, bleeding and fainting, I was lying among the foul straw with a line of friendly bars between me and the creature which ramped so frantically against them.

Too wounded to move, and too faint to be conscious of fear, I could only lie, more dead than alive, and watch it. It pressed its broad, black chest against the bars and angled for me with its crooked paws as I have seen a kitten do before a mouse-trap. It ripped my clothes, but, stretch as it would, it could not quite reach me. I have heard of the curious numbing effect produced by wounds from the great carnivora, and now I was destined to experience it, for I had lost all sense of personality, and was as interested in the cat's failure or success as if it were some game which I was watching. And then gradually my mind drifted away into strange vague dreams, always with that black face and red tongue coming back into them, and so I lost myself in the nirvana of delirium, the blessed relief of those who are too sorely tried.

Tracing the course of events afterwards, I conclude that I must have been insensible for about two hours. What roused me to consciousness once more was that sharp metallic click which had been the precursor of my terrible experience. It was the shooting back of the spring lock. Then, before my senses were clear enough to entirely apprehend what they saw, I was aware of the round, benevolent face of my cousin peering in through the open door. What he saw evidently amazed him. There was the cat crouching on the floor. I was stretched upon my back in my shirt-sleeves within the cage, my trousers torn to ribbons and a great pool of blood all round me. I can see his amazed face now, with the morning sunlight upon it. He peered at me, and peered again. Then he closed the door behind him and advanced to the cage to see if I were really dead.

I cannot undertake to say what happened. I was not in a fit state to witness or to chronicle such events. I can only say that I was suddenly conscious that his face was away from me – that he was looking towards the animal.

'Good old Tommy!' he cried. 'Good old Tommy!'

Then he came near the bars, with his back still towards me.

'Down, you stupid beast!' he roared. 'Down, sir! Don't you know your master?'

Suddenly even in my bemuddled brain a remembrance came of those words of his when he had said that the taste of blood would turn the cat into a fiend. My blood had done it, but he was to pay the price.

'Get away!' he screamed. 'Get away, you devil! Baldwin! Baldwin! Oh, my God!'

And then I heard him fall, and rise, and fall again, with a sound like the ripping of sacking. His screams grew fainter until they were lost in the worrying snarl. And then, after I thought that he was dead, I saw, as in a nightmare, a blinded, tattered, blood-soaked figure running wildly round the room – and that was the last glimpse which I had of him before I fainted once again.

I was many months in my recovery – in fact, I cannot say that I have ever recovered, for to the end of my days I shall carry a stick as a sign of my night with the Brazilian cat. Baldwin, the groom, and the other servants could not tell what had occurred, when, drawn by the death-cries of their master, they found me behind the bars, and his remains – or what they afterwards discovered to be his remains – in the clutch of the creature which he had reared. They stalled him off with hot irons, and afterwards shot him through the loophole of the door before they could finally extricate me. I was carried to my bedroom, and there, under the roof of my would-be murderer, I remained between life and death for several weeks. They had sent for a surgeon from Clipton and a nurse from London, and in a month I was able to be carried to the station, and so conveyed back once more to Grosvenor Mansions.

I have one remembrance of that illness, which might have been part of the ever-changing panorama conjured up by a delirious brain were it not so definitely fixed in my memory. One night, when the nurse was absent, the door of my chamber opened, and a tall woman in blackest mourning slipped into the room. She came across to me, and as she bent her sallow face I saw by the faint gleam of the night-light that it was the Brazilian woman whom my cousin had married. She stared intently into my face, and her expression was more kindly than I had ever seen it.

'Are you conscious?' she asked.

I feebly nodded – for I was still very weak.

'Well, then, I only wished to say to you that you have yourself to blame. Did I not do all I could for you? From the beginning I tried to drive you from the house. By every means, short of betraying my husband, I tried to save you from him. I knew that he had a reason for bringing you here. I knew that he would never let you get away again. No one knew him as I knew him, who had suffered from him so often. I did not dare to tell you all this. He would have killed me. But I did my best for you. As things have turned out, you have been the best friend that I have ever had. You have set me free, and I fancied that nothing but death would do that. I am sorry if you are hurt, but I cannot reproach myself. I told you that you were a fool – and a fool you have been.' She crept out of the room, the bitter, singular woman, and I was never destined to see her again. With what remained from her husband's property she went back to her native land, and I have heard that she afterwards took the veil at Pernambuco.

It was not until I had been back in London for some time that the doctors pronounced me to be well enough to do business. It was not a very welcome permission to me, for I feared that it would be the signal for an inrush of creditors; but it was Summers, my lawyer, who first took advantage of it.

'I am very glad to see that your lordship is so much better,' said he. 'I have been waiting a long time to offer my congratulations.'

'What do you mean, Summers? This is no time for joking.'

'I mean what I say,' he answered. 'You have been Lord Southerton for the last six weeks, but we feared that it would retard your recovery if you were to learn it.'

Lord Southerton! One of the richest peers in England! I could not believe my ears. And then suddenly I thought of the time which had elapsed, and how it coincided with my injuries.

'Then Lord Southerton must have died about the same time that I was hurt?'

'His death occurred upon that very day.' Summers looked hard at me as I spoke, and I am convinced – for he was a very shrewd fellow – that he had guessed the true state of the case. He paused for a moment as if awaiting a confidence with me, but I could not see what was to be gained by exposing such a family scandal.

'Yes, a very curious coincidence,' he continued, with the same knowing look. 'Of course, you are aware that your cousin Everard King was the next heir to the estates. Now, if it had been you instead of him who had been torn to pieces by this tiger, or whatever it was, then of course he would have been Lord Southerton at the present moment.'

'No doubt,' said I.

'And he took such an interest in it,' said Summers. 'I happen to know that the late Lord Southerton's valet was in his pay, and that he used to have telegrams from him every few hours to tell him how he was getting on. That would be about the time when you were down there. Was it not strange that he should wish to be so well informed, since he knew that he was not the direct heir?'

'Very strange,' said I. 'And now, Summers, if you will bring me my bills and a new cheque-book, we will begin to get things into order.'

Somerville and Ross
(Edith Anna Oenone Somerville and Violet Florence Martin)

Great-Uncle McCarthy

A resident Magistracy in Ireland is not an easy thing to come by nowadays; neither is it a very attractive job; yet on the evening when I first propounded the idea to the young lady who had recently consented to become Mrs Sinclair Yeates, it seemed glittering with possibilities. There was, on that occasion, a sunset, and a string band playing 'The Gondoliers', and there was also an ingenuous belief in the omnipotence of a godfather of Philippa's – (Philippa was the young lady) – who had once been a member of the Government.

I was then climbing the steep ascent of the Captains towards my Majority. I have no fault to find with Philippa's godfather; he did all and more than even Philippa had expected; nevertheless, I had attained to the dignity of mud major, and had spent a good deal on postage stamps, and on railway fares to interview people of influence, before I found myself in the hotel at Skebawn, opening long envelopes addressed to 'Major Yeats, R.M.'.

My most immediate concern, as anyone who has spent nine weeks at Mrs Raverty's hotel will readily believe, was to leave it at the earliest opportunity; but in those nine weeks I had learned, amongst other painful things, a little, a very little, of the methods of the artisan in the west of Ireland. Finding a house had been easy though. I had had my choice of several, each with some hundreds of acres of shooting, thoroughly poached, and a considerable portion of the roof intact. I had selected one; the one that had the largest extent of roof in proportion to the shooting, and had been assured by my landlord that in a fortnight or so it would be fit for occupation.

'There's a few little odd things to be done,' he said easily; 'a lick of paint here and there, and a slap of plaster —'

I am short-sighted; I am also of Irish extraction; both facts that make for toleration – but even I thought he was understating the case. So did the contractor.

At the end of three weeks the latter reported progress, which mainly consisted of the facts that the plumber had accused the carpenter of stealing sixteen feet of his inch-pipe to run a bell wire through, and that the carpenter had replied that he wished the devil might run the plumber through a wran's quill. The plumber having reflected upon the carpenter's parentage, the work of renovation had merged in battle, and at the next Petty Sessions I was reluctantly compelled to allot to each combatant seven days, without the option of a fine.

These and kindred difficulties extended in an unbroken chain through the summer months, until a certain wet and windy day in October, when, with my baggage, I drove over to establish myself at Shreelane. It was a tall, ugly house of three stories high, its wall faced with weather-beaten slates, its windows staring, narrow, and vacant. Round the house ran an area, in which grew some laurustinus and holly bushes among ash heaps, and nettles, and broken bottles. I stood on the steps, waiting for the door to be opened, while the rain sluiced upon me from a broken eaveshoot that had, amongst many other things, escaped the notice of my landlord. I thought of Philippa, and of her plan, broached in today's letter, of having the hall done up as a sitting-room.

The door opened, and revealed the hall. It struck me that I had perhaps overestimated its possibilities. Among them I had certainly not included a flagged floor, sweating with damp, and a reek of cabbage from the adjacent kitchen stairs. A large elderly woman, with a red face, and a cap worn helmet-wise on her forehead, swept me a magnificent curtsy as I crossed the threshold.

'Your honour's welcome —' she began, and then every door in the house slammed in obedience to the gust that drove through it. With something that sounded like 'Mend ye for a back door!' Mrs Cadogan abandoned her opening speech and made for the kitchen stairs. (Improbable as it may appear, my housekeeper was called Cadogan, a name made locally possible by being pronounced Caydogawn.)

Only those who have been through a similar experience can

know what manner of afternoon I spent. I am a martyr to colds in the head, and I felt one coming on. I made a laager in front of the dining-room fire, with a tattered leather screen and the dinner table, and gradually, with cigarettes and strong tea, baffled the smell of must and cats, and fervently trusted that the rain might avert a threatened visit from my landlord. I was then but super-ficially acquainted with Mr Florence McCarthy Knox and his habits.

At about 4.30, when the room had warmed up, and my cold was yielding to treatment, Mrs Cadogan entered and informed me that 'Mr Flurry' was in the yard, and would be thankful if I'd go out to him, for he couldn't come in. Many are the privileges of the female sex; had I been a woman I should unhesitatingly have said that I had a cold in my head.

My landlord was there on horseback, and with him there was a man standing at the head of a stout grey animal. I recognized with despair that I was about to be compelled to buy a horse.

'Good afternoon, Major,' said Mr Knox in his slow, sing-song brogue; 'it's rather soon to be paying you a visit, but I thought you might be in a hurry to see the horse I was telling you of.'

I could have laughed. As if I were ever in a hurry to see a horse! I thanked him, and suggested that it was rather wet for horse-dealing.

'Oh, it's nothing when you're used to it,' replied Mr Knox. His gloveless hands were red and wet, the rain ran down his nose, and his covert coat was soaked to a sodden brown. I thought that I did not want to become used to it. My relations with horses have been of a purely military character. I have endured the Sandhurst riding-school, I have galloped for an impetuous general, I have been steward at regimental races, but none of these feats has altered my opinion that the horse, as a means of locomotion, is obsolete. Nevertheless, the man who accepts a resident magis-tracy in the south-west of Ireland voluntarily retires into the prehistoric age; to institute a stable became inevitable.

'You ought to throw a leg over him,' said Mr Knox, 'and you're welcome to take him over a fence or two if you like. He's a nice flippant jumper.'

Even to my unexacting eye the grey horse did not seem to

promise flippancy, nor did I at all desire to find that quality in him. I explained that I wanted something to drive, and not to ride.

'Well, that's a fine raking horse in harness,' said Mr Knox, looking at me with his serious grey eyes, 'and you'd drive him with a sop of hay in his mouth. Bring him up here, Michael.'

Michael abandoned his efforts to kick the grey horse's forelegs into a becoming position, and led him up to me.

I regarded him from under my umbrella with a quite unreasonable disfavour. He had the dreadful beauty of a horse in a toy-shop, as chubby, as wooden, and as conscientiously dappled, but it was unreasonable to urge this as an objection, and I was incapable of finding any more technical drawbacks. Yielding to circumstance, I 'threw my leg' over the brute, and after pacing gravely round the quadrangle that formed the yard, and jolting to my entrance gate and back, I decided that as he had neither fallen down nor kicked me off, it was worth paying twenty-five pounds for him, if only to get in out of the rain.

Mr Knox accompanied me into the house and had a drink. He was a fair, spare young man, who looked like a stableboy among gentlemen, and a gentleman among stableboys. He belonged to a clan that cropped up in every grade of society in the county, from Sir Valentine Knox of Castle Knox down to the auctioneer Knox, who bore the attractive title of Larry the Liar. So far as I could judge, Florence McCarthy of that ilk occupied a shifting position about midway in the tribe. I had met him at dinner at Sir Valentine's, I had heard of him at an illicit auction, held by Larry the Liar, of brandy stolen from a wreck. They were 'Black Protestants', all of them, in virtue of their descent from a godly soldier of Cromwell, and all were prepared at any moment of the day or night to sell a horse.

'You'll be apt to find this place a bit lonesome after the hotel,' remarked Mr Flurry, sympathetically, as he placed his foot in its steaming boot on the hob, 'but it's a fine sound house anyway, and lots of rooms in it, though indeed, to tell you the truth, I never was through the whole of them since the time my great-uncle, Denis McCarthy, died here. The dear knows I had enough of it that time.' He paused, and lit a cigarette — one of my best, and quite thrown away upon him. 'Those top floors, now,' he resumed, 'I wouldn't make too free with them. There's some of them would jump under you like a spring bed. Many's the night I was in and out of those attics, following my poor uncle when he had a bad turn on him – the horrors, y'know – there were nights he never stopped walking through the house. Good Lord! will I ever forget the morning he said he saw the devil coming up the avenue! 'Look at the two horns on him', says he, and he out with his gun and shot him, and, begad, it was his own donkey!'

Mr Knox gave a couple of short laughs. He seldom laughed, having in unusual perfection the gravity of manner that is bred by horse-dealing, probably from the habitual repression of all emotion save disparagement.

The autumn evening, grey with rain, was darkening in the tall windows, and the wind was beginning to make bullying rushes among the shrubs in the area; a shower of soot rattled down the chimney and fell on the hearthrug.

'More rain coming,' said Mr Knox, rising composedly; 'you'll have to put a goose down these chimneys some day soon, it's the only way in the world to clean them. Well, I'm for the road. You'll come out on the grey next week, I hope; the hounds'll be meeting here. Give a roar at him coming in at his jumps.' He threw his cigarette into the fire and extended a hand to me. 'Goodbye, Major, you'll see plenty of me and my hounds before you're done. There's a power of foxes in the plantations here.'

This was scarcely reassuring for a man who hoped to shoot woodcock, and I hinted as much.

'Oh, is it the cock?' said Mr Flurry; 'b'leeve me, there never was a woodcock yet that minded hounds, now, no more than they'd mind rabbits! The best shoots ever I had here, the hounds were in it the day before.'

When Mr Knox had gone, I began to picture myself going across country roaring, like a man on a fire-engine, while Philippa put the goose down the chimney; but when I sat down to write to her I did not feel equal to being humorous about it. I dilated ponderously on my cold, my hard work, and my loneliness, and eventually went to bed at ten o'clock full of cold shivers and hot whisky-and-water.

After a couple of hours of feverish dozing, I began to understand what had driven Great-Uncle McCarthy to perambulate the house by night. Mrs Cadogan had assured me that the Pope of Rome hadn't a betther bed undher him than myself; wasn't I down on the new flog mattherass the old masther bought in Father Scanlan's auction? By the smell I recognized that 'flog' meant flock, otherwise I should have said my couch was stuffed with old boots. I have seldom spent a more wretched night. The rain drummed with soft fingers on my window panes; the house was full of noises. I seemed to see Great-Uncle McCarthy ranging the passages with Flurry at his heels; several times I thought I heard him. Whisperings seemed borne on the wind through my keyhole, boards creaked in the room overhead, and once I could have sworn that a hand passed, groping, over the panels of my door. I am, I may admit, a believer in ghosts; I even take in a paper that deals with their culture, but I cannot pretend that on that night I looked forward to a manifestation of Great-Uncle McCarthy with any enthusiasm.

The morning broke stormily, and I woke to find Mrs Cadogan's understudy, a grimy nephew of about eighteen, standing by my bedside, with a black bottle in his hand.

'There's no bath in the house, sir,' was his reply to my command; 'but me a'nt said, would ye like a taggeen?'

This alternative proved to be a glass of raw whisky. I declined it.

I look back to that first week of housekeeping at Shreelane as to a comedy excessively badly staged, and striped with lurid melodrama. Towards its close I was positively home-sick for Mrs Raverty's, and I had not a single clean pair of boots. I am not one of those who hold the convention that in Ireland the rain never ceases, day or night, but I must say that my first November at Shreelane was composed of weather of which my friend Flurry Knox remarked that you wouldn't meet a Christian out of doors, unless it was a snipe or a dispensary doctor. To this lamentable category might be added a resident magistrate. Daily, shrouded in mackintosh, I set forth for the Petty Sessions Courts of my wide district; daily, in the inevitable atmosphere of wet frieze and perjury, I listened to indictments of old women who plucked geese alive, of publicans whose hospitality to their friends broke forth uncontrollably on Sunday afternoons, of 'parties' who, in the language of the police sergeant, were subtly defined as 'not to say dhrunk, but in good fighting thrim'.

I got used to it all in time – I suppose one can get used to anything – I even became callous to the surprises of Mrs Cadogan's cooking. As the weather hardened and the woodcock came in, and one by one I discovered and nailed up the rat holes, I began to find life endurable, and even to feel some remote sensation of home-coming when the grey horse turned in at the gate of Shreelane.

The one feature of my establishment to which I could not become inured was the pervading subpresence of some thing or things which, for my own convenience, I summarized as Great-Uncle McCarthy. There were nights on which I was certain that I heard the inebriate shuffle of his foot overhead, the touch of his fumbling hand against the walls. There were dark times before the dawn when sounds went to and fro, the moving of weights, the creaking of doors, a far-away rapping in which was a workman-like suggestion of the undertaker, a rumble of wheels on the avenue. Once I was impelled to the perhaps imprudent measure of cross-examining Mrs Cadogan. Mrs Cadogan, taking the preliminary precaution of crossing herself, asked me fatefully what day of the week it was.

'Friday!' she repeated after me. 'Friday! The Lord save us! 'Twas a Friday the old masther was buried!'

At this point a saucepan opportunely boiled over, and Mrs Cadogan fled with it to the scullery, and was seen no more.

In the process of time I brought Great-Uncle McCarthy down to a fine point. On Friday nights he made coffins and drove hearses; during the rest of the week he rarely did more than patter and shuffle in the attics over my head.

One night, about the middle of December, I awoke, suddenly aware that some noise had fallen like a heavy stone into my dreams. As I felt for the matches it came again, the long, grudging groan and the uncompromising bang of the cross door at the head of the kitchen stairs. I told myself that it was a draught that had done it, but it was a perfectly still night. Even as I listened, a sound of wheels on the avenue shook the stillness. The thing was getting past a joke. In a few minutes I was stealthily groping my way down my own staircase, with a box of matches in my hand, enforced by scientific curiosity, but none the less armed with a stick. I stood in the dark at the top of the back stairs and listened; the snores of Mrs Cadogan and her nephew Peter rose tranquilly from their respective lairs. I descended to the kitchen and lit a candle; there was nothing unusual there, except a great portion of the Cadogan wearing apparel, which was arranged at the fire, and was being serenaded by two crickets. Whatever had opened the door, my household was blameless.

The kitchen was not attractive, yet I felt indisposed to leave it. None the less, it appeared to be my duty to inspect the yard. I put the candle on the table and went forth into the outer darkness. Not a sound was to be heard. The night was very cold, and so dark that I could scarcely distinguish the roofs of the stables against the sky; the house loomed tall and oppressive above me; I was conscious of how lonely it stood in the dumb and barren country. Spirits were certainly futile creatures, childish in their manifestations, stupidly content with the old machinery of raps and rumbles. I thought how fine a scene might be played on a stage like this; if I were a ghost, how bluely I would glimmer at the windows, how whimperingly chatter in the wind. Something whirled out of the darkness above me, and fell with a flop on the ground, just at my feet. I jumped backwards, in point of fact I made for the kitchen door, and, with my hand on the latch, stood still and waited. Nothing further happened; the thing that lay there did not stir. I struck a match. The moment of tension turned to pathos as the light flickered on nothing more fateful than a dead crow.

Dead it certainly was. I could have told that without looking at it; but why should it, at some considerable period after its death, fall from the clouds at my feet. But did it fall from the clouds? I struck another match, and stared up at the impenetrable face of the house. There was no hint of solution in the dark windows, but I determined to go up and search the rooms that gave upon the yard.

How cold it was! I can feel now the frozen musty air of those attics, with their rat-eaten floors and wallpapers furred with damp. I went softly from one to another, feeling like a burglar in my own house, and found nothing in elucidation of the mystery. The windows were hermetically shut, and sealed with cobwebs. There was no furniture, except in the end room, where a wardrobe without doors stood in a corner, empty save for the solemn presence of a monstrous tall hat. I went back to bed, cursing those powers of darkness that had got me out of it, and heard no more.

My landlord had not failed of his promise to visit my coverts with his hounds; in fact, he fulfilled it rather more conscientiously than seemed to me quite wholesome for the cock-shooting. I maintained a silence which I felt to be magnanimous on the part of a man who cared nothing for hunting and a great deal for shooting, and wished the hounds more success in the slaughter of my foxes than seemed to be granted to them. I met them all, one red frosty evening, as I drove down the long hill to my demesne gates, Flurry at their head, in his shabby pink coat and dingy breeches, the hounds trailing dejectedly behind him and his half-dozen companions.

'What luck?' I called out, drawing rein as I met them.

'None,' said Mr Flurry briefly. He did not stop, neither did he remove his pipe from the down-twisted corner of his mouth; his eye at me was cold and sour. The other members of the hunt passed me with equal hauteur; I thought they took their ill luck very badly.

On foot, among the last of the straggling hounds, cracking a carman's whip, and swearing comprehensively at them all, slouched my friend Slipper. Our friendship had begun in Court, the relative positions of the dock and the judgment-seat forming no obstacle to its progress, and had been cemented during several days' tramping after snipe. He was, as usual, a little drunk, and he hailed me as though I were a ship.

'Ahoy, Major Yeates!' he shouted, bringing himself up with a lurch against my cart; 'it's hunting you should be, in place of sending poor divils to gaol!'

'But I hear you had no hunting,' I said.

'Ye heard that, did ye?' Slipper rolled upon me an eye like that of a profligate pug. 'Well, begor, ye heard no more than the thruth.'

'But where are all the foxes?' said I.

'Begor, I don't know no more than your honour. And Shreelane – that there used to be as many foxes in it as there's crosses in a yard of check! Well, well, I'll say nothin' for it, only that it's quare! Here, Vaynus! Naygress!' Slipper uttered a yell, hoarse with whisky, in adjuration of two elderly ladies of the pack who had profited by our conversation to stray away into an adjacent cottage. 'Well, goodnight, Major. Mr Flurry's as cross as briars, and he'll have me ate!'

He set off at a surprisingly steady run, cracking his whip, and whooping like a madman. I hope that when I also am fifty I shall be able to run like Slipper.

That frosty evening was followed by three others like unto it, and a flight of woodcock came in. I calculated that I could do with five guns, and I dispatched invitations to shoot and dine on the following day to four of the local sportsmen, among whom was, of course, my landlord. I remember that in my letter to the latter I expressed a facetious hope that my bag of cock would be more successful than his of foxes had been.

The answers to my invitations were not what I expected. All, without so much as a conventional regret, declined my invitation; Mr Knox added that he hoped the bag of cock would be to my liking, and that I need not be 'afraid' that the hounds would trouble my coverts any more. Here was war! I gazed in stupefaction at the crooked scrawl in which my landlord had declared it. It was wholly and entirely inexplicable, and instead of going to sleep comfortably over the fire and my newspaper as a gentleman should, I spent the evening in irritated ponderings over this bewildering and exasperating change of front on the part of my friendly squireens.

My shoot the next day was scarcely a success. I shot the woods in company with my gamekeeper, Tim Connor, a gentleman whose duties mainly consisted in limiting the poaching privileges to his personal friends, and whatever my offence might have been, Mr Knox could have wished me no bitterer punishment than hearing the unavailing shouts of 'Mark cock!' and seeing my birds winging their way from the coverts, far out of shot. Tim Connor and I got ten couple between us; it might have been thirty if my neighbours had not boycotted me, for what I could only suppose was the slackness of their hounds.

I was dog-tired that night, having walked enough for three men, and I slept the deep, insatiable sleep that I had earned. It was somewhere about 3 a.m. that I was gradually awakened by a continuous knocking, interspersed with muffled calls. Great-Uncle McCarthy had never before given tongue, and I freed one ear from blankets to listen. Then I remembered that Peter had told me the sweep had promised to arrive that morning, and to arrive early. Blind with sleep and fury I went to the passage window, and thence desired the sweep to go the devil. It availed me little. For the remainder of the night I could hear him pacing round the house, trying the windows, banging at the doors, and calling upon Peter Cadogan as the priests of Baal called upon their god. At six o'clock I had fallen into a troubled doze, when Mrs Cadogan knocked at my door and imparted the information that the sweep had arrived. My answer need not be recorded, but in spite of it the door opened, and my housekeeper, in a weird *déshabille*, effectively lighted by the orange beams of her candle, entered my room.

'God forgive me, I never seen one I'd hate as much as that sweep!' she began; 'he's these three hours – arrah, what three hours! – no, but all night, raising tallywack and tandem round the house to get at the chimbleys.'

'Well, for Heaven's sake let him get at the chimneys and let me go to sleep,' I answered, goaded to desperation, 'and you may tell him from me that if I hear his voice again I'll shoot him!'

Mrs Cadogan silently left my bedside, and as she closed the door she said to herself, 'The Lord save us!'

Subsequent events may be briefly summarized. At seven-thirty I was awakened anew by a thunderous sound in the chimney, and a brick crashed into the fireplace, followed at a short interval by two dead jackdaws and their nests. At eight, I was informed by Peter that there was no hot water, and that he wished the divil would roast the same sweep. At nine-thirty, when I came down to breakfast, there was no fire anywhere, and my coffee, made in the coach-house, tasted of soot. I put on an overcoat and opened my letters. About fourth or fifth in the uninteresting heap came one in an egregiously disguised hand.

'Sir,' it began, 'this is to inform you your unsportsmanlike conduct has been discovered. You have been suspected this good while of shooting the Shreelane foxes, it is known now you do worse. Parties have seen your gamekeeper going regular to meet the Saturday early train at Salters Hill Station, with your grey horse under a cart, and your labels on the boxes, and we know as well as *your agent in Cork* what it is you have in those boxes. Be warned in time. – Your Wellwisher.'

I read this through twice before its drift became apparent, and I realized that I was accused of improving my shooting and my finances by the simple expedient of selling my foxes. That is to say, I was in a worse position than if I had stolen a horse, or murdered Mrs Cadogan, or got drunk three times a week in Skebawn.

For a few moments I fell into wild laughter, and then, aware that it was rather a bad business to let a lie of this kind get a start, I sat down to demolish the preposterous charge in a letter to Flurry Knox. Somehow, as I selected my sentences, it was born in upon me that, if the letter spoke the truth, circumstantial evidence was rather against me. Mere lofty repudiation would be unavailing, and by my infernal facetiousness about the woodcock I had effectively filled in the case against myself. At all events, the first thing to do was to establish a basis, and have it out with Tim Connor. I rang the bell.

'Peter, is Tim Connor about the place?'

'He is not, sir. I heard him say he was going west the hill to mend the bounds fence.' Peter's face was covered with soot, his eyes were red, and he coughed ostentatiously. 'The sweep's after breaking one of his brushes within in yer bedroom chimney, sir,' he went on, with all the satisfaction of his class in announcing domestic calamity; 'he's above on the roof now, and he'd be thankful to you to go up to him.'

I followed him upstairs in that state of simmering patience that any employer of Irish labour must know and sympathize with. I climbed the rickety ladder and squeezed through the dirty trap-door involved in the ascent to the roof, and was confronted by the hideous face of the sweep, black against the frosty blue sky. He had encamped with all his paraphernalia on the flat top of the roof, and was good enough to rise and put his pipe in his pocket on my arrival.

'Good morning, Major. That's a grand view you have up here,' said the sweep. He was evidently far too well bred to talk shop. 'I travelled every roof in this counthry, and there isn't one where you'd get as handsome a prospect!'

Theoretically he was right, but I had not come up to the roof to discuss scenery, and demanded brutally why he had sent for me. The explanation involved a recital of the special genius required to sweep the Shreelane chimneys; of the fact that the sweep had in infancy been sent up and down every one of them by Great-Uncle McCarthy; of the three ass-loads of soot that by his peculiar skill he had this morning taken from the kitchen chimney; of its present purity, the draught being such that it would 'dhraw up a young cat with it'. Finally – realizing that I could endure no more – he explained that my bedroom chimney had got what he called 'a wynd' in it, and he proposed to climb down a little way in the stack to try 'would he get to come at the brush'. The sweep was very small, the chimney very large. I stipulated that he should have a rope round his waist, and despite the illegality, I let him go. He went down like a monkey, digging his toes and fingers into the niches made for the purpose in the old chimney; Peter held the rope. I lit a cigarette and waited.

Certainly the view from the roof was worth coming up to look at. It was rough, heathery country on one side, with a string of little blue lakes running like a turquoise necklet round the base of a firry hill, and patches of pale green pasture were set amidst the rocks and heather. A silvery flash behind the undulations of the hills told where the Atlantic lay in immense plains of sunlight. I turned to survey with an owner's eye my own grey woods and straggling plantations of larch, and espied a man coming out of the western wood. He had something on his back, and he was walking very fast; a rabbit poacher no doubt. As he passed out of sight into the back avenue he was beginning to run. At the same instant I saw on the hill beyond my western boundaries half a dozen horsemen scrambling by zigzag ways down towards the wood. There was one red coat among them; it came first at the gap in the fence that Tim Connor had gone out to mend, and with the others was lost to sight in the covert, from which, in another instant, came clearly through the frosty air a shout of 'Gone to ground!' Tremendous horn blowings followed, then, all in the same moment, I saw the hounds break in full cry from the wood, and come stringing over the grass and up the back avenue towards the yard gate. Were they running a fresh fox into the stables?

I do not profess to be a hunting-man, but I am an Irishman, and so, it is perhaps superfluous to state, is Peter. We forgot the sweep as if he had never existed, and precipitated ourselves down the ladder, down the stairs, and out into the yard. One side of the yard is formed by the coach-house and a long stable, with a range of lofts above them, planned on the heroic scale in such matters that obtained in Ireland formerly. These join the house at the corner by the back door. A long flight of stone steps leads to the lofts, and up these, as Peter and I emerged from the back door, the hounds were struggling helter-skelter. Almost simultaneously there was a confused clatter of hoofs in the back avenue, and Flurry Knox came stooping at a gallop under the archway followed by three or four other riders. They flung themselves from their horses and made for the steps of the loft; more hounds pressed, yelling, on their heels, the din was indescribable, and justified Mrs Cadogan's subsequent remark that 'when she heard the noise she thought 'twas the end of the world and the divil collecting his own!'

I jostled in the wake of the party, and found myself in the loft, wading in hay, and nearly deafened by the clamour that was bandied about the high roof and walls. At the farther end of the loft the hounds were raging in the hay, encouraged thereto by the whoops and screeches of Flurry and his friends. High up in the gable of the loft, where it joined the main wall of the house, there was a small door, and I noted with a transient surprise that there was a long ladder leading up to it. Even as it caught my eye a hound fought his way out of a drift of hay and began to jump at the ladder, throwing his tongue vociferously, and even clambering up a few rungs in his excitement.

· 'There's the way he's gone!' roared Flurry, striving through hounds and hay towards the ladder. 'Trumpeter has him! What's up there, back of the door, Major? I don't remember it at all.'

My crimes had evidently been forgotten in the supremacy of the moment. While I was futilely asserting that had the fox gone up the ladder he could not possibly have opened the door and shut it after him, even if the door led anywhere which, to the best of my belief, it did not, the door in question opened, and to my amazement the sweep appeared at it. He gesticulated violently, and over the tumult was heard to asseverate that there was nothing above there, only a way into the flue, and anyone would be destroyed with the soot —

'Ah, go to blazes with your soot!' interrupted Flurry, already half-way up the ladder.

I followed him, the other men pressing up behind me. That Trumpeter had made no mistake was instantly brought home to our noses by the reek of fox that met us at the door. Instead of a chimney, we found ourselves in a dilapidated bedroom, full of people. Tim Connor was there, the sweep was there, and a squalid elderly man and woman on whom I had never set eyes before. There was a large open fireplace, black with the soot the sweep had brought down with him, and on the table stood a bottle of my own special Scotch whisky. In one corner of the room was a pile of broken packing-cases, and beside these on the floor lay a bag in which something kicked.

Flurry, looking more uncomfortable and nonplussed than I could have believed possible, listened in silence to the ceaseless harangue of the elderly woman. The hounds were yelling like lost spirits in the loft below, but her voice pierced the uproar like a bagpipe. It was an unspeakably vulgar voice, yet it was not the voice of a countrywoman, and there were frowsy remnants of respectability about her general aspect.

'And is it you, Flurry Knox, that's calling me a disgrace! Disgrace, indeed, am I? Me that was your poor mother's own uncle's daughter and as good a McCarthy as ever stood in Shreelane!'

What followed I could not comprehend, owing to the fact that the sweep kept up a perpetual undercurrent of explanation to me as to how he had got down the wrong chimney. I noticed that his breath stank of whisky – Scotch, not the native variety.

Never, as long as Flurry Knox lives to blow a horn, will he hear the last of the day that he ran his mother's first cousin to ground in the attic. Never, while Mrs Cadogan can hold a basting spoon, will she cease to recount how, on the same occasion, she plucked and roasted ten couple of woodcock in one torrid hour to provide luncheon for the hunt. In the glory of this achievement her confederacy with the stowaways in the attic is wholly slurred over, in much the same manner as the startling outburst of summons for trespass, brought by Tim Connor during the remainder of the shooting season, obscured the unfortunate episode of the bagged fox. It was, of course, zeal for my shooting that induced him to assist Mr Knox's disreputable relations in the deportation of my foxes; and I have allowed it to remain at that.

In fact, the only things not allowed to remain were Mr and Mrs McCarthy Gannon. They, as my landlord informed me, in the midst of vast apologies, had been permitted to squat at Shreelane until my tenancy began, and having then ostentatiously and abusively left the house, they had, with the connivance of the Cadogans, secretly returned to roost in the corner attic, to sell foxes under the ægis of my name, and to make inroads on my belongings. They retained connection with the outer world by means of the ladder and the loft, and with the house in general, and my whisky in particular, by a door into the other attics – a door concealed by the wardrobe in which reposed Great-Uncle McCarthy's tall hat.

It is with the greatest regret that I relinquish the prospect of writing a monograph on Great-Uncle McCarthy for a Spiritualistic Journal, but with the departure of his relations he ceased to manifest himself, and neither the nailing up of packing-cases, nor the rumble of the cart that took them to the station, disturbed my sleep for the future.

I understand that the task of clearing out the McCarthy Gannons' effects was of a nature that necessitated two glasses of whisky per man; and if the remnants of rabbit and jackdaw disinterred in the process were anything like the crow that was thrown out of the window at my feet, I do not grudge the restorative.

As Mrs Cadogan remarked to the sweep, 'A Turk couldn't stand it.'

George Gissing

THE SCRUPULOUS FATHER

It was market day in the little town; at one o'clock a rustic company besieged the table of the Greyhound, lured by savoury odours and the frothing of amber ale. Apart from three frequenters of the ordinary, in a small room prepared for overflow, sat two persons of a different stamp – a middle-aged man, bald, meagre, unimpressive, but wholly respectable in bearing and apparel, and a girl, evidently his daughter, who had the look of the latter twenties, her plain dress harmonizing with a subdued charm of feature and a timidity of manner not ungraceful. Whilst waiting for their meal they conversed in an undertone; their brief remarks and ejaculations told of a long morning's ramble from the seaside resort some miles away; in their quiet fashion they seemed to have enjoyed themselves, and dinner at an inn evidently struck them as something of an escapade. Rather awkwardly the girl arranged a handful of wild flowers which she had gathered, and put them for refreshment into a tumbler of water; when a woman entered with viands, silence fell upon the two; after hesitations and mutual glances, they began to eat with nervous appetite.

Scarcely was their modest confidence restored, when in the doorway sounded a virile voice, gaily humming, and they became aware of a tall young man, red-headed, anything but handsome, flushed and perspiring from the sunny road; his open jacket showed a blue cotton shirt without waistcoat, in his hand was a shabby straw hat, and thick dust covered his boots. One would have judged him a tourist of the noisier class, and his rather loud 'Good morning!' as he entered the room seemed a serious menace to privacy; on the other hand, the rapid buttoning of his coat, and the quiet choice of a seat as far as possible from the two guests whom his arrival disturbed, indicated a certain tact. His greeting had met with the merest murmur of reply; their eyes on their plates, father and daughter resolutely disregarded him; yet he ventured to speak again.

'They're busy here today. Not a seat to be had in the other room.'

It was apologetic in intention, and not rudely spoken. After a moment's delay the bald, respectable man made a curt response.

'This room is public, I believe.'

The intruder held his peace. But more than once he glanced at the girl, and after each furtive scrutiny his plain visage manifested some disturbance, a troubled thoughtfulness. His one look at the mute parent was from beneath contemptuous eyebrows.

Very soon another guest appeared, a massive agricultural man, who descended upon a creaking chair and growled a remark about the hot weather. With him the red-haired pedestrian struck into talk. Their topic was beer. Uncommonly good, they agreed, the local brew, and each called for a second pint. What, they asked in concert, would England be without her ale? Shame on the base traffickers who enfeebled or poisoned this noble liquor! And how cool it was – ah! The right sort of cellar! He of the red hair hinted at a third pewter.

These two were still but midway in their stout attack on meat and drink, when father and daughter, having exchanged a few whispers, rose to depart. After leaving the room, the girl remembered that she had left her flowers behind; she durst not return for them, and, knowing her father would dislike to do so, said nothing about the matter.

'A pity!' exclaimed Mr Whiston (that was his respectable name) as they strolled away. 'It looked at first as if we should have such a nice quiet dinner.'

'I enjoyed it all the same,' replied his companion, whose name was Rose.

'That abominable habit of drinking!' added Mr Whiston austerely. He himself had quaffed water, as always. 'Their ale, indeed! See the coarse, gross creatures it produces!'

He shuddered. Rose, however, seemed less consentient than usual. Her eyes were on the ground; her lips were closed with a certain firmness. When she spoke, it was on quite another subject.

They were Londoners. Mr Whiston held the position of draughtsman in the office of a geographical publisher; though his income was small, he had always practised a rigid economy, and the possession of a modest private capital put him beyond fear of reverses. Profoundly conscious of social limits, he felt it a subject for gratitude that there was nothing to be ashamed of in his calling, which he might fairly regard as a profession, and he nursed this sense of respectability as much on his daughter's behalf as on his own. Rose was an only child; her mother had been dead for years; her kinsfolk on both sides laid claim to the title of gentlefolk, but supported it on the narrowest margin of independence. The girl had grown up in an atmosphere unfavourable to mental development, but she had received a fairly good education, and nature had dowered her with intelligence. A sense of her father's conscientiousness and of his true affection forbade her to criticise openly the principles on which he had directed her life; hence a habit of solitary meditation, which half fostered, yet half opposed, the gentle diffidence of Rose's character.

Mr Whiston shrank from society, ceaselessly afraid of receiving less than his due; privately, meanwhile, he deplored the narrowness of the social opportunities granted to his daughter, and was for ever forming schemes for her advantage – schemes which never passed beyond the stage of nervous speculation. They inhabited a little house in a western suburb, a house illumined with every domestic virtue; but scarcely a dozen persons crossed the threshold within a twelve-month. Rose's two or three friends were, like herself, mistrustful of the world. One of them had lately married after a very long engagement, and Rose still trembled from the excitement of that occasion, still debated fearfully with herself on the bride's chances of happiness. Her own marriage was an event so inconceivable that merely to glance at the thought appeared half immodest and wholly irrational.

Every winter Mr Whiston talked of new places which he and Rose would visit when the holidays came round; every summer he shrank from the thought of adventurous novelty, and ended by proposing a return to the same western seaside-town, to the familiar lodgings. The climate suited neither him nor his daughter, who both needed physical as well as moral bracing; but they only thought of this on finding themselves at home again, with another long year of monotony before them. And it was so good to feel welcome, respected; to receive the smiling reverences of tradesfolk; to talk with just a little well-bred condescension, sure that it would be appreciated. Mr Whiston savoured these things, and Rose in this respect was not wholly unlike him.

Today was the last of their vacation. The weather had been magnificent throughout; Rose's cheeks were more than touched by the sun, greatly to the advantage of her unpretending comeliness. She was a typical English maiden, rather tall, shapely rather than graceful, her head generally bent, her movements always betraying the diffidence of solitary habit. The lips were her finest feature, their perfect outline indicating sweetness without feebleness of character. Such a girl is at her best towards the stroke of thirty. Rose had begun to know herself; she needed only opportunity to act upon her knowledge.

A train would take them back to the seaside. At the railway station Rose seated herself on a shaded part of the platform, whilst her father, who was exceedingly short of sight, peered over publications on the bookstall. Rather tired after her walk, the girl was dreamily tracing a pattern with the point of her parasol, when some one advanced and stood immediately in front of her. Startled, she looked up, and recognised the red-haired stranger of the inn.

'You left these flowers in a glass of water on the table. I hope I'm not doing a rude thing in asking whether they were left by accident.'

He had the flowers in his hand, their stems carefully protected by a piece of paper. For a moment Rose was incapable of replying; she looked at the speaker; she felt her cheeks burn; in utter embarrassment she said she knew not what.

'Oh! —thank you! I forgot them. It's very kind.'

Her hand touched his as she took the bouquet from him. Without another word the man turned and strode away.

Mr Whiston had seen nothing of this. When he approached, Rose held up the flowers with a laugh.

'Wasn't it kind? I forgot them, you know, and some one from the inn came looking for me.'

'Very good of them, very,' replied her father graciously. 'A very nice inn that. We'll go again – some day. One likes to encourage such civility. It's rare nowadays'.

He of the red hair travelled by the same train though not in the same carriage. Rose caught sight of him at the seaside station. She was vexed with herself for having so scantily acknowledged his kindness; it seemed to her that she had not really thanked him at all; how absurd, at her age, to be incapable of common self-command! At the same time she kept thinking of her father's phrase, 'coarse, gross creatures', and it vexed her even more than her own ill behaviour. The stranger was certainly not coarse, far from gross. Even his talk about beer (she remembered every word of it) had been amusing rather than offensive. Was he a 'gentleman'? The question agitated her; it involved so technical a definition, and she felt so doubtful as to the reply. Beyond doubt he had acted in a gentlemanly way; but his voice lacked something. Coarse? Gross? No, no, no! Really, her father was very severe, not to say uncharitable. But perhaps he was thinking of the heavy agricultural man; oh, he must have been!

Of a sudden she felt very weary. At the lodgings she sat down in her bedroom, and gazed through the open window at the sea. A sense of discouragement, hitherto almost unknown, had fallen upon her; it spoilt the blue sky and the soft horizon. She thought rather drearily of the townward journey tomorrow, of her home in the suburbs, of the endless monotony that awaited her. The flowers lay on her lap; she smelt them, dreamed over them. And then – strange incongruity – she thought of beer!

Between tea and supper she and her father rested on the beach. Mr Whiston was reading. Rose pretended to turn the leaves of a book. Of a sudden, as unexpectedly to herself as to her companion, she broke silence.

'Don't you think, father, that we are too much afraid of talking with strangers?'

'Too much afraid?'

Mr Whiston was puzzled. He had forgotten all about the incident at the dinner-table.

'I mean – what harm is there in having a little conversation when one is away from home? At the inn today, you know, I can't help thinking we were rather – perhaps a little too silent.'

'My dear Rose, did you want to talk about beer?'

She reddened, but answered all the more emphatically.

'Of course not. But, when the first gentleman came in, wouldn't it have been natural to exchange a few friendly words? I'm sure he wouldn't have talked of beer to *us*.'

'The *gentleman*? I saw no gentleman, my dear. I suppose he was a small clerk, or something of the sort, and he had no business whatever to address us.'

'Oh, but he only said good morning, and apologized for sitting at our table. He needn't have apologized at all.'

'Precisely. That is just what I mean,' said Mr Whiston with self-satisfaction. 'My dear Rose, if I had been alone, I might perhaps have talked a little, but with you it was impossible. One cannot be too careful. A man like that will take all sorts of liberties. One has to keep such people at a distance.'

A moment's pause, then Rose spoke with unusual decision –

'I feel quite sure, father, that he would not have taken liberties. It seems to me that he knew quite well how to behave himself.'

Mr Whiston grew still more puzzled. He closed his book to meditate this new problem.

'One has to lay down rules,' fell from him at length, sententiously. 'Our position, Rose, as I have often explained, is a delicate one. A lady in circumstances such as yours cannot exercise too much caution. Your natural associates are in the world of wealth; unhappily, I cannot make you wealthy. We have to guard our self-respect, my dear child. Really, it is not *safe* to talk with strangers – least of all at an inn. And you have only to remember that disgusting conversation about beer!'

Rose said no more. Her father pondered a little, felt that he had delivered his soul, and resumed the book.

The next morning they were early at the station to secure good places for the long journey to London. Up to almost the last moment it seemed that they would have a carriage to themselves. Then the door suddenly opened, a bag was flung on to the seat, and after it came a hot, panting man, a red-haired man, recognized immediately by both the travellers.

'I thought I'd missed it!' ejaculated the intruder merrily.

Mr Whiston turned his head away, disgust transforming his countenance. Rose sat motionless, her eyes cast down. And the stranger mopped his forehead in silence.

He glanced at her; he glanced again and again; and Rose was aware of every look. It did not occur to her to feel offended. On the contrary, she fell into a mood of tremulous pleasure, enhanced by every turn of the stranger's eyes in her direction. At him she did not look, yet she saw him. Was it a coarse face? she asked herself. Plain, perhaps, but decidedly not vulgar. The red hair, she thought, was not disagreeably red; she didn't dislike that shade of colour. He was humming a tune; it seemed to be his habit, and it argued healthy cheerfulness. Meanwhile Mr Whiston sat stiffly in his corner, staring at the landscape, a model of respectable muteness.

At the first stop another man entered. This time, unmistakably, a commercial traveller. At once a dialogue sprang up between him and Rufus. The traveller complained that all the smoking compartments were full.

'Why,' exclaimed Rufus, with a laugh, 'that reminds me that I wanted a smoke. I never thought about it till now; jumped in here in a hurry.'

The traveller's 'line' was tobacco; they talked tobacco – Rufus with must gusto. Presently the conversation took a wider scope.

'I envy you,' cried Rufus, 'always travelling about. I'm in a beastly office, and get only a fortnight off once a year. I enjoy it, I can tell you! Time's up today, worse luck! I've a good mind to emigrate. Can you give me a tip about the colonies?'

He talked of how he had spent his holiday. Rose missed not a word, and her blood pulsed in sympathy with the joy of freedom which he expressed. She did not mind his occasional slang; the tone was manly and right-hearted; it evinced a certain simplicity of feeling by no means common in men, whether gentle or other. At a certain moment the girl was impelled to steal a glimpse of his face. After all, was it really so plain? The features seemed to her to have a certain refinement which she had not noticed before.

'I'm going to try for a smoker,' said the man of commerce, as the train slackened into a busy station.

Rufus hesitated. His eye wandered.

'I think I shall stay where I am,' he ended by saying.

In that same moment, for the first time, Rose met his glance. She saw that his eyes did not at once avert themselves; they had a singular expression, a smile which pleaded pardon for its audacity. And Rose, even whilst turning away, smiled in response.

The train stopped. The commercial traveller alighted. Rose, leaning towards her father, whispered that she was thirsty; would he get her a glass of milk or of lemonade? Though little disposed to rush on such errands, Mr Whiston had no choice but to comply; he sped at once for the refreshment-room.

And Rose knew what would happen; she knew perfectly. Sitting rigid, her eyes on vacancy, she felt the approach of the young man, who for the moment was alone with her. She saw him at her side: she heard his voice.

'I can't help it. I want to speak to you. May I?'

Rose faltered a reply.

'It was so kind to bring the flowers. I didn't thank you properly.'

'It's now or never,' pursued the young man in rapid, excited tones. 'Will you let me tell you my name? Will you tell me yours?'

Rose's silence consented. The daring Rufus rent a page from a pocket-book, scribbled his name and address, gave it to Rose. He rent out another page, offered it to Rose with the pencil, and in a moment had secured the precious scrap of paper in his pocket. Scarce was the transaction completed when a stranger jumped in. The young man bounded to his own corner, just in time to see the return of Mr Whiston, glass in hand.

During the rest of the journey Rose was in the strangest state of mind. She did not feel in the least ashamed of herself. It seemed to her that what had happened was wholly natural and simple. The extraordinary thing was that she must sit silent and with cold countenance at the distance of a few feet from a person with whom she ardently desired to converse. Sudden illumination had wholly changed the aspect of life. She seemed to be playing a part in a grotesque comedy rather than living in a world of grave realities. Her father's dignified silence struck her as intolerably absurd. She could have burst into laughter; at moments she was indignant, irritated, tremulous with the spirit of revolt. She detected a glance of frigid superiority with which Mr Whiston chanced to survey the other occupants of the compartment. It amazed her. Never had she seen her father in such an alien light. He bent forward and addressed to her some commonplace remark; she barely deigned a reply. Her views of conduct, of character, had undergone an abrupt and extraordinary change. Having justified without shadow of argument her own incredible proceeding, she judged everything and everybody by some new standard, mysteriously attained. She was no longer the Rose Whiston of yesterday. Her old self seemed an object of compassion. She felt an unspeakable happiness, and at the same time an encroaching fear.

The fear predominated; when she grew aware of the streets of London looming on either hand it became a torment, an anguish. Small-folded, crushed within her palm, the piece of paper with its still unread inscription seemed to burn her. Once, twice, thrice she met the look of her friend. He smiled cheerily, bravely, with evident purpose of encouragement. She knew his face better than that of any oldest acquaintance; she saw in it a manly beauty. Only by a great effort of self-control could she refrain from turning aside to unfold and read what he had written. The train slackened speed, stopped. Yes, it was London. She must arise and go. Once more their eyes met. Then, without recollection of any interval, she was on the Metropolitan Railway, moving towards her suburban home.

A severe headache sent her early to bed. Beneath her pillow lay a scrap of paper with a name and address she was not likely to forget. And through the night of broken slumbers Rose suffered a martyrdom. No more self-glorification! All her courage gone, all her new vitality! She saw herself with the old eyes, and was shame-stricken to the very heart.

Whose the fault? Towards dawn she argued it with the bitterness of misery. What a life was hers in this little world of choking respectabilities! Forbidden this, forbidden that; permitted – the pride of ladyhood. And she was not a lady, after all. What lady would have permitted herself to exchange names and addresses with a strange man in a railway carriage – furtively, too, escaping her father's observation? If not a lady, what *was* she? It meant the utter failure of her breeding and education. The sole end for which she had lived was frustrate. A common, vulgar young woman – well mated, doubtless, with an impudent clerk, whose noisy talk was of beer and tobacco!

This arrested her. Stung to the defence of her friend, who, clerk though he might be, was neither impudent nor vulgar, she found herself driven back upon self-respect. The battle went on for hours; it exhausted her; it undid all the good effects of sun and sea, and left her flaccid, pale.

'I'm afraid the journey yesterday was too much for you,' remarked Mr Whiston, after observing her as she sat mute the next evening.

'I shall soon recover,' Rose answered coldly.

The father meditated with some uneasiness. He had not forgotten Rose's singular expression of opinion after their dinner at the inn. His affection made him sensitive to changes in the girl's demeanour. Next summer they must really find a more bracing resort. Yes, yes; clearly Rose needed bracing. But she was always better when the cool days came round.

On the morrow it was his daughter's turn to feel anxious. Mr Whiston all at once wore a face of indignant severity. He was absent-minded; he sat at table with scarce a word; he had little nervous movements, and subdued mutterings as of wrath. This continued on a second day, and Rose began to suffer an intolerable agitation. She could not help connecting her father's strange behaviour with the secret which tormented her heart.

Had something happened? Had her friend seen Mr Whiston, or written to him?

She had awaited with tremors every arrival of the post. It was probable – more than probable – that *he* would write to her; but as yet no letter came. A week passed, and no letter came. Her father was himself again; plainly she had mistaken the cause of his perturbation. Ten days, and no letter came.

It was Saturday afternoon. Mr Whiston reached home at tea-time. The first glance showed his daughter that trouble and anger once more beset him. She trembled, and all but wept, for suspense had overwrought her nerves.

'I find myself obliged to speak to you on a very disagreeable subject' – thus began Mr Whiston over the tea-cups – 'a very unpleasant subject indeed. My one consolation is that it will probably settle a little argument we had down at the seaside.'

As his habit was when expressing grave opinions (and Mr

Whiston seldom expressed any other), he made a long pause and ran his fingers through his thin beard. The delay irritated Rose to the last point of endurance.

'The fact is,' he proceeded at length, 'a week ago I received a most extraordinary letter – the most impudent letter I ever read in my life. It came from that noisy, beer-drinking man who intruded upon us at the inn – you remember. He began by explaining who he was, and – if you can believe it – had the impertinence to say that he wished to make my acquaintance! An amazing letter! Naturally, I left it unanswered – the only dignified thing to do. But the fellow wrote again, asking if I had received his proposal. I now replied, briefly and severely, asking him, first, how he came to know my name; secondly, what reason I had given him for supposing that I desired to meet him again. His answer to this was even more outrageous than the first offence. He bluntly informed me that in order to discover my name and address he had followed us home that day from Paddington Station! As if this was not bad enough, he went on to – really, Rose, I feel I must apologise to you, but the fact is I seem to have no choice but to tell you what he said. The fellow tells me, really, that he wants to know *me* only that he may come to know *you*! My first idea was to go with this letter to the police. I am not sure that I shan't do so even yet; most certainly I shall if he writes again. The man may be crazy – he may be dangerous. Who knows but he may come lurking about the house? I felt obliged to warn you of this unpleasant possibility.'

Rose was stirring her tea; also she was smiling. She continued to stir and to smile, without consciousness of either performance.

'You make light of it?' exclaimed her father solemnly.

'O father, of course I am sorry you have had this annoyance.'

So little was there of manifest sorrow in the girl's tone and countenance that Mr Whiston gazed at her rather indignantly. His pregnant pause gave birth to one of those admonitory axioms which had hitherto ruled his daughter's life.

'My dear, I advise you never to trifle with questions of proprie-ty. Could there possibly be a better illustration of what I have so often said – that in self-defence we are bound to keep strangers at a distance?'

'Father —'

Rose began firmly, but her voice failed.

'You were going to say, Rose?'

She took her courage in both hands.

'Will you allow me to see the letters?'

'Certainly. There can be no objection to that.'

He drew from his pocket the three envelopes, held them to his daughter. With shaking hand Rose unfolded the first letter; it was written in clear commercial character, and was signed 'Charles James Burroughs.' When she had read all, the girl said quietly –

'Are you quite sure, father, that these letters are impertinent?'

Mr Whiston stopped in the act of finger-combing his beard.

'What doubt can there be of it?'

'They seem to me,' proceeded Rose nervously, 'to be very respectful and very honest.'

'My dear, you astound me! Is it respectful to force one's acquaintance upon an unwilling stranger? I really don't understand you. Where is your sense of propriety, Rose? A vulgar, noisy fellow, who talks of beer and tobacco – a petty clerk! And he has the audacity to write to me that he wants to – to make friends with my daughter! Respectful? Honest? Really!'

When Mr Whiston became sufficiently agitated to lose his decorous gravity, he began to splutter, and at such moments he was not impressive. Rose kept her eyes cast down. She felt her strength once more, the strength of a wholly reasonable and half-passionate revolt against that tyrannous propriety which Mr Whiston worshipped.

'Father —'

'Well, my dear?'

'There is only one thing I dislike in these letters – and that is a falsehood.'

'I don't understand.'

Rose was flushing. Her nerves grew tense; she had wrought herself to a simple audacity which overcame small embarrassments.

'Mr Burroughs says that he followed us home from Paddington to discover our address. That is not true. He asked me for my name and address in the train, and gave me his.'

The father gasped.

'He *asked* —? You *gave* —?'

'It was whilst you were away in the refreshment-room,' proceeded the girl, with singular self-control, in a voice almost
matter-of-fact. 'I ought to tell you, at the same time, that it was Mr
Burroughs who brought me the flowers from the inn, when I
forgot them. You didn't see him give them to me in the station.'

The father stared.

'But, Rose, what does all this mean? You – you overwhelm me!
Go on, please. What next?'

'Nothing, father.'

And of a sudden the girl was so beset with confusing emotions
that she hurriedly quitted her chair and vanished from the room.

Before Mr Whiston returned to his geographical drawing on
Monday morning, he had held long conversations with Rose, and
still longer with himself. Not easily could he perceive the justice of
his daughter's quarrel with propriety; many days were to pass,
indeed, before he would consent to do more than make inquiries
about Charles James Burroughs, and to permit that aggressive
young man to give a fuller account of himself in writing. It was by
silence that Rose prevailed. Having defended herself against the
charge of immodesty, she declined to urge her own inclination or
the rights of Mr Burroughs; her mute patience did not lack its
effect with the scrupulous but tender parent.

'I am willing to admit, my dear,' said Mr Whiston one evening,
à propos of nothing at all, 'that the falsehood in that young man's
letter gave proof of a certain delicacy.'

'Thank you, father,' replied Rose, very quietly and simply.

It was next morning that the father posted a formal, proper,
self-respecting note of invitation, which bore results.

Baroness (Emmuska) Orczy

THE MYSTERIOUS DEATH ON THE UNDERGROUND RAILWAY

DRAMATIS PERSONAE

THE MAN
who explains each mystery to
THE LADY JOURNALIST
whilst at lunch at an A.B.C.
MR HAZELDENE
(shipping agent).
MRS HAZELDENE
(his wife, found dead on the Underground Railway).
FRANK ERRINGTON
(suspected of her murder).
MR ANDREW CAMPBELL   MR JAMES VERNER
(witnesses before the Magistrates at Bow Street).

I

'Will you be good enough to give me a description of the man who sat next to you just now, while you were having your cup of coffee and scone?' said the man in the corner to me that day.

He had been sitting in his accustomed place when I came into the A.B.C. shop, but had made no remark all the time that I was partaking of my modest luncheon. I was just in the act of thinking how rude he was not to have said 'Good morning', when his abrupt remark caused me to look up.

'Do you know at all if he was tall or short, dark or fair?' he insisted, seemingly not the least disconcerted by my somewhat rude survey of his eccentric personality, 'Can you tell me at all what he was like?'

'Of course I can,' I rejoined impatiently, 'but I don't see that my description of one of the customers of an A.B.C. shop can have the slightest importance.'

He was silent for a minute, while his nervous fingers fumbled about in his capacious pockets in search of the inevitable piece of string. When he had found this necessary 'adjunct to thought', he viewed me again through his half-closed lids, and added maliciously:

'But supposing it were of paramount importance that you should give an accurate description of a man who sat next to you for half-an-hour today, how would you proceed?'

'I should say that he was of medium height—'

'Five foot eight, nine, or ten?' he interrupted quietly.

'How can one tell to an inch or two?' I rejoined crossly. 'He was between colours.'

'What's that?' he inquired blandly.

'Neither fair nor dark – his nose—'

'Well, what was his nose like? Will you sketch it?'

'I am not an artist. His nose was fairly straight – his eyes—'

'Were neither dark nor light – his hair had the same striking peculiarity – he was neither short nor tall – his nose was neither aquiline nor snub —" he recapitulated sarcastically.

'No,' I retorted; 'he was just ordinary-looking.'

'Would you know him again – say tomorrow, and among a number of other men who were "neither tall nor short, dark nor fair, aquiline nor snub-nosed," etc?'

'I don't know – I might – he was certainly not striking enough to be specially remembered.'

'Exactly,' he said, while he leant forward excitedly, for all the world like a jack-in-the-box let loose. 'Precisely; and you are a novelist – call yourself one, at least – and it should be part of your business to notice and describe people. I don't mean only the wonderful personage with the clear Saxon features, the fine blue eyes, the noble brow and classic face, but the ordinary person – the person who represents ninety out of every hundred of his own kind – the average Englishman, say, of the middle classes, who is neither very tall nor very short, who wears a moustache which is neither fair nor dark, but which masks his mouth, and a top hat which hides the shape of his head and brow, a man, in fact, who dresses like hundreds of his fellow creatures, moves like them, speaks like them, has no peculiarity

'Try to describe *him*, to recognise him, say a week hence, among his other eighty-nine doubles; worse still, to swear his life away, if he happened to be implicated in some crime, wherein *your* recognition of him would place the halter round his neck.

'Try that, I say, and having utterly failed you will more readily understand how one of the greatest scoundrels unhung is still at large, and why the mystery on the Underground Railway was never cleared up.

'I think it was the only time in my life that I was seriously tempted to give the police the benefit of my own views upon the matter. You see, though I admire the brute for his cleverness, I did not see that his being unpublished could possibly benefit anyone.

'The Central London Railway had just been opened a few days, and the old Underground was being deserted for the time being for the sake of the novelty of the other line. Anyway, when that particular train steamed into Aldgate at about 4 p.m. on June 18th last, the first-class carriages were all but empty.

'The guard marched up and down the platform looking into all the carriages to see if anyone had left a halfpenny evening paper behind for him, and opening the door of one of the first class compartments, he noticed a lady sitting in the further corner, with her head turned away towards the window evidently oblivious of the fact that on this line, Aldgate is the terminal station.

' "Where are you for, lady?" he said.

'The lady did not move, and the guard stepped into the carriage, thinking that perhaps the lady was asleep. He touched her arm lightly and looked into her face. In his own poetic language he was "struck all of a 'eap." In the glassy eyes, the ashen colour of the cheeks, the rigidity of the head, there was the unmistakable look of death.

'Hastily the guard, having carefully locked the carriage door, summoned a couple of porters, and sent one of them off to the police station, and the other in search of the stationmaster.

'Fortunately at this time of day the up platform is not very crowded, all the traffic tending westward in the afternoon. It was only when an inspector and two police constables, accompanied by a detective in plain clothes and a medical officer, appeared upon the scene, and stood round a first-class railway compartment, that a few idlers realised that something unusual had occurred, and crowded round, eager and curious.

'Thus it was that the later editions of the evening papers, under the sensational heading, "Mysterious Suicide on the Underground Railway", had already an account of the extraordinary event. The medical officer had very soon come to the decision that the guard had not been mistaken, and that life was indeed extinct.

'The lady was young, and must have been very pretty, before the look of fright and horror had so terribly distorted her features. She was very elegantly dressed, and the more frivolous papers were able to give their feminine readers a detailed account of the unfortunate woman's gown, her shoes, hat, and gloves.

'It appears that one of the latter, the one on the right hand, was partly off, leaving the thumb and wrist bare. That hand held a small satchel, which the police opened, with a view to the possible identification of the deceased, but which was found to contain only a little loose silver, some smelling salts, and a small empty bottle which was handed over to the medical officer for purposes of analysis.

'It was the presence of that small bottle which had caused the report to circulate freely that the mysterious case on the Underground Railway was one of suicide. Certain it was that neither about the lady's person, nor in the appearance of the railway carriage, was there the slightest sign of struggle or even of resistance. Only the look in the poor woman's eyes spoke of sudden terror, of the rapid vision of an unexpected and violent death, which probably only lasted an infinitesimal fraction of a second, but which had left its indelible mark upon the face, otherwise so placid and so still.'

II

'The body of the deceased was conveyed to the mortuary. So far, of course, not a soul had been able to identify her, or to throw the slightest light upon the mystery which hung around her death.

'Against that, quite a crowd of idlers – genuinely interested or not – obtained admission to view the body, on the pretext of having lost or mislaid a relative or a friend. At about 8.30 a young man, very well dressed, drove up to the station in a hansom, and sent in his card to the superintendent. It was Mr Hazeldene, shipping agent, of 11, Crown Lane, E.C., and No. 19, Addison Row, Kensington.

'The young man looked in a pitiable state of mental distress; his hand clutched nervously a copy of the *St James's Gazette*, which contained the fatal news. He said very little to the superintendent except that a person who was very dear to him had not returned home that evening.

'He had not felt really anxious until half-an-hour ago, when suddenly he thought of looking at his paper. The description of the deceased lady, though vague, had terribly alarmed him. He had jumped into a hansom, and now begged permission to view the body, in order that his worst fears might be allayed.

'You know what followed, of course,' continued the man in the corner, 'the grief of the young man was truly pitiable. In the woman lying there in a public mortuary before him, Mr Hazeldene had recognised his wife.

'I am waxing melodramatic,' said the man in the corner who looked up at me with a mild and gentle smile, while his nervous fingers vainly endeavoured to add another knot on the scrappy bit of string with which he was continually playing, 'and I fear that your story will savour this time of the penny novelette, but you must admit, and no doubt you remember, that it was an intensely pathetic and truly dramatic moment.

'The unfortunate young husband of the deceased lady was not much worried with questions that night. As a matter of fact he was not in a fit condition to make any coherent statement. It was at the coroner's inquest on the following day, that certain facts came to light, which for the time being seemed to clear up the mystery surrounding Mrs Hazeldene's death, only to plunge that same mystery, later on, into denser gloom than before.

'The first witness at the inquest was, of course, Mr Hazeldene himself. I think everyone's sympathy went out to the young man, as he stood before the coroner and tried to throw what light he could upon the mystery. He was well dressed as he had been the day before, but he looked terribly ill and worried, and no doubt the fact that he had not shaved gave his face a careworn and neglected air.

'It appears that he and the deceased had been married some six years or so, and that they had always been happy in their married life. They had no children. Mrs Hazeldene seemed to enjoy the best of health till lately, when she had had a slight attack of influenza, in which Dr Arthur Jones had attended her. The doctor was present at this moment and would no doubt explain to the coroner and the jury whether he thought that Mrs Hazeldene had the slightest tendency to heart disease, which might have had a sudden and fatal ending.

'The coroner was, of course, very considerate to the bereaved husband. He tried by circumlocution to get at the point he wanted, namely, Mrs Hazeldene's mental condition lately. Mr Hazeldene seemed loth to talk about this. No doubt he had been warned as to the existence of the small bottle found in his wife's satchel.

'It certainly did seem to me at times,' he at last reluctantly admitted, 'that my wife did not seem quite herself. She used to be very gay and bright, and lately, I often saw her in the evening sitting, as if brooding over some matters, which evidently she did not care to communicate to me.'

'Still the coroner insisted, and suggested the small bottle.

'I know, I know,' replied the young man with a short, heavy sigh. 'You mean – the question of suicide – I cannot understand it at all – it seems so sudden and so terrible – she certainly had seemed listless and troubled lately – but only at times – and yesterday morning, when I went to business, she appeared quite herself again, and I suggested that we should go to the opera in the evening. She was delighted, I know, and told me she would do some shopping, and pay a few calls in the afternoon.'

' "Do you know at all where she intended to go when she got into the Underground Railway?"

' "Well, not with certainty. You see she may have meant to get out at Baker Street, and go down to Bond Street to do her shopping. Then again, she sometimes goes to a shop in St Paul's Churchyard, in which case, she would take a ticket to Aldersgate Street; but I cannot say."

' "Now, Mr Hazeldene," said the coroner at last very kindly, "will you try to tell me if there was anything in Mrs Hazeldene's life which you know of, and which might in some measure explain the cause of the distressed state of mind, which you yourself had noticed? Did there exist any financial difficulty which might have preyed upon Mrs Hazeldene's mind; was there any friend – to whose intercourse with Mrs Hazeldene – you – er – at any time took exception to. In fact," added the coroner, as if thankful that he had got over an unpleasant moment, "can you give me the slightest indication which would tend to confirm the suspicion that the unfortunate lady, in a moment of mental anxiety or derangement, may have wished to take her own life."

'There was silence in the court for a few moments. Mr Hazeldene seemed to everyone there present to be labouring under some terrible moral doubt. He looked very pale and wretched, and twice attempted to speak, before he at last said in scarcely audible tones.

"No; there were no financial difficulties of any sort. My wife had an independent fortune of her own – she had no extravagant tastes —"

' "Nor any friend you at any time objected to?" insisted the coroner.

' "Nor any friend, I – at any time objected to," stammered the unfortunate young man, evidently speaking with an effort.

'I was present at the inquest,' resumed the man in the corner, after he had drunk a glass of milk, and ordered another, 'and I can assure you that the most obtuse person there plainly realized that Mr Hazeldene was telling a lie. It was pretty plain to the meanest intelligence that the unfortunate lady had not fallen into a state of morbid dejection for nothing, and that perhaps there existed a third person who could throw more light on her strange and sudden death than the unhappy, bereaved young widower.

'That the death was more mysterious even than it had at first appeared, became very soon apparent. You read the case at the time, no doubt, and must remember the excitement in the public mind caused by the evidence of the two doctors. Dr Arthur Jones, the lady's usual medical man, who had not attended her in a last very slight illness, but who had seen her in a professional capacity fairly recently, declared most emphatically that Mrs Hazeldene suffered from no organic complaint which could possibly have

been the cause of sudden death. Moreover, he had assisted Mr
Andrew Thorton, the district medical officer, in making a postmortem examination, and together they had come to the conclusion that death was due to the action of prussic acid, which had
caused instantaneous failure of the heart, but how the drug had
been administered neither he nor his colleague were at present
able to state.

' "Do I understand, then, Dr Jones, that the deceased died,
poisoned with prussic acid?"

' "Such is my opinion," replied the doctor.

' "Did the bottle found in her satchel contain prussic acid?"

' "It had contained some at one time, certainly."

' "In your opinion, then, the lady caused her own death by
taking a dose of that drug?"

' "Pardon me, I never suggested such a thing; the lady died
poisoned by the drug, but how the drug was administered we
cannot say. By injection of some sort, certainly. The drug certainly was not swallowed; there was not a vestige of it in the
stomach.

' "Yes," added the doctor in reply to another question from the
coroner, "death had probably followed the injection in this case
almost immediately; say within a couple of minutes, or perhaps
three. It was quite possible, that the body would not have more
than one quick and sudden convulsion, perhaps not that; death in
such cases is absolutely sudden and crushing."

'I don't think that at the time anyone in the room realised how
important the doctor's statement was, a statement which, by the
way, was confirmed in all its details by the district medical officer,
who had conducted the postmortem. Mrs Hazeldene had died
suddenly from an injection of prussic acid, administered no one
knew how or when. She had been travelling in a first-class railway
carriage, in a busy time of the day. That young and elegant
woman must have had singular nerve and coolness to go through
the process of a self-inflicted injection of a deadly poison in the
presence of perhaps two or three other persons.

'Mind you, when I say that no one there realised the importance
of the doctor's statement at that moment, I am wrong; there were
three persons, who fully understood at once the gravity of the

situation, and the astounding development which the case was beginning to assume.

'Of course, I should have put myself out of the question,' added my strange interlocutor, with that inimitable self-conceit peculiar to himself. 'I guessed then and there in a moment where the police were going wrong, and where they would go on going wrong until the mysterious death on the Underground Railway had sunk into oblivion, together with the other cases which they mismanage from time to time.

'I said there were three persons who understood the gravity of the two doctors' statements – the other two were, firstly, the detective who had originally examined the railway carriage, a young man of energy and plenty of misguided intelligence, the other was Mr Hazeldene.

'At this point the interesting element of the whole story was first introduced into the proceedings, and this was done through the humble channel of Emma Funnel, Mrs Hazeldene's maid, who, as far as was known then, was the last person who had seen the unfortunate lady alive and had spoken to her.

' "Mrs Hazeldene lunched at home," explained Emma, who was shy, and spoke almost in a whisper, "she seemed well and cheerful. She went out at about half-past three, and told me she was going to Spence's in St Paul's Churchyard, to try on her new tailor-made gown. Mrs Hazeldene had meant to go there in the morning, but was prevented as Mr Errington called."

' "Mr Errington?" asked the coroner casually. "Who is Mr Errington?"

'But this, Emma found difficult to explain. "Mr Errington was – Mr Errington, that's all."

' "Mr Errington was a friend of the family. He lived in a flat in the Albert Mansions. He very often came to Addison Crescent, and generally stayed late."

'Pressed still further with questions, Emma at last stated that latterly Mrs Hazeldene had been to the theatre several times with Mr Errington, and that on those nights the master looked very gloomy, and was very cross.

'Recalled, the young widower was strangely reticent. He gave forth his answers very grudgingly, and the coroner was evidently absolutely satisfied with himself at the marvellous way in which, after a quarter of an hour of firm, yet very kind questionings, he had elicited from the witness what information he wanted.

'Mr Errington was a friend of his wife. He was a gentleman of means, and seemed to have a great deal of time at his command. He himself did not particularly care about Mr Errington, but he certainly had never made any observations to his wife on the subject.

' "But who is Mr Errington?" repeated the coroner once more. "What does he do? What is his business or profession?"

' "He has no business or profession."

' "What is his occupation, then?"

' "He has no special occupation. He has ample private means. But he has a great and very absorbing hobby."

' "What is that?"

' "He spends all his time in chemical experiments, and is, I believe, as an amateur, a very distinguished toxicologist." '

III

'Did you ever see Mr Errington, the gentleman so closely connected with the mysterious death on the Underground Railway?' asked the man in the corner as he placed one or two of his little snapshot photos before me. 'There he is, to the very life. Fairly good-looking, a pleasant face enough, but ordinary, absolutely ordinary.

'It was this absence of any peculiarity which very nearly, but not quite, placed the halter round Mr Errington's neck. But I am going too fast, and you will lose the thread.

'The public, of course, never heard how it actually came about that Mr Errington, the wealthy bachelor of Albert Mansions, of the Grosvenor, and other young dandies' clubs, one fine day found himself before the magistrates at Bow Street charged with being concerned in the death of Mary Beatrice Hazeldene, late of No. 19, Addison Row.

'I can assure you both press and public were literally flabbergasted. You see Mr Errington was a well-known and very popular member of a certain smart section of London society. He was a constant visitor at the opera, the racecourse, the Park, and the Carlton, he had a great many friends, and there was consequently quite a large attendance at the police court that morning.

'What had transpired was this:

'After the very scrappy bits of evidence which came to light at the inquest, two gentlemen bethought themselves that perhaps they had some duty to perform towards the State and the public generally. Accordingly, they had come forward in order to offer to throw what light they could upon the mysterious affair on the Underground Railway.

'The police naturally felt that their information, such as it was, came rather late in the day, but as it proved of paramount importance, and the two gentlemen, moreover, were of undoubtedly good position in the world, they were thankful for what they could get, and acted accordingly; they accordingly brought Mr Errington up before the Magistrate on a charge of murder.

'The accused looked pale and worried when I first caught sight of him in the Court that day, which was not to be wondered at, considering the terrible position in which he found himself.

'He had been arrested at Marseilles, where he was preparing to start for Colombo.

'I don't think he realised how terrible his position really was, until later in the proceedings when all the evidence relating to the arrest had been heard, and Emma Funnel had repeated her statement as to Mr Errington's call at 19, Addison Row in the morning, and Mrs Hazeldene starting off for St Paul's Church-yard at 3:30 in the afternoon.

'Mr Hazeldene had nothing to add to the statements he had made at the coroner's inquest. He had last seen his wife alive on the morning of the fatal day. She had seemed very well and cheerful. I think everyone present understood that he was trying to say as little as possible that could in any way couple his deceased wife's name with that of the accused.

'And yet, from the servant's evidence, it undoubtedly leaked out that Mrs Hazeldene, who was young, pretty, and evidently fond of admiration, had once or twice annoyed her husband by somewhat open, yet perfectly innocent, flirtations with Mr Errington.

'I think everyone was most agreeably impressed by the widower's moderate and dignified attitude. You will see his photo there, among this bundle. That is just how he appeared in court. In deep black, of course, but without any sign of ostentation in his mourning. He had allowed his beard to grow lately, and wore it closely cut in a point. After his evidence, the sensation of the day occurred. A tall dark-haired man with the word "City" written metaphorically all over him, had kissed the book, and was waiting to tell the truth, and nothing but the truth.

'He gave his name as Andrew Campbell, head of the firm of Campbell & Co., brokers, of Throgmorton Street.

'In the afternoon of June 18th Mr Campbell, travelling on the Underground Railway, had noticed a very pretty woman in the same carriage as himself. She had asked him if she was in the right train for Aldersgate. Mr Campbell replied in the affirmative, and then buried himself in the Stock Exchange quotations of his evening paper. At Gower Street, a gentleman in a tweed suit and bowler hat got into the carriage, and took a seat opposite the lady.

'She seemed very much astonished at seeing him, but Mr Andrew Campbell did not recollect the exact words she said.

'The two talked to one another a good deal, and certainly the lady appeared animated and cheerful. Witness took no notice of them; he was very much engrossed in some calculations, and finally got out at Farringdon Street. He noticed that the man in the tweed suit also got out close behind him, having shaken hands with the lady, and said in a pleasant way: '*Au revoir!* Don't be late tonight.' Mr Campbell did not hear the lady's reply, and soon lost sight of the man in the crowd.

'Everyone was on tenterhooks, and eagerly waiting for the palpitating moment when witness would describe and identify the man who last had seen and spoken to the unfortunate woman, within five minutes probably of her strange and unaccountable death. Personally, I knew what was coming before the Scotch stockbroker spoke. I could have jotted down the graphic and lifelike description he would give of a probable murderer. It would have fitted equally well the man who sat and had luncheon at this table just now; it would certainly have described five out of every ten young Englishmen you know.

'The individual was of medium height, he wore a moustache which was not very fair nor yet very dark, his hair was between colours. He wore a bowler hat, and a tweed suit, and – and – that was all – Mr Campbell might perhaps know him again, but then again, he might not – he was not paying much attention – the gentleman was sitting on the same side of the carriage as himself – and he had his hat on all the time. He himself was busy with his newspaper – yes – he might know him but he really could not say –

'Mr Andrew Campbell's evidence was not worth very much, you will say. No. It was not in itself, and would not have justified any arrest were it not for the additional statements made by Mr James Verner, manager of Messrs Rodney & Co., colour printers.

'Mr Verner is a personal friend of Mr Andrew Campbell, and it appears that at Farringdon Street, where he was waiting for his train, he saw Mr Campbell get out of a first-class railway carriage. Mr Verner spoke to him for a second, and then, just as the train was moving off, he stepped into the same compartment which had just been vacated by the stockbroker, and the man in the tweed suit. He vaguely recollects a lady sitting in the opposite corner to his own with her face turned away from him, apparently asleep, but he paid no special attention to her. He was like nearly all business men when they are travelling – engrossed in his paper. Presently a special quotation interested him; he wished to make a note of it, took out a pencil from his waistcoat pocket, and seeing a clean piece of paste-board on the floor, he picked it up, and scribbled on it the memoranda he wished to keep. He then slipped the card into his pocketbook.

' "It was only two or three days later," added Mr Verner in the midst of breathless silence, "that I had occasion to refer to these same notes again. In the meanwhile the papers had been full of the mysterious death on the Underground Railway, and the names of those connected with it were pretty familiar to me. It was, therefore, with much astonishment that on looking at the paste-board which I had casually picked up in the railway carriage I saw the name on it 'Frank Errington'." '

'There was no doubt that the sensation in Court was almost unprecedented. Never since the days of the Fenchurch Street mystery and the trial of Smethurst had I seen so much excitement. Mind you, I was not excited – I knew by now every detail of that crime as if I had committed it myself. In fact, I could not have done it better, although I have been a student of crime for many years now. Many people there – his friends, mostly – believed that Errington was doomed. I think he thought so too, for I could see that his face was terribly white, and he now and then passed his tongue over his lips, as if they were parched.

'You see he was in the awful dilemma – a perfectly natural one, by the way – of being absolutely incapable of *proving* an alibi. The crime – if crime there was – had been committed three weeks ago. A man about town like Mr Frank Errington might remember that he spent certain hours of a special afternoon at his club, or in the Park, but it is very doubtful in nine cases out of ten if he can find a friend who could positively swear as to having seen him there. No! no! Mr Errington was in a tight corner and he knew it. You see, there were – besides the evidence – two or three circumstances which did not improve matters for him. His hobby in the direction of toxicology, to begin with. The police had found in his room every description of poisonous substances, incuding prussic acid.

'Then, again, that journey to Marseilles, the start for Colombo, was, though perfectly innocent, a very unfortunate one. Mr Errington had gone on an aimless voyage, but the public thought that he had fled terrified at his own crime. Sir Arthur Inglewood, however, here again displayed his marvellous skill on behalf of his client by the masterly way in which he literally turned all the witnesses for the Crown inside out.

'Having first got Mr Andrew Campbell to state positively that in the accused he certainly did *not* recognise the man in the tweed suit, the eminent lawyer, after twenty minutes' cross-examination, had so completely upset the stockbroker's equanimity that it is very likely he would not have recognised his own office boy.

'But through all his flurry and all his annoyance Mr Andrew Campbell remained very sure of one thing; namely, that the lady was alive and cheerful, and talking pleasantly with the man in the tweed suit up to the moment when the latter, having shaken hands with her, left her with a pleasant "*Au revoir!* Don't be late tonight." He had heard neither scream nor struggle, and in his opinion, if the individual in the tweed suit had administered a dose of poison to his companion, it must have been with her own knowledge and free will; and the lady in the train most emphatically neither looked nor spoke like a woman prepared for a sudden and violent death.

'Mr James Verner, against that, swore equally positively that he had stood in full view of the carriage door, from the moment that Mr Campbell got out until he himself stepped into the compartment, that there was no one else in that carriage between Farringdon Street and Aldgate, and that the lady, to the best of his belief, had made no movement during the whole of that journey.

IV

'No; Frank Errington was *not* committed for trial on the capital charge,' said the man in the corner with one of his sardonic smiles, 'thanks to the cleverness of Sir Arthur Inglewood, his lawyer. He absolutely denied his identity with the man in the tweed suit, and swore he had not seen Mrs Hazeldene since eleven o'clock in the morning of that fatal day. There was no *proof* that he had; moreover, according to Mr Campbell's opinion, the man in the tweed suit was in all probability not the murderer. Common sense would not admit that a woman could have a deadly poison injected into her without her knowledge, while chatting pleasantly to her murderer.

'Mr Errington lives abroad now. He is about to marry. I don't think any of his real friends for a moment believed that he committed the dastardly crime. The police think they know better. They do know this much, that it could not have been a case of suicide, that if the man who undoubtedly travelled with Mrs· Hazeldene on that fatal afternoon had no crime upon his conscience he would long ago have come forward and thrown what light he could upon the mystery.

'As to who that man was, the police in their blindness have not the faintest doubt. Under the unshakable belief that Errington is guilty they have spent the last few months in unceasing labour to try and find further and strong proofs of his guilt. But they won't find them, because there are none. There are no positive proofs against the actual murderer, for he was one of those clever blackguards who think of everything, forsee every eventuality, who know human nature well, and can foretell exactly what evidence will be brought against them, and act accordingly.

'This blackguard from the first kept the figure, the personality, of Frank Errington before his mind. Frank Errington was the dust which the scoundrel threw metaphorically in the eyes of the police, and you must admit that he succeeded in blinding them – to the extent even of making them entirely forget the one simple little sentence, overheard by Mr Andrew Campbell, and which was, of course, the clue to the whole thing – the only slip the cunning rogue made – '*Au revoir!* Don't be late tonight.' Mrs Hazeldene was going that night to the opera with her husband —

'You are astonished?' he added with a shrug of the shoulders, 'you do not see the tragedy yet, as I have seen it before me all along. The frivolous young wife, the flirtation with the friend? – all a blind, all pretence. I took the trouble which the police should have taken immediately, of finding out something about the finances of the Hazeldene *ménage*. Money is in nine cases out of ten the keynote to a crime. I found that the will of Mary Beatrice Hazeldene had been proved by the husband, her sole executor, the estate being sworn at £15,000. I found out, moreover, that Mr Edward Sholto Hazeldene was a poor shipper's clerk when he married the daughter of a wealthy builder in Kensington – and then I made note of the fact that the disconsolate widower had allowed his beard to grow since the death of his wife.

'There's no doubt that he was a clever rogue,' added the strange creature leaning excitedly over the table, and peering into my face. 'Do you know how that deadly poison was injected into the poor woman's system? By the simplest of all means, one known to every scoundrel in Southern Europe. A ring – yes! a ring, which has a tiny hollow needle capable of holding a sufficient quantity of prussic acid to have killed two persons instead of one. The man in the tweed suit shook hands with his fair companion – probably she hardly felt the prick, not sufficiently in any case to make her utter a scream. And, mind you, the scoundrel had every facility, through his friendship with Mr Errington, of procuring what poison he required, not to mention his friend's visiting card. We cannot gauge how many months ago he began to try and copy Frank Errington in his style of dress, the cut of his moustache, his general appearance, making the change probably so gradual, that no one in his own *entourage* would notice it. He selected for his model a man his own height and build, with the same coloured hair.'

'But there was the terrible risk of being identified by his fellow-traveller in the Underground,' I suggested.

'Yes, there certainly was that risk; he chose to take it, and he was wise. He reckoned that several days would in any case elapse before that person, who, by the way, was a business man absorbed in his newspaper, would actually see him again. The great secret of successful crime is to study human nature,' added the man in the corner, as he began looking for his hat and coat. 'Edward Hazeldene knew it well.'

'But the ring?' I said.

'He may have bought that when he was on his honeymoon,' he suggested with a grim chuckle, 'the tragedy was not planned in a week; it may have taken years to mature. But you will own that there goes a frightful scoundrel unhung. I have left you his photograph as he was a year ago, and as he is now. You will see he has shaved his beard again, but also his moustache. I fancy he is a friend now of Mr Andrew Campbell.'

He left me wondering. I don't know what I did believe; his whole story sounded so farfetched and strange. Was he really giving me the results of continued thought, or was he experimenting as to exactly how far the credulity of a lady novelist could go?

Joseph Conrad

AMY FOSTER

Kennedy is a country doctor, and lives in Colebrook, on the shores of Eastbay. The high ground rising abruptly behind the red roofs of the little town crowds the quaint High Street against the wall which defends it from the sea. Beyond the sea-wall there curves for miles in a vast and regular sweep the barren beach of shingle, with the village of Brenzett standing out darkly across the water, a spire in a clump of trees; and still further out the perpendicular column of a lighthouse, looking in the distance no bigger than a lead-pencil, marks the vanishing-point of the land. The country at the back of Brenzett is low and flat; but the bay is fairly well sheltered from the seas, and occasionally a big ship, windbound or through stress of weather, makes use of the anchoring ground a mile and a half due north from you as you stand at the back door of the 'Ship Inn' in Brenzett. A dilapidated windmill near by lifting its shattered arms from a mound no loftier than a rubbish-heap, and a Martello tower squatting at the water's edge half a mile to the south of the Coastguard cottages, are familiar to the skippers of small craft. These are the official sea-marks for the patch of trustworthy bottom represented on the Admiralty charts by an irregular oval of dots enclosing several figures six, with a tiny anchor engraved among them, and the legend 'mud and shells' over all.

The brow of the upland overtops the square tower of the Colebrook Church. The slope is green and looped by a white road. Ascending along this road, you open a valley broad and shallow, a wide green trough of pastures and hedges merging inland into a vista of purple tints and flowing lines closing the view.

In this valley down to Brenzett and Colebrook and up to Darnford, the market town fourteen miles away, lies the practice of my friend Kennedy. He had begun life as surgeon in the Navy, and afterwards had been the companion of a famous traveller, in the days when there were continents with unexplored interiors. His papers on the fauna and flora made him known to scientific societies. And now he had come to a country practice – from choice. The penetrating power of his mind, acting like a corrosive fluid, had destroyed his ambition, I fancy. His intelligence is of a scientific order, of an investigating habit, and of that unappeasable curiosity which believes that there is a particle of a general truth in every mystery.

A good many years ago now, on my return from abroad, he invited me to stay with him. I came readily enough, and as he could not neglect his patients to keep me company, he took me on his rounds – thirty miles or so of an afternoon, sometimes. I waited for him on the roads; the horse reached after the leafy twigs, and, sitting high in the dogcart, I could hear Kennedy's laugh through the half-open door of some cottage. He had a big, hearty laugh that would have fitted a man twice his size, a brisk manner, a bronzed face, and a pair of grey, profoundly attentive eyes. He had the talent of making people talk to him freely, and an inexhaustible patience in listening to their tales.

One day, as we trotted out of a large village into a shady bit of road, I saw on our left hand a low, black cottage, with diamond panes in the windows, a creeper on the end wall, a roof of shingle, and some roses climbing on the rickety trellis-work of the tiny porch. Kennedy pulled up to a walk. A woman, in full sunlight, was throwing a dripping blanket over a line stretched between two old apple-trees. And as the bob-tailed, long-necked chestnut, trying to get his head, jerked the left hand, covered by a thick dogskin glove, the doctor raised his voice over the hedge: 'How's your child, Amy?'

I had the time to see her dull face, red, not with a mantling blush, but as if her flat cheeks had been vigorously slapped, and to take in the squat figure, the scanty, dusty brown hair drawn into a tight knot at the back of the head. She looked quite young. With a distinct catch in her breath, her voice sounded low and timid.

'He's well, thank you.'

We trotted again. 'A young patient of yours?' I said; and the doctor, flicking the chestnut absently, muttered, 'Her husband used to be.'

'She seems a dull creature,' I remarked listlessly.

'Precisely,' said Kennedy. 'She is very passive. It's enough to look at the red hands hanging at the end of those short arms, at those slow, prominent brown eyes to know the inertness of her mind – an inertness that one would think made it everlastingly safe from all the surprises of imagination. And yet which of us is safe? At any rate, such as you see her, she had enough imagination to fall in love. She's the daughter of one Isaac Foster, who from a small farmer has sunk into a shepherd; the beginning of his misfortunes dating from his runaway marriage with the cook of his widowed father – a well-to-do, apoplectic grazier, who passionately struck his name off his will, and had been heard to utter threats against his life. But this old affair, scandalous enough to serve as a motive for a Greek tragedy, arose from the similarity of their characters. There are other tragedies, less scandalous and of a subtler poignancy, arising from irreconcilable differences and from that fear of the Incomprehensible that hangs over all our heads – over all our heads. . . .'

The tired chestnut dropped into a walk; and the rim of the sun, all red in a speckless sky, touched familiarly the smooth top of a ploughed rise near the road as I had seen it times innumerable touch the distant horizon of the sea. The uniform brownness of the harrowed field glowed with a rosy tinge, as though the powdered clods had sweated out in minute pearls of blood the toil of uncounted ploughmen. From the edge of a copse a wagon with two horses was rolling gently along the ridge. Raised above our heads upon the skyline, it loomed up against the red sun, triumphantly big, enormous, like a chariot of giants drawn by two slow-stepping steeds of legendary proportions. And the clumsy figure of the man plodding at the head of the leading horse projected itself on the background of the Infinite with a heroic uncouthness. The end of his carter's whip quivered high up in the blue. Kennedy discoursed.

'She's the eldest of a large family. At the age of fifteen they put her out to service at the New Barns Farm. I attended Mrs Smith, the tenant's wife, and saw that girl there for the first time. Mrs Smith, a genteel person with a sharp nose, made her put on a black dress every afternoon. I don't know what induced me to notice her at all. There are faces that call your attention by a curious want of definiteness in their whole aspect, as, walking in a mist, you peer attentively at a vague shape which, after all, may be nothing more curious or strange than a signpost. The only peculiarity I perceived in her was a slight hesitation in her utterance, a sort of preliminary stammer which passes away with the first word. When sharply spoken to, she was apt to lose her head at once; but her heart was of the kindest. She had never been heard to express a dislike for a single human being, and she was tender to every living creature. She was devoted to Mrs Smith, to Mr Smith, to their dogs, cats, canaries; and as to Mrs Smith's grey parrot, its peculiarities exercised upon her a positive fascination. Nevertheless, when that outlandish bird, attacked by the cat, shrieked for help in human accents, she ran out into the yard stopping her ears, and did not prevent the crime. For Mrs Smith this was another evidence of her stupidity; on the other hand, her want of charm, in view of Smith's well-known frivolousness, was a great recommendation. Her short-sighted eyes would swim with pity for a poor mouse in a trap, and she had been seen once by some boys on her knees in the wet grass helping a toad in difficulties. If it's true, as some German fellow has said, that without phosphorous there is no thought, it is still more true that there is no kindness of heart without a certain amount of imagination. She had some. She had even more than is necessary to understand suffering and to be moved by pity. She fell in love under circumstances that leave no room for doubt in the matter; for you need imagination to form a notion of beauty at all, and still more to discover your ideal in an unfamiliar shape.

'How this aptitude came to her, what it did feed upon, is an inscrutable mystery. She was born in the village, and had never been further away from it than Colebrook or perhaps Darnford. She lived for four years with the Smiths. New Barns is an isolated farmhouse a mile away from the road, and she was content to look day after day at the same fields, hollows, rises; at the trees and the hedgerows; at the faces of the four men about the farm, always the same – day after day, month after month, year after year. She never showed a desire for conversation, and, as it seemed to me, she did not know how to smile. Sometimes of a fine

Sunday afternoon she would put on her best dress, a pair of stout boots, a large grey hat trimmed with a black feather (I've seen her in that finery), seize an absurdly slender parasol, climb over two stiles, tramp over three fields and along two hundred yards of road – never further. There stood Foster's cottage. She would help her mother to give their tea to the younger children, wash up the crockery, kiss the little ones, and go back to the farm. That was all. All the rest, all the change, all the relaxation. She never seemed to wish for anything more. And then she fell in love. She fell in love silently, obstinately – perhaps helplessly. It came slowly, but when it came it worked like a powerful spell; it was love as the Ancients understood it: an irresistible and fateful impulse – a possession! Yes, it was in her to become haunted and possessed by a face, by a presence, fatally, as though she had been a pagan worshipper of form under a joyous sky – and to be awakened at last from that mysterious forgetfulness of self, from that enchantment, from that transport, by a fear resembling the unaccountable terror of a brute. . . .'

With the sun hanging low on its western limit, the expanse of the grass-lands framed in the counterscarps of the rising ground took on a gorgeous and sombre aspect. A sense of penetrating sadness, like that inspired by a grave strain of music disengaged itself from the silence of the fields. The men we met walked past, slow, unsmiling, with downcast eyes, as if the melancholy of an over-burdened earth had weighted their feet, bowed their shoulders, borne down their glances.

'Yes,' said the doctor to my remark, 'one would think the earth is under a curse, since of all her children these that cling to her the closest are uncouth in body and as leaden of gait as if their very hearts were loaded with chains. But here on this same road you might have seen amongst these heavy men a being lithe, supple and long-limbed, straight like a pine, with something striving upwards in his appearance as though the heart within him had been buoyant. Perhaps it was only the force of the contrast, but when he was passing one of these villagers here, the soles of his feet did not seem to me to touch the dust of the road. He vaulted over the stiles, paced these slopes with a long elastic stride that made him noticeable at a great distance, and had lustrous black eyes. He was so different from the mankind around that, with his freedom of movement, his soft – a little startled – glance, his olive complexion and graceful bearing, his humanity suggested to me the nature of a woodland creature. He came from there.'

The doctor pointed with his whip, and from the summit of the descent seen over the rolling tops of the trees in a park by the side of the road, appeared the level sea far below us, like the floor of an immense edifice inlaid with bands of dark ripple, with still trails of glitter, ending in a belt of glassy water at the foot of the sky. The light blurr of smoke, from an invisible steamer, faded on the great clearness of the horizon like the mist of a breath on a mirror; and, inshore, the white sails of a coaster, with the appearance of disentangling themselves slowly from under the branches, floated clear of the foliage of the trees.

'Shipwrecked in the bay?' I said.

'Yes; he was a castaway. A poor emigrant from Central Europe bound to America and washed ashore here in a storm. And for him, who knew nothing of the earth, England was an undiscovered country. It was some time before he learned its name; and for all I know he might have expected to find wild beasts or wild men here, when, crawling in the dark over the sea-wall, he rolled down the other side into a dyke, where it was another miracle he didn't get drowned. But he struggled instinctively like an animal under a net, and this blind struggle threw him out into a field. He must have been, indeed, of a tougher fibre than he looked to withstand without expiring such buffetings, the violence of his exertions, and so much fear. Later on, in his broken English that resembled curiously the speech of a young child, he told me himself that he put his trust in God, believing he was no longer in this world. And truly – he would add – how was he to know? He fought his way against the rain and the gale on all fours, and crawled at last among some sheep huddled close under the lee of a hedge. They ran off in all directions, bleating in the darkness, and he welcomed the first familiar sound he heard on these shores. It must have been two in the morning then. And this is all we know of the manner of his landing, though he did not arrive unattended by any means. Only his grisly company did not begin to come ashore till much later in the day. . . .'

The doctor gathered the reins, clicked his tongue; we trotted down the hill. Then turning, almost directly, a sharp corner into the High Street, we rattled over the stones and were home.

Late in the evening, Kennedy, breaking a spell of moodiness that had come over him, returned to the story. Smoking his pipe, he paced the long room from end to end. A reading-lamp concentrated all its light upon the papers on his desk; and, sitting by the open window, I saw, after the windless, scorching day, the frigid splendour of a hazy sea lying motionless under the moon. Not a whisper, not a splash, not a stir of the shingle, not a footstep, not a sigh came up from the earth below – never a sign of life but the scent of climbing jasmine: and Kennedy's voice, speaking behind me, passed through the wide casement, to vanish outside in a chill and sumptuous stillness.

'. . . The relations of shipwrecks in the olden time tell us of much suffering. Often the castaways were only saved from drowning to die miserably from starvation on a barren coast; others suffered violent death or else slavery, passing through years of precarious existence with people to whom their strangeness was an object of suspicion, dislike or fear. We read about these things, and they are very pitiful. It is indeed hard upon a man to find himself a lost stranger, helpless, incomprehensible, and of a mysterious origin, in some obscure corner of the earth. Yet amongst all the adventurers shipwrecked in all the wild parts of the world, there is not one, it seems to me, that ever had to suffer a fate so simply tragic as the man I am speaking of, the most innocent of adventurers cast out by the sea in the bight of this bay, almost within sight from this very window.

'He did not know the name of his ship. Indeed, in the course of time we discovered he did not even know that ships had names – "like Christian people"; and when, one day, from the top of the Talfourd Hill, he beheld the sea lying open to his view, his eyes roamed afar, lost in an air of wild surprise, as though he had never seen such a sight before. And probably he had not. As far as I could make out, he had been hustled together with many others on board an emigrant-ship lying at the mouth of the Elbe, too bewildered to take note of his surroundings, too weary to see anything, too anxious to care. They were driven below into the 'tween-deck and battened down from the very start. It was a low timber dwelling – he would say – with wooden beams overhead, like the houses in his country, but you went into it down a ladder. It was very large, very cold, damp and sombre, with places in the manner of wooden boxes where people had to sleep one above another, and it kept on rocking all ways at once all the time. He crept into one of these boxes and lay down there in the clothes in which he had left his home many days before, keeping his bundle and his stick by his side. People groaned, children cried, water dripped, the lights went out, the walls of the place creaked, and everything was being shaken so that in one's little box one dared not lift one's head. He had lost touch with his only companion (a young man from the same valley, he said), and all the time a great noise of wind went on outside and heavy blows fell – boom! boom! An awful sickness overcame him, even to the point of making him neglect his prayers. Besides, one could not tell whether it was morning or evening. It seemed always to be night in that place.

'Before that he had been travelling a long, long time on the iron track. He looked out of the window, which had a wonderfully clear glass in it, and the trees, the houses, the fields, and the long roads seemed to fly round and round about him till his head swam. He gave me to understand that he had on his passage beheld uncounted multitudes of people – whole nations – all dressed in such clothes as the rich wear. Once he was made to get out of the carriage, and slept through a night on a bench in a house of bricks with his bundle under his head; and once for many hours he had to sit on a floor of flat stones dozing, with his knees up and with his bundle between his feet. There was a roof over him, which seemed made of glass, and was so high that the tallest mountain-pine he has ever seen would have had room to grow under it. Steam-machines rolled in at one end and out at the other. People swarmed more than you can see on a feast-day round the miraculous Holy Image in the yard of the Carmelite Convent down in the plains where, before he left his home, he drove his mother in a wooden cart: – a pious old woman who wanted to offer prayers and make a vow for his safety. He could not give me an idea of how large and lofty and full of noise and smoke and gloom, and clang of iron, the place was, but some one had told him it was called Berlin. Then they rang a bell, and another steam-machine came in, and again he was taken on and on through a land that wearied his eyes by its flatness without a single bit of a hill to be seen anywhere. One more night he spent shut up in a building like a good stable with a litter of straw on the floor, guarding his bundle amongst a lot of men, of whom not one could understand a single word he said. In the morning they were all led down to the stony shores of an extremely broad muddy river, flowing not between hills but between houses that seemed immense. There was a steam-machine that went on the water and they all stood upon it packed tight, only now there were with them many women and children who made much noise. A cold rain fell, the wind blew in his face; he was wet through, and his teeth chattered. He and the young man from the same valley took each other by the hand.

'They thought they were being taken to America straight away, but suddenly the steam-machine bumped against the side of a thing like a great house on the water. The walls were smooth and black, and there uprose, growing from the roof as it were, bare trees in the shape of crosses, extremely high. That's how it appeared to him then, for he had never seen a ship before. This was the ship that was going to swim all the way to America. Voices shouted, everything swayed; there was a ladder dipping up and down. He went up on his hands and knees in mortal fear of falling into the water below, which made a great splashing. He got separated from his companion, and when he descended into the bottom of that ship his heart seemed to melt suddenly within him.

'It was then also, as he told me, that he lost contact for good and all with one of those three men who the summer before had been going about through all the little towns in the foothills of his country. They would arrive on market-days driving in a peasant's cart, and would set up an office in an inn or some other Jew's house. There were three of them, of whom one with a long beard looked venerable; and they had red cloth collars round their necks and gold lace on their sleeves like Government officials. They sat proudly behind a long table; and in the next room, so that the common people shouldn't hear, they kept a cunning telegraph machine, through which they could talk to the Emperor of America. The fathers hung about the door, but the young men of the mountains would crowd up to the table asking many questions, for there was work to be got all the year round at three dollars a day in America, and no military service to do.

'But the American Kaiser would not take everybody. Oh no! He himself had a great difficulty in getting accepted, and the venerable man in uniform had to go out of the room several times to work the telegraph on his behalf. The American Kaiser engaged him at last at three dollars, he being young and strong. However, many able young men backed out, afraid of the great distance; besides, those only who had some money could be taken. There were some who sold their huts and their land because it cost a lot of money to get to America; but then, once there, you had three dollars a day, and if you were clever you could find places where true gold could be picked up on the ground. His father's house was getting over full. Two of his brothers were married and had children. He promised to send money home from America by post twice a year. His father sold an old cow, a pair of piebald mountain ponies of his own raising, and a cleared plot of fair pasture land on the sunny slope of a pine-clad pass to a Jew inn-keeper, in order to pay the people of the ship that took men to America to get rich in a short time.

'He must have been a real adventurer at heart, for how many of the greatest enterprises in the conquest of the earth had for their beginning just such a bargaining away of the paternal cow for the mirage of true gold far away! I have been telling you more or less in my own words what I learned fragmentarily in the course of two or three years, during which I seldom missed an opportunity of a friendly chat with him. He told me this story of his adventure with many flashes of white teeth and lively glances of black eyes, at first in a sort of anxious baby-talk, then, as he acquired the language, with great fluency, but always with that singing, soft, and at the same time vibrating intonation that instilled a strangely penetrating power into the sound of the most familiar English words, as if they had been the words of an unearthly language. And he always would come to an end, with many emphatic shakes of his head, upon that awful sensation of his heart melting within him directly he set foot on board that ship. Afterwards there seemed to come for him a period of blank ignorance, at any rate as to facts. No doubt he must have been abominably seasick and abominably unhappy – this soft and passionate adventurer, taken thus out of his knowledge, and feeling bitterly as he lay in his emigrant bunk his utter loneliness; for his was a highly sensitive nature. The next thing we know of him for certain is that he had been hiding in Hammond's pig-pound by the side of the road to Norton, six miles, as the crow flies, from the sea. Of these experiences he was unwilling to speak: they seemed to have seared into his soul a sombre sort of wonder and indignation. Through the rumours of the countryside, which lasted for a good many days after his arrival, we know that the fisherman of West Colebrook had been disturbed and startled by heavy knocks against the walls of weatherboard cottages, and by a voice crying piercingly strange words in the night. Several of them turned out even, but, no doubt, he had fled in sudden alarm at their rough angry tones hailing each other in the darkness. A sort of frenzy must have helped him up the steep Norton hill. It was he, no doubt, who early the following morning had been seen lying (in a swoon, I should say) on the roadside grass by the Brenzett carrier, who actually got down to have a nearer look, but drew back, intimidated by the perfect immobility, and by something queer in the aspect of that tramp, sleeping so still under the showers. As the day advanced, some children came dashing into school at Norton in such a fright that the schoolmistress went out and spoke indignantly to a "horrid-looking man" on the road. He edged away, hanging his head, for a few steps, and then suddenly ran off with extraordinary fleetness. The driver of Mr Bradley's milk-cart made no secret of it that he had lashed with his whip at a hairy sort of gipsy fellow who, jumping up at a turn of the road by the Vents, made a snatch at the pony's bridle. And he caught him a good one too, right over the face, he said, that made him drop down in the mud a jolly sight quicker than he had jumped up; but it was a good half a mile before he could stop the pony. Maybe that in his desperate endeavours to get help, and in need to get in touch with some one, the poor devil had tried to stop the cart. Also three boys confessed afterwards to throwing stones at a funny tramp, knocking about all wet and muddy, and, it seemed, very drunk, in the narrow deep lane by the limekilns. All this was the talk of three villages for days; but we have Mrs Finn's (the wife of Smith's waggoner) unimpeachable testimony that she saw him get over the low wall of Hammond's pig-pound and lurch straight at her, babbling aloud in a voice that was enough to make one die of fright. Having the baby with her in a perambulator, Mrs Finn called out to him to go away, and as he persisted in coming nearer, she hit him courageously with her umbrella over the head, and, without once looking back, ran like the wind with the perambulator as far as the first house in the village. She stopped then, out of breath, and spoke to old Lewis, hammering there at a heap of stones; and the old chap, taking off his immense black wire goggles, got up on his shaky legs to look where she pointed. Together they followed with their eyes the figure of the man running over a field; they saw him fall down, pick himself up, and run on again, staggering and waving his long arms above his head, in the direction of the New Barns Farm. From that moment he is plainly in the toils of his obscure and touching destiny. There is no doubt after this of what happened to him. All is certain now: Mrs Smith's intense terror; Amy Foster's stolid conviction held against the other's nervous attack, that the man "meant no harm"; Smith's exasperation (on his return from Darnford Market) at finding the dog barking himself into a fit, the back-door locked, his wife in hysterics; and all for an unfortunate dirty tramp, supposed to be even then lurking in his stackyard. Was he? He would teach him to frighten women.

'Smith is notoriously hot-tempered, but the sight of some nondescript and miry creature sitting cross-legged amongst a lot of loose straw, and swinging itself to and fro like a bear in a cage, made him pause. Then this tramp stood up silently before him, one mass of mud and filth from head to foot. Smith, alone amongst his stacks with this apparition, in the stormy twilight ringing with the infuriated barking of the dog, felt the dread of an inexplicable strangeness. But when that being, parting with his black hands the long matted locks that hung before his face, as you part the two halves of a curtain, looked out at him with glistening, wild, black-and-white eyes, the weirdness of this silent encounter fairly staggered him. He has admitted since (for the story has been a legitimate subject of conversation about here for years) that he made more than one step backwards. Then a sudden burst of rapid, senseless speech persuaded him at once that he had to do with an escaped lunatic. In fact, that impression never wore off completely. Smith has not in his heart given up his secret conviction of the man's essential insanity to this very day.

'As the creature approached him, jabbering in a most discomposing manner, Smith (unaware that he was being addressed as "gracious lord", and adjured in God's name to afford food and shelter) kept on speaking firmly but gently to it, and retreating all the time into the other yard. At last, watching his chance, by a sudden charge he bundled him headlong into the wood-lodge, and instantly shot the bolt. Thereupon he wiped his brow, though the day was cold. He had done his duty to the community by shutting up a wandering and probably dangerous maniac. Smith isn't a hard man at all, but he had room in his brain only for that one idea of lunacy. He was not imaginative enough to ask himself whether the man might not be perishing with cold and hunger. Meantime, at first, the maniac made a great deal of noise in the lodge. Mrs Smith was screaming upstairs, where she had locked herself in her bedroom; but Amy Foster sobbed piteously at the kitchen-door, wringing her hands and muttering, "Don't! don't!" I daresay Smith had a rough time of it that evening with one noise and another, and this insane, disturbing voice crying obstinately through the door only added to his irritation. He couldn't possibly have connected this troublesome lunatic with the sinking of a ship in Eastbay, of which there had been a rumour in the Darnford market-place. And I daresay the man inside had been very near to insanity on that night. Before his excitement collapsed and he became unconscious he was throwing himself violently about in the dark, rolling on some dirty sacks, and biting his fists with rage, cold, hunger, amazement, and despair.

'He was a mountaineer of the eastern range of the Carpathians, and the vessel sunk the night before in Eastbay was the Hamburg emigrant-ship *Herzogin Sophia-Dorothea*, of appalling memory.

'A few months later we could read in the paper the accounts of the bogus "Emigration Agencies" among the Sclavonian peasantry in the more remote provinces of Austria. The object of these scoundrels was to get hold of the poor ignorant people's homesteads, and they were in league with the local usurers. They exported their victims through Hamburg mostly. As to the ship, I had watched her out of this very window, reaching close-hauled under short canvas into the bay on a dark, threatening afternoon. She came to an anchor, correctly by the chart, off the Brenzett Coastguard station. I remember before the night fell looking out again at the outlines of her spars and rigging that stood out dark and pointed on a background of ragged, slaty clouds like another and a slighter spire to the left of the Brenzett church-tower. In the evening the wind rose. At midnight I could hear in my bed the terrific gusts and the sounds of a driving deluge.

'About that time the Coastguardmen thought they saw the lights of a steamer over the anchoring-ground. In a moment they vanished; but it is clear that another vessel of some sort had tried for shelter in the bay on that awful, blind night, had rammed the German ship amidships (a breach – as one of the divers told me afterwards – "that you could sail a Thames barge through"), and then had gone out either scathless or damaged, who shall say; but had gone out, unknown, unseen, and fatal, to perish mysteriously at sea. Of her nothing ever came to light, and yet the hue and cry that was raised all over the world would have found her out if she had been in existence anywhere on the face of the waters.

'A completeness without a clue, and a stealthly silence as of a neatly executed crime, characterize this murderous disaster, which, as you may remember, had its gruesome celebrity. The wind would have prevented the loudest outcries from reaching the shore; there had been evidently no time for signals of distress. It was death without any sort of fuss. The Hamburg ship, filling all at once, capsized as she sank, and at daylight there was not even the end of a spar to be seen above water. She was missed, of course, and at first the Coastguardmen surmised that she had either dragged her anchor or parted her cable some time during the night, and had been blown out to sea. Then, after the tide turned, the wreck must have shifted a little and released some of the bodies, because a child – a little fair-haired child in a red frock – came ashore abreast of the Martello tower. By the afternoon you could see along three miles of beach dark figures with bare legs dashing in and out of the tumbling foam, and rough-looking men, women with hard faces, children, mostly fair-haired, were being carried, stiff and dripping, on stretchers, on wattles, on ladders, in a long procession past the door of the "Ship Inn", to be laid out in a row under the north wall of the Brenzett Church.

'Officially, the body of the little girl in the red frock is the first thing that came ashore from that ship. But I have patients amongst the seafaring population of West Colebrook, and, unofficially, I am informed that very early that morning two brothers, who went down to look after their cobble hauled up on the beach, found, a good way from Brenzett, an ordinary ship's hencoop lying high and dry on the shore, with eleven drowned ducks inside. Their families ate the birds, and the hencoop was split into firewood with a hatchet. It is possible that a man (supposing he happened to be on the deck at the time of the accident) might have floated ashore on that hencoop. He might. I admit it is improbable, but there was the man — and for days, nay, for weeks — it didn't enter our heads that we had amongst us the only living soul that had escaped from that disaster. The man himself, even when he learned to speak intelligibly, could tell us very little. He remembered he had felt better (after the ship had anchored, I suppose), and that the darkness, the wind, and the rain took his breath away. This looks as if he had been on deck some time during that night. But we mustn't forget he had been taken out of his knowledge, that he had been sea-sick and battened down below for four days, that he had no general notion of a ship or of the sea, and therefore could have no definite idea of what was happening to him. The rain, the wind, the darkness he knew; he understood the bleating of the sheep, and he remembered the pain of his wretchedness and misery, his heartbroken astonishment that it was neither seen nor understood, his dismay at finding all the men angry and all the women fierce. He had approached them as a beggar, it is true, he said; but in his country, even if they gave nothing, they spoke gently to beggars. The children in his country were not taught to throw stones at those who asked for compassion. Smith's strategy overcame him completely. The wood-lodge presented the horrible aspect of a dungeon. What would be done to him next? . . . No wonder that Amy Foster appeared to his eyes with the aureole of an angel of light. The girl had not been able to sleep for thinking of the poor man, and in the morning, before the Smiths were up, she slipped out across the back yard. Holding the door of the wood-lodge ajar, she looked in and extended to him half a loaf of white bread – "such bread as the rich eat in my country", he used to say.

'At this he got up slowly from amongst all sorts of rubbish, stiff, hungry, trembling, miserable, and doubtful. "Can you eat this?" she asked in her soft and timid voice. He must have taken her for a "gracious lady". He devoured ferociously, and tears were falling on the crust. Suddenly he dropped the bread, seized her wrist, and imprinted a kiss on her hand. She was not frightened. Through his forlorn condition she had observed that he was good-looking. She shut the door and walked back slowly to the kitchen. Much later on, she told Mrs Smith, who shuddered at the bare idea of being touched by that creature.

'Through this act of impulsive pity he was brought back again within the pale of human relations with his new surroundings. He never forgot it – never.

'That very same morning old Mr Swaffer (Smith's nearest neighbour) came over to give his advice, and ended by carrying him off. He stood, unsteady on his legs, meek, and caked over in half-dried mud, while the two men talked around him in an incomprehensible tongue. Mrs Smith had refused to come downstairs till the madman was off the premises; Amy Foster, from far within the dark kitchen, watched through the open back door; and he obeyed the signs that were made to him to the best of his ability. But Smith was full of mistrust. "Mind, sir! It may be all his cunning," he cried repeatedly in a tone of warning. When Mr Swaffer started the mare, the deplorable being sitting humbly by his side, through weakness, nearly fell out over the back of the high two-wheeled cart. Swaffer took him straight home. And it is then that I come upon the scene.

'I was called in by the simple process of the old man beckoning to me with his forefinger over the gate of his house as I happened to be driving past. I got down, of course.

' "I've got something here," he mumbled, leading the way to an outhouse at a little distance from his other farm-buildings.

'It was there that I saw him first, in a long low room taken upon the space of that sort of coach-house. It was bare and whitewashed, with a small square aperture glazed with one cracked, dusty pane at its further end. He was lying on his back upon a straw pallet; they had given him a couple of horse-blankets, and he seemed to have spent the remainder of his strength in the exertion of cleaning himself. He was almost speechless; his quick breathing under the blankets pulled up to his chin, his glittering, restless black eyes reminded me of a wild bird caught in a snare. While I was examining him, old Swaffer stood silently by the door, passing the tips of his fingers along his shaven upper lip. I gave some directions, promised to send a bottle of medicine, and naturally made some inquiries.

' "Smith caught him in the stackyard at New Barns," said the old chap in his deliberate, unmoved manner, and as if the other had been indeed a sort of wild animal, "That's how I came by him. Quite a curiosity, isn't it? Now tell me, doctor — you've been all over the world — don't you think that's a bit of a Hindoo we've got hold of here?"

'I was greatly surprised. His long black hair scattered over the straw bolster contrasted with the olive pallor of his face. It occurred to me he might be a Basque. It didn't necessarily follow that he should understand Spanish; but I tried him with the few words I know, and also with some French. The whispered sounds I caught by bending my ear to his lips puzzled me utterly. That afternoon the young ladies from the rectory (one of them read Goethe with a dictionary, and the other had struggled with Dante for years), coming to see Miss Swaffer, tried their German and Italian on him from the doorway. They retreated, just the least bit scared by the flood of passionate speech which, turning on his pallet, he let out at them. They admitted that the sound was pleasant, soft, musical — but, in conjunction with his looks perhaps, it was startling — so excitable, so utterly unlike anything one had ever heard. The village boys climbed up the bank to have a peep through the little square aperture. Everybody was wondering what Mr Swaffer would do with him.

'He simply kept him.

'Swaffer would be called eccentric were he not so much respected. They will tell you that Mr Swaffer sits up as late as ten o'clock at night to read books, and they will tell you also that he can write a cheque for two hundred pounds without thinking twice about it. He himself would tell you that the Swaffers had owned land between this and Darnford for these three hundred years. He must be eighty-five today, but he does not look a bit older than when I first came here. He is a great breeder of sheep, and deals extensively in cattle. He attends market days for miles around in every sort of weather, and drives sitting bowed low over the reins, his lank grey hair curling over the collar of his warm coat, and with a green plaid rug round his legs. The calmness of advanced age gives a solemnity to his manner. He is clean-shaved; his lips are thin and sensitive; something rigid and monarchial in the set of his features lends a certain elevation to the character of his face. He has been known to drive miles in the rain to see a new kind of rose in somebody's garden, or a monstrous cabbage grown by a cottager. He loves to hear tell of or to be shown something what he calls "outlandish". Perhaps it was just that outlandishness of the man which influenced old Swaffer. Perhaps it was only an inexplicable caprice. All I know is that at the end of three weeks I caught sight of Smith's lunatic digging in Swaffer's kitchen garden. They had found out he could use a spade. He dug barefooted.

'His black hair flowed over his shoulders. I suppose it was Swaffer who had given him the striped old cotton shirt; but he wore still the national brown cloth trousers (in which he had been washed ashore) fitting to the leg almost like tights; was belted with a broad leathern belt studded with little brass discs; and had never yet ventured into the village. The land he looked upon seemed to him kept neatly, like the grounds round a landowner's house; the size of the cart-horses struck him with astonishment; the roads resembled garden walks, and the aspect of the people, especially on Sundays, spoke of opulence. He wondered what made them so hardhearted and their children so bold. He got his food at the back door, carried it in both hands, carefully, to his outhouse, and, sitting alone on his pallet, would make the sign of the cross before he began. Beside the small pallet, kneeling in the early darkness of the short days, he recited aloud the Lord's Prayer before he slept. Whenever he saw old Swaffer he would bow with veneration from the waist, and stand erect while the old man, with his fingers over his upper lip, surveyed him silently. He bowed also to Miss Swaffer, who kept house frugally for her father – a broad-shouldered, big-boned woman of forty-five, with the pocket of her dress full of keys, and a grey, steady eye. She was Church – as people said (while her father was one of the trustees of the Baptist Chapel) – and wore a little steel cross at her waist. She dressed severely in black, in memory of one of the innumerable Bradleys of the neighbourhood, to whom she had been engaged some twenty-five years ago – a young farmer who broke his neck out hunting on the eve of the wedding-day. She had the unmoved countenance of the deaf, spoke very seldom, and her lips, thin like her father's, astonished one sometimes by a mysteriously ironic curl.

'These were the people to whom he owed allegiance, and an overwhelming loneliness seemed to fall from the leaden sky of that winter without sunshine. All the faces were sad. He could talk to no one, and had no hope of ever understanding anybody. It was as if these had been the faces of people from the other world – dead people – he used to tell me years afterwards. Upon my word, I wonder he did not go mad. He didn't know where he was. Somewhere very far from his mountains – somewhere over the water. Was this America? he wondered.

'If it hadn't been for the steel cross at Miss Swaffer's belt he would not, he confessed, have known whether he was in a Christian country at all. He used to cast stealthy glances at it, and feel comforted. There was nothing here the same as in his country! The earth and the water were different; there were no images of the Redeemer by the roadside. The very grass was different, and the trees. All the trees but the three old Norway pines on the bit of lawn before Swaffer's house, and these reminded him of his country. He had been detected once, after dusk, with his forehead against the trunk of one of them, sobbing, and talking to himself. They had been like brothers to him at that time, he affirmed. Everything else was strange. Conceive you the kind of an existence over-shadowed, oppressed, by the everyday material appearances, as if by the visions of a nightmare. At night, when he could not sleep, he kept on thinking of the girl who gave him the first piece of bread he had eaten in this foreign land. She had been neither fierce nor angry, nor frightened. Her face he remembered as the only comprehensible face amongst all these faces that were as closed, as mysterious, and as mute as the faces of the dead who are possessed of a knowledge beyond the comprehension of the living. I wonder whether the memory of her compassion prevented him from cutting his throat. But there! I suppose I am an old sentimentalist, and forget the instinctive love of life which it takes all the strength of an uncommon despair to overcome.

'He did the work which was given him with an intelligence which surprised old Swaffer. By-and-by it was discovered that he could help at the ploughing, could milk the cows, feed the bullocks in the cattle-yard, and was of some use with the sheep. He began to pick up words, too, very fast; and suddenly, one fine morning in spring, he rescued from an untimely death a grandchild of old Swaffer.

'Swaffer's younger daughter is married to Wilcox, a solicitor and the Town Clerk of Colebrook. Regularly twice a year they come to stay with the old man for a few days. Their only child, a little girl not three years old at the time, ran out of the house alone in her little white pinafore, and, toddling across the grass of a terraced garden, pitched herself over a low wall head first into the horsepond in the yard below.

'Our man was out with the waggoner and the plough in the field nearest to the house, and as he was leading the team round to begin a fresh furrow, he saw, through the gap of a gate, what for anybody else would have been a mere flutter of something white. But he had straight-glancing, quick, far-reaching eyes, that only seemed to flinch and lose their amazing power before the immensity of the sea. He was bare-footed, and looking as outlandish as the heart of Swaffer could desire. Leaving the horses on the turn, to the inexpressible disgust of the waggoners he bounded off, going over the ploughed ground in long leaps, and suddenly appeared before the mother, thrust the child into her arms, and strode away.

'The pond was not very deep; but still, if he had not had such good eyes, the child would have perished – miserably suffocated in the foot or so of sticky mud at the bottom. Old Swaffer walked out slowly into the field, waited till the plough came over to his side, had a good look at him, and without saying a word went back to the house. But from that time they laid out his meals on the kitchen table; and at first, Miss Swaffer, all in black and with an inscrutable face, would come and stand in the doorway of the living-room to see him make a big sign of the cross before he fell to. I believe that from that day, too, Swaffer began to pay him regular wages.

'I can't follow step by step his development. He cut his hair short, was seen in the village and along the road going to and fro to his work like any other man. Children ceased to shout after him. He became aware of social differences, but remained for a long time surprised at the bare poverty of the churches among so much wealth. He couldn't understand either why they were kept shut up on week-days. There was nothing to steal in them. Was it to keep people from praying too often? The rectory took much notice of him about that time, and I believe the young ladies attempted to prepare the ground for his conversion. They could not, however, break him of his habit of crossing himself, but he went so far as to take off the string with a couple of brass medals the size of a sixpence, a tiny metal cross, and a square sort of scapulary which he wore round his neck. He hung them on the wall by the side of his bed, and he was still to be heard every evening reciting the Lord's Prayer, in incomprehensible words and in a slow, fervent tone, as he had heard his old father do at the head of all the kneeling family, big and little, on every evening of his life. And though he wore corduroys at work, and a slop-made pepper-and-salt suit on Sundays, strangers would turn round to look after him on the road. His foreignness had a peculiar and indelible stamp. At last people became used to seeing him. But they never became used to him. His rapid, skimming walk; his swarthy complexion; his hat cocked on the left ear; his habit, on warm evenings, of wearing his coat over one shoulder, like a hussar's dolman; his manner of leaping over the stiles, not as a feat of agility, but in the ordinary course of progression – all these peculiarities were, as one may say, so many causes of scorn and offence to the inhabitants of the village. *They* wouldn't in their dinner hour lie flat on their backs on the grass to stare at the sky. Neither did they go about the fields screaming dismal tunes. Many times have I heard his high-pitched voice from behind the ridge of some sloping sheep-walk, a voice light and soaring, like a lark's, but with a melancholy human note, over our fields that hear only the song of birds. And I would be startled myself. Ah! He was different: innocent of heart, and full of good will, which nobody wanted, this castaway, that, like a man transplanted into another planet, was separated by an immense space from his past and by an immense ignorance from his future. His quick, fervent utterance positively shocked everybody. "An excitable devil", they called him. One evening, in the tap-room of the Coach and Horses (having drunk some whisky), he upset them all by singing a love-song of his country. They hooted him down, and he was pained; but Preble, the lame wheelwright, and Vincent, the fat blacksmith, and the other notables too, wanted to drink their evening beer in peace. On another occasion he tried to show them how to dance. The dust rose in clouds from the sanded floor; he leaped straight up amongst the deal tables, struck his heels together, squatted on one heel in front of old Preble, shooting out the other leg, uttered wild and exulting cries, jumped up to whirl one foot, snapping his fingers above his head – and a strange carter who was having a drink in there began to swear, and cleared out with his half-pint in his hand into the bar. But when suddenly he sprang upon a table and continued to dance among the glasses, the landlord interfered. He didn't want any "acrobat tricks in the tap-room". They laid their hands on him. Having had a glass or two, Mr Swaffer's foreigner tried to expostulate: was ejected forcibly: got a black eye.

'I believe he felt the hostility of his human surroundings. But he was tough – tough in spirit, too, as well as in body. Only the memory of the sea frightened him, with that vague terror that is left by a bad dream. His home was far away; and he did not want now to go to America. I had often explained to him that there is no place on earth where true gold can be found lying ready and to be got for the trouble of the picking up. How then, he asked, could he ever return home with empty hands when there had been sold a cow, two ponies, and a bit of land to pay for his going? His eyes would fill with tears, and, averting them from the immense shimmer of the sea, he would throw himself face down on the grass. But sometimes, cocking his hat with a little conquering air, he would defy my wisdom. He had found his bit of true gold. That was Amy Foster's heart; which was "a golden heart, and soft to people's misery", he would say in the accents of overwhelming conviction.

'He was called Yanko. He had explained that this meant Little John; but as he would also repeat very often that he was a mountaineer (some word sounding in the dialect of his country like Goorall) he got it for his surname. And this is the only trace of him that the succeeding ages may find in the marriage register of the parish. There it stands – Yanko Goorall – in the rector's handwriting. The crooked cross made by the castaway, a cross whose tracing no doubt seemed to him the most solemn part of the whole ceremony, is all that remains now to perpetuate the memory of his name.

'His courtship had lasted some time – ever since he got his precarious footing in the community. It began by his buying for Amy Foster a green satin ribbon in Darnford. This was what you did in his country. You bought a ribbon at a Jew's stall on a fair-day. I don't suppose the girl knew what to do with it, but he seemed to think that his honourable intentions could not be mistaken.

'It was only when he declared his purpose to get married that I fully understood how, for a hundred futile and inappreciable reasons, how – shall I say odious? – he was to all the countryside. Every old woman in the village was up in arms. Smith, coming upon him near the farm, promised to break his head for him if he found him about again. But he twisted his little black moustache with such a bellicose air and rolled such big, black fierce eyes at Smith that this promise came to nothing. Smith, however, told the girl that she must be mad to take up with a man who was surely wrong in his head. All the same, when she heard him in the gloaming whistle from beyond the orchard a couple of bars of a weird and mournful tune, she would drop whatever she had in her hand – she would leave Mrs Smith in the middle of a sentence –

and she would run out to his call. Mrs Smith called her a shameless hussy. She answered nothing. She said nothing at all to anybody, and went on her way as if she had been deaf. She and I alone in all the land, I fancy, could see his very real beauty. He was very good-looking, and most graceful in his bearing, with that something wild as of a woodland creature in his aspect. Her mother moaned over her dismally whenever the girl came to see her on her day out. The father was surly, but pretended not to know; and Mrs Finn once told her plainly that "this man, my dear, will do you some harm some day yet". And so it went on. They could be seen on the roads, she tramping stolidly in her finery – grey dress, black feather, stout boots, prominent white cotton gloves that caught your eye a hundred yards away; and he, his coat slung picturesquely over one shoulder, pacing by her side, gallant of bearing and casting tender glances upon the girl with the golden heart. I wonder whether he saw how plain she was. Perhaps among types so different from what he had seen, he had not the power to judge; or perhaps he was seduced by the divine quality of her pity.

'Yanko was in great trouble meantime. In his country you get an old man for an ambassador in marriage affairs. He did not know how to proceed. However, one day in the midst of sheep in a field (he was now Swaffer's under-shepherd with Foster) he took off his hat to the father and declared himself humbly. "I daresay she's fool enough to marry you," was all Foster said. "And then," he used to relate, "he puts his hat on his head, looks black at me as if he wanted to cut my throat, whistles the dog, and off he goes, leaving me to do the work." The Fosters, of course, didn't like to lose the wages the girl earned: Amy used to give all her money to her mother. But there was in Foster a very genuine aversion to that match. He contended that the fellow was very good with sheep, but was not fit for any girl to marry. For one thing, he used to go along the hedges muttering to himself like a dam' fool; and then, these foreigners behave very queerly to women sometimes. And perhaps he would want to carry her off somewhere – or run off himself. It was not safe. He preached it to his daughter that the fellow might ill-use her in some way. She made no answer. It was, they said in the village, as if the man had done something to her.

People discussed the matter. It was quite an excitement, and the two went on "walking out" together in the face of opposition. Then something unexpected happened.

'I don't know whether old Swaffer ever understood how much he was regarded in the light of a father by his foreign retainer. Anyway the relation was curiously feudal. So when Yanko asked formally for an interview – "and the Miss too" (he called the severe, deaf Miss Swaffer simply *Miss*) – it was to obtain their permission to marry. Swaffer heard him unmoved, dismissed him by a nod, and then shouted the intelligence into Miss Swaffer's best ear. She showed no surprise, and only remarked grimly, in a veiled blank voice, "He certainly won't get any other girl to marry him."

'It is Miss Swaffer who has all the credit of the munificence: but in a very few days it came out that Mr Swaffer had presented Yanko with a cottage (the cottage you've seen this morning) and something like an acre of ground – had made it over to him in absolute property. Willcox expedited the deed, and I remember him telling me he had a great pleasure in making it ready. It recited: "In consideration of saving the life of my beloved grand-child Bertha Willcox."

'Of course, after that no power on earth could prevent them from getting married.

'Her infatuation endured. People saw her going out to meet him in the evening. She stared with unblinking, fascinated eyes up the road where he was expected to appear, walking freely, with a swing from the hip, and humming one of the love-tunes of his country. When the boy was born, he got elevated at the "Coach and Horses", essayed again a song and a dance, and was again ejected. People expressed their commiseration for a woman married to that Jack-in-the-box. He didn't care. There was a man now (he told me boastfully) to whom he could sing and talk in the language of his country, and show how to dance by-and-by.

'But I don't know. To me he appeared to have grown less springy of step, heavier in body, less keen of eye. Imagination, no doubt; but it seems to me now as if the net of fate had been drawn closer round him already.

'One day I met him on the footpath over the Talfourd Hill. He told me that "women were funny". I had heard already of domestic differences. People were saying that Amy Foster was beginning to find out what sort of man she had married. He looked upon the sea with indifferent, unseeing eyes. His wife had snatched the child out of his arms one day as he sat on the doorstep crooning to it a song such as the mothers sing to babies in his mountains. She seemed to think he was doing it some harm. Women are funny. And she had objected to him praying aloud in the evening. Why? He expected the boy to repeat the prayer aloud after him by-and-by, as he used to do after his old father when he was a child – in his own country. And I discovered he longed for their boy to grow up so that he could have a man to talk with in that language that to our ears sounded so disturbing, so passionate, and so bizarre. Why his wife should dislike the idea he couldn't tell. But that would pass, he said. And tilting his head knowingly, he tapped his breastbone to indicate that she had a good heart: not hard, not fierce, open to compassion, charitable to the poor!

'I walked away thoughtfully; I wondered whether his difference, his strangeness, were not penetrating with repulsion that dull nature they had begun by irresistibly attracting. I wondered. . . .'

The doctor came to the window and looked out at the frigid splendour of the sea, immense in the haze, as if enclosing all the earth with all the hearts lost among the passions of love and fear.

'Physiologically now,' he said, turning away abruptly, 'it was possible. It was possible.'

He remained silent. Then went on –

'At all events, the next time I saw him he was ill – lung trouble. He was tough, but I daresay he was not acclimatized as well as I had supposed. It was a bad winter; and, of course, these mountaineers do get fits of homesickness; and a state of depression would make him vulnerable. He was lying half dressed on a couch downstairs.

'A table covered with a dark oilcloth took up all the middle of the little room. There was a wicker cradle on the floor, a kettle spouting steam on the hob, and some child's linen lay drying on the fender. The room was warm, but the door opens right into the garden, as you noticed, perhaps.

'He was very feverish, and kept on muttering to himself. She sat on a chair and looked at him fixedly across the table with her brown, blurred eyes. "Why don't you have him upstairs?" I asked. With a start and a confused stammer she said, "Oh! ah! I couldn't sit with him upstairs, sir."

'I gave her certain directions; and going outside, I said again that he ought to be in bed upstairs. She wrung her hands. "I couldn't. I couldn't. He keeps on saying something—I don't know what." With the memory of all the talk against the man that had been dinned into her ears, I looked at her narrowly. I looked into her short-sighted eyes, at her dumb eyes that once in her life had seen an enticing shape, but seemed, staring at me, to see nothing at all now. But I saw she was uneasy.

' "What's the matter with him?" she asked in a sort of vacant trepidation. "He doesn't look very ill. I never did see anybody look like this before. . . ."

' "Do you think," I asked indignantly, "he is shamming?"

' "I can't help it, sir," she said stolidly. And suddenly she clasped her hands and looked right and left. "And there's the baby. I am so frightened. He wanted me just now to give him the baby. I can't understand what he says to it."

' "Can't you ask a neighbour to come in tonight?" I asked.

' "Please, sir, nobody seems to care to come," she muttered, dully resigned all at once.

'I impressed upon her the necessity of the greatest care, and then had to go. There was a good deal of sickness that winter. "Oh, I hope he won't talk!" she exclaimed softly just as I was going away.

'I don't know how it is I did not see — but I didn't. And yet, turning in my trap, I saw her lingering before the door, very still, and as if meditating a flight up the miry road.

'Towards the night his fever increased.

'He tossed, moaned, and now and then muttered a complaint. And she sat with the table between her and the couch, watching every movement and every sound, with the terror, the unreasonable terror, of that man she could not understand creeping over her. She had drawn the wicker cradle close to her feet. There was nothing in her now but the maternal instinct and that unaccountable fear.

'Suddenly coming to himself, parched, he demanded a drink of water. She did not move. She had not understood, though he may have thought he was speaking in English. He waited, looking at her, burning with fever, amazed at her silence and immobility, and then he shouted impatiently. "Water! Give me water!"

'She jumped to her feet, snatched up the child, and stood still. He spoke to her, and his passionate remonstrances only increased her fear of that strange man. I believe he spoke to her for a long time, entreating, wondering, pleading, ordering I suppose. She says she bore it as long as she could. And then a gust of rage came over him.

'He sat up and called out terribly one word – some word. Then he got up as though he hadn't been ill at all, she says. And as in fevered dismay, indignation, and wonder he tried to get to her round the table, she simply opened the door and ran out with the child in her arms. She heard him call twice after her down the road in a terrible voice – and fled. . . . Ah! but you should have seen stirring behind the dull, blurred glance of these eyes the spectre of the fear which had hunted her on that night three miles and a half to the door of Foster's cottage! I did the next day.

'And it was I who found him lying face down and his body in a puddle, just outside the little wicker-gate.

'I had been called out that night to an urgent case in the village, and on my way home at daybreak passed by the cottage. The door stood open. My man helped me to carry him in. We laid him on the couch. The lamp smoked, the fire was out, the chill of the stormy night oozed from the cheerless yellow paper on the wall. "Amy!" I called aloud, and my voice seemed to lose itself in the emptiness of this tiny house as if I had cried in a desert. He opened his eyes. "Gone!" he said, distinctly. "I had only asked for water – only for a little water. . . ."

'He was muddy. I covered him up and stood waiting in silence, catching a painfully gasped word now and then. They were no longer in his own language. The fever had left him, taking with it the heat of life. And with his panting breast and lustrous eyes he reminded me again of a wild creature under the net; of a bird caught in a snare. She had left him. She had left him – sick – helpless – thirsty. The spear of the hunter had entered his very soul. "Why?" he cried, in the penetrating and indignant voice of a man calling to a responsible Maker. A gust of wind and a swish of rain answered.

'And as I turned away to shut the door he pronounced the word "Merciful!" and expired.

'Eventually I certified heart-failure as the immediate cause of death. His heart must have indeed failed him, or else he might have stood this night of storm and exposure, too. I closed his eyes and drove away. Not very far from the cottage I met Foster walking sturdily between the dripping hedges with his collie at his heels.

' "Do you know where your daughter is?" I asked.

' "Don't I!" he cried. "I am going to talk to him a bit. Frightening a poor woman like this."

' "He won't frighten her any more," I said. "He is dead."

'He struck with his stick at the mud.

' "And there's the child."

'Then, after thinking deeply for a while—

' "I don't know that it isn't for the best."

'That's what he said. And she says nothing at all now. Not a word of him. Never. Is his image as utterly gone from her mind as his lithe and striding figure, his carolling voice are gone from our fields? He is no longer before her eyes to excite her imagination into a passion of love or fear; and his memory seems to have vanished from her dull brain as a shadow passes away upon a white screen. She lives in the cottage and works for Miss Swaffer. She is Amy Foster for everybody, and the child is "Amy Foster's boy". She calls him Johnny – which means Little John.

'It is impossible to say whether this name recalls anything to her. Does she ever think of the past? I have seen her hanging over the boy's cot in a very passion of maternal tenderness. The little fellow was lying on his back, a little frightened at me, but very still, with his big black eyes, with his fluttered air of a bird in a snare. And looking at him I seemed to see again the other one – the father, cast out mysteriously by the sea to perish in the supreme disaster of loneliness and despair.'

Biographical Notes

Douglas William Jerrold (1803–1857). The son of an actor, and himself an amateur thespian, Jerrold wrote some forty plays. Among the melodramas, farces, and comedies that earned him a reputation was *Black-eyed Susan, or All in the Downs* (1829), which ran for more than 400 performances. He co-managed the Strand Theatre; edited half-a-dozen periodicals; wrote several novels; contributed both light and serious pieces to numerous magazines and newspapers (he was a surprisingly astringent social critic for *Punch*); and perhaps scored his greatest success with *Mrs Caudle's Curtain Lectures* (1846), a series of unsentimental, witty monologues addressed by a complexly characterized woman to her long-suffering husband after she has extinguished the night-candle.

William Schwenk Gilbert (1836–1911). The story that Gilbert was ransomed from kidnappers in Naples when he was two years old is true; a distorted version may be found in *The Pirates of Penzance*. Gilbert supplied illustrations for several of his father's novels, and found that, by comparison, the duties of a clerk in the Privy Council Office (1857–61) were dull. He moved to the Inner Temple, and was called to the Bar in 1864. Undiscouraged by rejections from editors, he wrote sketches and light verse, signing his ballads 'Bab' (a dialectal form of 'Babe'). From the mid-1860s, he served as dramatic critic for the *Illustrated Times*, and contributed countless short pieces to *Fun*, *Cornhill*, *London Society*, *Tinsley's*, *Temple Bar*, and *Punch*. He also wrote commercially successful comedies and romantic dramas, both before and during the celebrated collaboration (lasting a full two decades) with Arthur Seymour Sullivan. His librettos – fresh, witty, and beautifully constructed – were instant successes. Nevertheless, he liked writing short stories more than plays, and thought of them as his major literary achievement. He continued to write them till the end of his life. He died of heart failure at the age of 75 when he attempted, gallantly, to rescue a woman from drowning in his swimming-lake at Grim's Dyke, Harrow Weald, Middlesex.

Charles Dickens (1812–1870). Successor to Scott as the most widely read and influential novelist of the century, Dickens developed as a human being against long odds. His family background was troubled (his father, unable to live within his income, went to prison for debt), his education haphazard, his childhood employments humiliating. A diligent student of shorthand, he became a successful parliamentary reporter and well-known journalist before scoring his first great success with *The Pickwick Papers* (1836–37). His fourteen hugely popular novels, published in 'parts', permanently changed relationships between publishers and authors. He also served as the energetic and brilliant editor of *Household Words* (1850–59) and *All the Year Round* (1859–67), two of the most widely read family magazines of the Victorian Age. Increasingly sombre and more pointed in its sociological criticism, the art of Dickens darkened significantly during his last two decades. Though he wrote more than seventy short stories, he used terms like 'tale', 'sketch', 'romance', and 'story' interchangeably. He achieved success in amateur theatricals. One of several demanding tours, on which he gave dramatic readings, led to exhaustion and premature death.

Joseph Sheridan Le Fanu (1814–1873). A master of the short story, he emphasized form more than any of his Irish predecessors (William Carleton, for example, exploited the oral tradition in casual ways that did not differentiate between spoken and shaped narratives), Le Fanu never practised law, his chosen profession. He had to scramble in the underpaid world of pamphlets and newspapers to stay afloat. He wrote for several periodicals, and was part-time owner of newspapers that were sued for libel on several occasions (he lost some expensive judgments). A number of grim novels about Irish life, expressing mordant views on nineteenth-century science, religion, political injustice, and the sharing of guilt by several social classes, followed. Though not the first writer of stories dealing with terror and the supernatural, he exerted a significant influence on generations of writers in the British Isles. His most important single collection, *In a Glass Darkly* (1872), still retains the power to change a reader's attitude toward the possibility of vengeful ghosts and the lurking dangers of darkness in both city streets and one's own home.

Robert Louis Stevenson (1850–1894). The sickly son of a well-known Scottish meteorologist and engineer, Stevenson acquired an excellent but not always appropriate education (engineering and law) in Edinburgh. His interests were far-flung; his first book described his travels with a donkey in the Cevennes, and indeed his travel essays won him a wide following. But he also wrote accounts of life in America's still-untamed West, gracefully erudite essays in an eighteenth-century tradition, highly personal literary criticism, an extraordinary series of articles on what he already perceived to be an outmoded colonialism in the South Pacific, and one of the century's most popular gatherings of poetry written from a child's perspective, *A Child's Garden of Verses* (1885). Stevenson's plays, some written in collaboration with W.E. Henley, were unsuccessful both as art and as commercial undertakings. But his novels (*Treasure Island*, 1883; *The Strange Case of Dr Jekyll and Mr Hyde*, 1886; *Kidnapped*, 1886; *The Master of Ballantrae*, 1888; and a magnificent fragment, *The Weir of Hermiston*, left unfinished at his death) and his short stories, which include some of the finest 'crawlers' – horror-inspiring narratives – in the language, earned him the reputation of a master romancer that he has never lost during this century.

Oscar Wilde (1854–1900). The word 'genius', often loosely applied, was willingly conceded to Wilde even by his enemies, of which he had many during his lifetime. His education, acquired in part at Trinity College, Dublin, and Magdalen College, Oxford, combined with his native Irish wit to establish, early on, his leadership of the notorious aesthetic movement of the 1880s and 90s. His poetry illustrates several key interests of romantic literature at century's end: a piling-up of verbal effects, the exploitation of turbulently erotic and even 'decadent' emotions, and occasionally brilliant musings on the impossibility of sustaining spiritual faith in the modern world. He was also, for several years, England's most successful architect of commercially successful drawing-room comedies: *Lady Windermere's Fan* (1893), *A Woman of No Importance* (1894), *The Importance of Being Earnest* (1895), and *An Ideal Husband* (1895). From his prison experiences of 1895–97 (the result of a lawsuit attempting to clear his reputation of the charge of homosexual practices) emerged the deeply moving *The Ballad of Reading Gaol* (1898) and the prose work *De Profundis* (partially published in 1905). Wilde's short stories, often written for children, display a delicacy and haunting beauty of phrase that made them instant favourites on both sides of the Atlantic.

Rudyard Kipling (1865–1936). Born in Bombay, Kipling was sent to England at an early age, primarily to avoid problems of health; but his childhood years, spent at Southsea, were desperately unhappy (as recounted in 'Baa, Baa, Black Sheep'). More exciting, and richer as a treasury for future memories (immortalized in *Stalky & Co.*), were his adolescent years at the United Services College at Westward Ho! Devon. Returning to India and a job on the *Civil and Military Gazette* of Lahore, Kipling, from the age of seventeen on, established a reputation as a poet of original themes and unforgettable metrical beats (*Department Ditties*, 1886) and as an author of 'turnovers', short stories that began on one page and concluded on another (*Plain Tales from the Hills*, 1888). Kipling's work as editor of the weekly edition of the *Pioneer* (Allahabad) further developed his story-telling talent; before he died he was to write some 350 short stories. The history of Kipling's triumphant reception in both England and the U.S. has been told many times, and provides impressive documentation of the importance of literature in middle-class cultural pursuits at the turn of the century. After three years in America, Kipling returned to England, and finally settled at Bateman's, a seventeenth century estate in Burwash, East Sussex. His novels, stories written about and expressly for children, polemical speeches, journalistic pieces on an astonishingly wide cross-section of subject-matter, as well as a distinguished history of *The Irish Guards in the Great War* (his son John served in the Guards), helped to win for him the Nobel Prize for Literature (1907) and countless additional honours. He is best remembered for his short stories. These, in his final decades, became extraordinarily complex, subtle, and dark-hued with intimations of mortality.

Thomas Hardy (1840–1928). Often referred to as 'a man of Wessex', Hardy lived most of his life within a ten-mile radius of his birthplace, Higher Bockhampton, near Dorchester in Dorset; but he believed that the lives of his fellow-countrymen contained passions as intense and as potentially fascinating as any that had animated the heroes of Greek tragedy, or, for that matter, King Lear. (Hardy believed that Lear had once roamed Egdon Heath in Wessex.) Hardy's education was intermittent and largely self-acquired, but eclectic and always well-informed. He began as a poet, and always regarded poetry as a higher art than the art of the novel. Indeed, after a sour reception given by some critics to *Jude the Obscure* (1895), Hardy renounced novel-writing, and spent his final three decades writing *The Dynasts* (1903–1908), an epic-drama commemorating the Napoleonic decade between 1805 and 1815, and more than nine-hundred poems that exerted tremendous influence on younger writers such as W.H. Auden, C. Day Lewis and Philip Larkin. Hardy wrote fourteen novels, almost all of them both commercial and critical successes (he tended to exaggerate critical hostility). Chief among them are *Far* *from the Madding Crowd* (1874), *The Return of the Native* (1878), *The Mayor of Casterbridge* (1886), *The Woodlanders* (1887), *Tess of the d'Urbervilles* (1891), and *Jude the Obscure*. His short stories, published in a wide variety of periodicals, specialized in Gothic effects, star-crossed loves, and a brooding sense of man's inability to control his destiny. Though he did not regard them as major efforts, they contain some of his finest work in fiction.

Henry James (1843–1916). Son of a highly intellectual father who attempted to adapt Swedenborgian ideas to an American context, and brother of one of America's most original philosophers, Henry James acquired his education, for the most part, in Europe. He studied law briefly at Harvard, but his interests from the beginning were concentrated on the craft of fiction. Some of his earliest essays, written during his early 'twenties, assessed the writings of Flaubert and Turgenev. A firm believer in the artistic possibilities of the novel, he disliked the 'baggy' fictions of Tolstoy, and emphasized – in his own novels and stories – the tight control of a consistent point of view, elliptical dialogue that suggested far more than it stated explicitly, and the importance of 'felt life'. Though an expatriate, one who in his final years became a British citizen to express support of the Allied cause in the Great War, James wrote much of the time on the theme of internationalism. Some of his finest work posits the irreconcilable nature of the conflict between American innocence and European experience. As in 'The Real Thing', he often debated the nature of the vast gulf which separates appearances from reality. James's influence, both as practitioner and as aesthetician, can be seen in the stories of William Dean Howells, Joseph Howells, and Edith Wharton. In a larger sense, he has defined the language whereby all of us describe rooms in the house of fiction.

'George Egerton' (Mary Chavelita Dunne), (1860–1945). Miss Dunne married three times, and the changes in her name have confused librarians as well as general readers; but she had a distinct personality in her own right. She was born in Australia, and educated privately. She knew well at least five languages, and compiled a multi-lingual vocabulary of fishing terms and translated a number of critical essays from Norwegian. Her first book, *Keynotes* (1893), was published by the Bodley Head, and for it Aubrey Beardsley devised a monogram of her name. Her second book, *Discords* (1894), like the first, treated with a disturbing and sometimes savage candour the relationship between men and women. She was not much impressed by the new generation which, she said, she knew not and 'mainly' prized not. A pioneer in feminist thinking, she published in the *Yellow Book*. Today she is remembered for a number of acid-etched portraits of unhappy wives. Henry James satirized her, in 'Death of a Lion', as Guy Walsingham, a woman writer of the 1890s who used a male pen-name in order to investigate 'the larger latitude'.

Hubert Crackanthorpe (1870–1895). His father was a well-known politician and lawyer, his mother a famous hostess and writer. George Gissing tutored him, but he lasted less than a year at Cambridge University because of a quarrel with the authorities. Yet his brief literary career had real momentum. He edited the *Albermarle* (1892–93), and published strikingly realistic stories in *Wreckage* (1893), *Sentimental Studies and a Set of Village Tales* (1895), *Last Studies* (1895), and *Vignettes* (1896). His death in Paris, near the Quai Voltaire, has never been satisfactorily explained (some called it a suicide, others murder). His vigorous style firmly rejected sentimentality. At the time of his death he was negotiating to become the editor of the *Savoy*, and to win a wider audience for his theories of fiction and art. Some have called him the English Maupassant, but his compassion for the downtrodden was probably stronger than that of his French predecessor.

Herbert George Wells (1866–1946). Born in Kent, Wells picked up an oddly irregular education, and spent several unhappy years apprenticed to different trades. Perhaps his first decisive step forward came with the awarding of a scholarship to the Normal School of Science, South Kensington; there his biology and zoology teacher turned out to be the great Thomas Henry Huxley. Bad health prevented Wells from continuing a career as science teacher, but his knowledge of trends in current scientific research coloured his choice of subject-matter when he turned to the career of professional writing. In fiction he made an early, unforgettable mark with such stories as *The Time Machine* (1895), *The Island of Dr Moreau* (1896), *The Invisible Man* (1897), *The War of the Worlds* (1898), and *When the Sleeper Awakes* (1899). Dozens of short stories were so successful that, by the mid-1890s, he was one of the highest-paid writers in England. Conrad, his neighbour, envied (and was baffled by) Wells's commercial triumph at the expense of any concern for art. Nevertheless, Wells turned into something more than a scientific romancer; with *Kipps* (1905), *Tono-Bungay* (1908), and *The History of Mr Polly* (1910), he emerged as an Edwardian master of the novel genre. He began to concentrate on social problems (some considered off-limits for lending-library patrons). His disregard of the need for cultivating a sense of style irritated Henry James, and the two quarrelled noisily in 1915. Wells's interest in popularizing the findings of the scientists he so much respected led to the writing of *The Outline of History* (1920) and *The Science of Life* (1930); the latter was written in collaboration with his son and with Julian Huxley. Although he coined the best-known slogan of the Great War when he titled a pamphlet, 'The War That Will End War', his training in Darwinian principles, his observation of trends in totalitarian governments around the world, and his personal exhaustion led to despair and the writing of a final book, *Mind at the End of Its Tether* (1945).

Arthur Conan Doyle (1859–1930). An Edinburgh-trained doctor who practised for eight years before launching his literary career, Doyle wrote – in addition to the Sherlock Holmes stories that made him famous – dozens of short stories on boxing, piracy, and themes of terror, as well as numerous historical romances. *A Study in Scarlet* was published in 1887, but Doyle's concentration on the exploits of the most successful character-creation in detective fiction did not truly begin until the rise of *The Strand Magazine* in the early 1890s, which soon reached a circulation of 500,000 copies a month. Doyle's effort to kill off his hero, in 'The Adventure of the Final Problem' (1893) led many in the City to don mourning-bands. Public demand led to Holmes's resurrection. Later, William Gillette's dramatization fixed even more deeply in the public consciousness the image of a pipe-smoking, lean-faced thinking machine. Doyle's ardent advocacy of the English side in the Boer War led to knighthood. His propaganda on behalf of the Allied Cause (1914–18) reached millions of readers in more than a dozen countries. Intensely interested in psychic phenomena, he held, in his final years, a firm faith in spiritualism.

Edith Anna Oenone Somerville (1858–1949) and **Violet Florence Martin** (1862–1915). Cousins to each other, and members of an Anglo-Irish Ascendancy class fated to be destroyed by Irish independence, Somerville and Ross wrote in such close harmony that their styles, and even their scripts, are indistinguishable. They began with *An Irish Cousin* (1889), continued with fourteen books (including *The Real Charlotte*, 1894, one of the best Irish novels of the century), and won their widest audience – beginning in 1899 – with *Some Experiences of an Irish R.M.* These stories, about the frustrations encountered by a conventionally respectable, retired English major who has come to the home of his ancestors to settle down, are less patronizing than has been assumed by some Irish readers. Their main moral, that the English and Irish can benefit tremendously from each other's folk wisdom if they are willing to live and let live, is presented with wit, and narrative powers of the first rank. Somerville continued to use the names of 'Somerville and Ross' for decades after Martin's death, on the ground that the collaboration was continuing in full strength.

George Gissing (1857–1903). A brilliant student at both a Quaker boarding-school and Owens College, Manchester, Gissing lived briefly in Boston and Chicago before returning to England in 1877. His two unhappy marriages (to a prostitute and a servant girl) forced him into writing for minimal wages in order to survive. These years of misery are unforgettably described in *New Grub Street* (1891) and *The Private Papers of Henry Ryecroft* (1903). Gissing wanted to write a series of naturalistic novels in the tradition of Balzac. Another early hero is the subject of one of his finest books, *Charles Dickens, A Critical Study* (1898). Although underestimated to this day, Gissing's realistic fictions, written over a quarter-century, are illuminating treatments of the lives of members of the lower-middle class, perhaps the best written during the final years of the Victorian Age. Gissing wrote with sympathy and understanding about the plight of women. H.G. Wells admired his skills, but accurately assessed the limitations of his appeal to contemporary readers. Gissing's final relationship with a woman, Mlle Gabrielle Fleury, turned out happily.

Baroness (Emmuska) Orczy (1865–1947). She was born in Hungary, daughter to Baron Felix Orczy, a distinguished composer and conductor. Because she became a wildly successful romantic novelist, it is not often remembered that she began her career as an artist, and that she exhibited at the Royal Academy. Her historical novel about a dashing hero's smuggling of condemned prisoners away from the guillotine of the French Revolution, entitled *The Scarlet Pimpernel* (1905), led to the writing of sequels and a number of novels dealing with the same period. Her short stories about crime and detection, ranked by many as among the best written by the successors to Arthur Conan Doyle, first began in the last year of Queen Victoria's reign, and included *Lady Molly of Scotland Yard* (1910) and *Unravelled Knots* (1925).

Joseph Conrad (1857–1924). A Polish writer brought up in the midst of a bitterly hated Russian culture, Conrad was deeply influenced by the example of his father, a poet who helped to organize the Polish insurrection against Russian rule (1863), and who, as a consequence, was exiled to Vologda, in northern Russia. His father translated English classics, and Conrad's reading tastes were permanently affected. When his father died, Conrad was taken under the wing of his maternal uncle, Tadeusz Bobrowski. In 1874 Conrad oined the French merchant marine. Obscure episodes of gun-running followed, as well as voyages that served as the basis of *Youth* (1898) and *The Nigger of the Narcissus*, his first novel (1897). The extraordinary voyage that led to the writing of *Heart of Darkness*, his finest novella, took place in 1890–91. Three years later his life as a sailor came to an end, and, with determination and an amazing linguistic adaptability, he turned to the career of an author. His best novels are, by critical consensus, *Lord Jim* (1900), *Nostromo* (1904), *The Secret Agent* (1907), and *Under Western Eyes* (1911). He also wrote some fine essays and some striking literary criticism. Popular acclaim caught up with him during the Great War, but by then he was tired, and too often wrote to eliminate debts rather than to define further his sombre and unsettling personal vision. Conrad's short stories are seldom as brief as 'Amy Foster', but his longer short stories, i.e. his novellas, are fully as distinguished as his contributions to the novel genre.

Acknowledgments

The Cone by H.G. Wells is reprinted by permission of A.P. Watt Ltd on behalf of The Literary Executors of the Estate of H.G. Wells.

Great-Uncle McCarthy by Somerville and Ross is reprinted from *The Irish R.M.* by permission of John Farquharson Ltd on behalf of Sphere Books Ltd.

The Mysterious Death on the Underground Railway by Baroness Orczy is reprinted by permission of A.P. Watt Ltd on behalf of Joan Orczy-Barstow.